THE

CORN LAWS

The Formation of Popular Economics in Britain

Edited by

ALON KADISH

VOLUME II

WHIG FREE TRADE II

FREE TRADE AND IRISH NATIONALISM I

Routledge
Taylor & Francis Group
LONDON AND NEW YORK

First published 1996 by Pickering & Chatto (Publishers) Limited

Published 2016 by Routledge
2 Park Square, Milton Park, Abingdon, Oxon OX14 4RN
605 Third Avenue, New York, NY 10017

Routledge is an imprint of the Taylor & Francis Group, an informa business

BRITISH LIBRARY CATALOGUING IN PUBLICATION DATA
Corn Laws: Formation of Popular Economics
in Britain
I. Kadish, Alon
941.081

Set ISBN 1 85196 410 X
ISBN 13: 978-1-13875-887-2 (hbk) (Vol-02)

LIBRARY OF CONGRESS CATALOGING-IN-PUBLICATION DATA
Kadish, Alon, 1950–
The corn laws : the formation of popular economics in Britain / Alon Kadish.
p. cm.
Includes bibliographical references and index.
ISBN 1–85196–410–X (set)
1. Corn laws (Great Britain) 2. Free trade––Great Britain.
3. Anti-Corn-Law League. I. Title.
HF2044.K33 1996
v. 1. Whig free trade I –– v. 2. Whig free trade II : Free trade and Irish nationalism I –– v. 3. Free trade and Irish nationalism I : James Wilson and the economist –– v. 4. Free trade and religion –– v. 5. Provincial free trade I –– v. 6. Provincial free trade II : Free trade farmers.
382.7'3'0942––dc20 98–1232
CIP

CONTENTS

REFLECTIONS

ON THE

OPERATION

OF THE

PRESENT SCALE OF DUTY

FOR REGULATING THE

IMPORTATION OF FOREIGN CORN,

ADDRESSED TO THE

BORDERS OF KENT AND SUSSEX AGRICULTURAL ASSOCIATION.

By DAVID SALOMONS, Esq.

LONDON:
PELHAM RICHARDSON, 23, CORNHILL.

1839.

David Salomons (1797–1873)

David Salomons, the second son of Levy Salomons, underwriter of Lloyd's was born in Bury Street, St Mary Axe, in the City of London. The Salomons were Jewish merchants who had settled in England early in the eighteenth century. David Salomons had been privately educated. In 1823 he became a member of the Stock Exchange, in 1834 an underwriter at Lloyd's, and in 1836 a subscriber to Lloyd's. In 1834 Salomons joined the newly-founded joint stock London and Westminster Bank, and became a member of the original board of directors when formally established in 1835. He was also chairman of the Reading, Guildford, and Reigate Railway Company, director of the South Australian Land Company, and trustee of the London Life Association. In 1847 Salomons retired from business.

David Salomons developed an early passion for public life. In 1831 he became a liveryman of the Coopers Company and thus a freeman of the City of London. In 1835 Salomons became a member of the Court of Assistants of the Company, and in 1841 a Master. In 1835 he was also elected one of the Sheriffs of London and with it Sheriff of Middlesex. In 1835 and again in 1844 he was elected alderman of the City of London, but it was not until 1847, following the Jewish Disabilities Removal Act (1845), that upon his election for the ward of Cordwainers that he was admitted member of the Court of Aldermen. And in September 1855 he was elected by the Court of Aldermen the first Jewish Lord Mayor.

Salomons contested unsuccessfully Shoreham 1837, Maidstone 1841, and Greenwich 1847. He was finally elected as Liberal MP for Greenwich in 1851 but was not allowed to take his seat in the House, and lost it in the elections of 1852. Following the Oaths Act and the Jewish Relief Act (1858) Salomons was elected again for Greenwich, and held the seat until his death. In 1869 he was created baronet.

Salomons was largely associated with the struggle for Jewish political emancipation. According to his biographer:

> He felt most fervently that a man's religious opinions were his private concern, and so long as they were not immoral or otherwise contrary to the interests of the State or of the people as a whole, whatever they might be they should not restrict his liberty or interfere with his inherent right to serve the State and the community in whatever capacity opportunity might give him. Every step in the extension of the liberties of Nonconformists from the State Church therefore aroused his enthusiastic approval.[1]

But Salomons was no radical. In 1825 he married Jeannette, daughter of

[1] Albert M. Hyamson, *David Salomons*, London: Methuen, 1939, p. 51.

Solomon Cohen of Grove Street, Canonbury, and in 1829 Salomons purchased by auction Broomhill, a small estate of 36 acres near Tunbridge Wells, and close to his father's country place at Frant. David Salomons and his heir increased the estate to 621 acres, built a new house, and added to their holdings the neighbouring estate of Burrswood which was sold in 1852.

According to his biographer: 'In Kent, Salomons lived the life of a country gentleman.'[1] He was appointed in 1838 magistrate for Kent, for Sussex and for Middlesex, appointments which led him to read law. Salomons was called to the Bar by the Middle Temple in 1849. He was also appointed Sheriff of Kent for 1839–40 and Deputy Lieutenant for Kent and Middlesex. Finally, Salomons was President of the Groombridge Agricultural Society 'which held under his auspices a number of its most useful and practical meetings.'[2] Hence in view of his political alliance with the Whigs in Parliament over the issue of Jews' political rights, and his country lifestyle it is not surprising that the banker and City politician should write on the corn laws as would a Whig free trade landowner.

Salomons' publications on free trade are:

Reflections on the Operation of the Present Scale of Duty for regulating the importation of foreign corn, addressed to the Borders of Kent and Sussex Agricultural Association, London: Pelham Richardson, 1839. 2nd edition with a supplement, 1840.

The Corn Laws. Their effects on the Trade of the Country considered, with suggestions for a Compromise, 1841.

[1] Ibid., p. 105.
[2] Ibid.

TO THE

EARL OF DELAWARR,

PRESIDENT,

THE

VICE-PRESIDENTS, AND COMMITTEE

OF THE

BORDERS OF KENT AND SUSSEX

AGRICULTURAL ASSOCIATION.

MY LORDS AND GENTLEMEN,

EVER since the meeting of the Association held last spring to petition Parliament against any alteration of the Corn Laws, I have been desirous of communicating my views on the degree of protection which is required by the agriculture of the country. The vicissitudes which the farmers have experienced during the last few years incline me to believe that the notion so prevalent of the concord between agricultural prosperity and the maintenance of the present Corn Laws is somewhat fallacious. In the following pages I have endeavoured to shew the defective operation of the fluctuating scale of duty, and the advantages offered to the country by adopting a fixed and uniform rate for regulating the importation of foreign grain.

In entering the field of Corn Law discussion, I trust that my friends and neighbours will believe that I have ventured upon it only from a wish to convey to them the opinions I hold on this important and intricate subject. Whether these opinions be approved of or not, your Lordship and the other Members of the Association may feel assured of my anxious desire for the welfare of this district, and of my ready co-operation in any measure having for its object the improvement of the system of agriculture, or the increase of the comforts of the labouring population.

I have the honour to be,

My Lords and Gentlemen,

Your most obedient Servant,

DAVID SALOMONS.

Broom Hill, Nov. 20th, 1839.

REFLECTIONS, &c.

The regulations which affect the prices of the necessaries of life afford a wide field for discussion even in ordinary periods; but more particularly so when their value has been enhanced by an apprehended scarcity. The Corn Laws must, therefore, necessarily occupy a considerable share of public attention. It is to be lamented that a settlement of this question is surrounded by so many difficulties. Party feeling is introduced with the view of awakening popular prejudice, and attempts are made to incite the multitude against the agricultural body, who are represented as being determined, from base and selfish motives, to resist every change, and anxious to enrich themselves at the expense of the rest of the people. Political bitterness and opposing interests, therefore, render this question still more complicated, and the feelings of the parties whose pecuniary interests are involved becoming excited, little hope remains of the subject being considered in a calm and moderate spirit. I cannot, therefore, but lament the agitation now in progress for the purpose of creating animosity between the manufacturing and rural population,—a course of conduct which appears to me to deserve the severest reprobation.

My object in the following pages is to draw attention to the imperfection of our Corn-law policy, and by exhibiting its defects to shew the necessity of such an alteration as may remove some of its commercial and social evils. The legislature has been called upon to invent methods by which it was hoped a protection for the Corn-grower might be secured without subjecting the consumer to any serious disadvantage. A retrospect of the various enactments which have received the sanction of Parliament for the regulation of the Corn-trade will shew that the attempts to limit the price for the quarter of wheat by means of a complicated system have hitherto proved unsuccessful. It is, therefore, our duty to call in aid the further experience which the last few years may have afforded us, and to see if the object we have in view may not be accomplished by other and more simple means.

I subjoin a brief sketch of the enactments for regulating the importation of corn from the year 1814 to 1828, but my observations will be limited to the system in operation since the latter year for regulating the Corn-trade.

On the termination of the continental war, a committee of the House of Lords was appointed on the subject of the trade in corn. The principal feature of the second Report of the Committee was the recommendation, that so long as the average price of wheat was under 80s. the ports should be completely closed against supplies from other countries. The prohibitive price suggested by the witnesses connected with agriculture examined by the committee, varied from 72s. to 96s. On the 23rd of March 1815, a Bill received the Royal Assent to the following effect, viz., that until the average price of wheat rose to 80s. the ports should be effectually closed. Colonial wheat was admitted when the average prices reached 67s. per quarter. Such were the leading features of the new Act. But the mode in which the average prices were determined greatly increased its stringency. An average was struck quarterly, on the 15th of February, May, August, and November, from the aggregate prices of the six preceding weeks; but it was provided that if, during the six weeks subsequent to any of these dates, the average prices, which might be at 80s., should fall below that price, no supplies should be admitted for home consumption from any ports between the rivers Eyder and Bidassoa,—that is, from Denmark to Spain inclusive.

In 1816, 1817, and 1818, the harvests were very deficient. Prices rose above the rate at which foreign supplies were admitted, and in these years a considerable importation of foreign corn took place. From January 1816 to June 1817, prices rose from 59s. 2d. to 120s. 6d. From June to September 1817, they fell from 120s. 6d. to 74s. 4d.; but three years afterwards, in 1821 and 1822, the agriculturists endured the most severe distress.

The following table shows the highest and lowest prices from 1815 to 1822:—

Years.	Highest.		Lowest.		Years.	Highest.		Lowest.	
	s.	d.	s.	d.		s.	d.	s.	d.
1815	70	3	55	8	1819	79	7	65	10
1816	113	2	56	9	1820	80	3	55	5
1817	120	6	74	4	1821	75	0	52	1
1818	93	1	75	4	1822	58	3	38	4

On the 15th July, 1822, a new Act received the Royal Assent, entitled, "An Act to amend the laws relating to the importation of corn." It alters and amends the 55 George III. c. 26 (the Act of 1815,) and enacts that "as soon as foreign wheat shall have been admitted for home consumption under the provisions of the said Act, the scale of prices, at which the home consumption of foreign corn, meal, or flour, is permitted by the said Act, shall cease and determine." The new scale was as follows:—Wheat at or above 70s., duty 12s.; and for the first three months of the ports being open, an additional duty of 5s. per quarter; above 70s. and under 80s., the "first low duty" of 5s.; above 80s. and under 85s., the "second low duty" of 1s. This Act did not come into operation, as prices never reached 80s.

In 1825 the trade in corn and grain to the British colonies in North America was placed on a more favourable footing. Instead of the scale by which the importation of wheat was regulated by the 55 Geo. III. c. 26, and 3 and 4 Geo. IV. c. 60, *a permanent duty of* 5s. *per quarter was imposed.*

In 1825 was also passed another Act, entitled "An Act to allow, until the 15th of August, 1825, the entry of warehoused corn, grain, and wheaten flour for home consumption on payment of duty;" that is, at a duty lower than that payable under the previous law. This Act provided that foreign corn secured in warehouse before May 13th, 1822, and wheaten flour warehoused under 5 Geo. IV. c. 70, might be taken out of bond under the following regulations:—Between the 15th June and 15th July, half the quantity warehoused might be liberated; and the remainder between the 15th July and 15th August, at a duty of 10s. Other descriptions of grain were permitted to be liberated on corresponding terms.

In the following year the Government took a still more decisive step to correct the operations of the Corn-law; and on the 1st of September an Order in Council was issued, by which certain descriptions of grain for home consumption were admitted, until forty days after the next meeting of Parliament, at an almost nominal rate of duty, on the ground that, "if the importation, for home consumption, of oats and oatmeal, and of rye, peas, and beans, be not immediately permitted, there is great cause to fear that much distress may ensue to all classes of his Majesty's subjects."

In 1827 Mr. Canning introduced certain resolutions in the House of Commons, founded upon which a Bill was brought in fixing a duty of 1s. on foreign wheat when the average price was 70s. per quarter; a duty of 2s. being imposed for the reduction of each shilling in the averages. In respect to colonial wheat, the duty was fixed at 6d. when the averages were 65s. per quarter. The Bill was not carried through the House of Lords. An Act, however, was passed during this session to permit corn, meal, &c. warehoused on the 1st of July, 1827, to be entered for home consumption upon payment of duties according to a scale which enabled the importer to introduce his stock at a duty of 1s. when the average prices of wheat in the home market were at 62s. and not under 61s., the duty falling 2s. for every rise of an additional shilling in the average price.

In 1828 Mr. Charles Grant (now Lord Glenelg) introduced a series of resolutions slightly differing from those moved by Mr. Canning, which were eventually embodied in a Bill which obtained the Royal Assent on the 15th of July. This measure is entitled "An Act to amend the Laws relating to the importation of Corn," and repeals 65 Geo. III. c. 26 (1815); 3 Geo. IV. c. 60 (1822); and 7 and 8 Geo. IV. c. 58 (1827). In one hundred and fifty towns in England and Wales mentioned in the Act, corn-dealers are required to make a declaration that they will return an accurate account of their purchases. (In London the sellers make the return.) In each of these towns inspectors are appointed who transmit returns to the receiver of the Corn Department of the Board of Trade, whose duty it is to compute the average weekly price of each description of grain, and the aggregate average price for the previous six weeks, and to transmit a certified copy to the collectors of customs at the different outports.

This Act constitutes the present Corn-law, and the following is the scale by which importation is regulated:—

When the Average of six Weeks per Quarter is s.	The Duty per Quarter is s. d.	Shewing an increase of s. d.
73 or above	1 0	
72 and under 73	2 8	1 8
71 ,, 72	6 8	4 0
70 ,, 71	10 8	4 0
69 ,, 70	13 8	3 0
68 ,, 69	16 8	3 0
67 ,, 68	18 8	2 0
66 ,, 67	20 8	2 0
65 ,, 66	21 8	1 0
64 ,, 65	22 8	1 0
63 ,, 64	23 8	1 0
62 ,, 63	24 8	1 0
61 ,, 62	25 8	1 0
60 ,, 61	26 8	1 0

and so on, increasing 1s. per quarter duty as the price of the wheat decreases 1s. per quarter.*

If the prices of corn during the last ten years be referred to, and it be recollected that in this interval parliamentary committees have sat, at the solicitation of the landed interest, to devise means for their relief, it may be assumed that the Corn-laws have failed in producing those good effects which their promoters so fondly anticipated. It appears that in good seasons the method adopted to regulate, or rather to prevent importation, has not proved so serviceable to the landowner as he expected, for prices have been extremely depressed, whilst in seasons of apprehended deficiency their operation has fallen with unmitigated severity on the consumer. The agriculturists of Great Britain ought not to require more than fair protection from foreign competition. The capital and property employed in the cultivation of the soil are entitled to protection; and the policy of awarding it must be admitted, although differences of opinion may exist as to the most eligible or efficient means by which it may be accomplished.

* Colonial wheat is admitted at a duty of 6d. when the averages are at or above 67s; and when below 67s. the duty is 5s.

The question for your consideration is, whether the Corn-laws have conferred on the landowner and farmer the advantages anticipated by their framers; and if they have not, whether an amended system may not be introduced, which shall afford adequate protection to the agriculturist in favourable seasons, and at the same time relieve the rest of the community from the heavy charges to which they are liable in unproductive ones. A code of laws under which corn has fallen to an extreme point of depression in productive seasons, and again reached to a very high price in unproductive ones, can neither be wise in theory nor useful in practice. In proof of this let me call to mind the abundant harvests commencing with 1832 and ending with 1836, during which period the average price of wheat gradually fell as low as 36s. per quarter, and to contrast with them the effect produced by the short crops in the last and present years, when the price rose to upwards of 75s., with apprehensions of further advance should the present harvest prove as unfavorable as many persons anticipate.

On an average of years we probably raise a quantity of wheat sufficient for the support of our population, but from the variations in the seasons we do not every year grow an average crop. Although an average supply may be yielded throughout a long period of years, the produce of some seasons will be under, and that of others above, our usual wants. The experience of late years has demonstrated that a succession of good harvests lowers the price of corn too much for the well-doing of the farmer, and that bad ones raise prices too high for the consumers. From the year 1833 to 1836 the complaints of the landed interest assumed a loud tone, and the cry of agricultural distress was universal. It is ascertained that the low prices then prevailing caused much soil to be withdrawn from the cultivation of wheat, and that a great deal of land was laid down in grass, or devoted to other modes of tillage, and hence the effects of the first unproductive year were more seriously felt. Since the advance in the prices of corn during the past and present years, fresh land has been brought into cultivation, and this will most probably so augment the supplies in the first favorable season, as again to bring down the price of agricultural produce to a low rate.

Allowing that the Corn-laws were framed with a view to protect the grower, the occurrences of the last few years prove that the cultivators of the soil have been subjected to the extremes of high and low prices, a condition by no means desirable for the farmer, and inconsistent with the welfare of the rest of the community. The commercial, manufacturing, and agricultural bodies should be linked together as one interest; the tendency of the present Corn-laws is to disunite them, and to split them into parties and factions, promoting discord instead of harmony, fostering a spirit of jealousy and discontent, and causing endeavours on the part of each to prosper at the expense of the others. But the position of either of these great interests cannot be regarded with indifference. The corn-grower furnishes the great staple of human subsistence; the manufacturer is engaged in producing fabrics required either at home or abroad; while the attention and enterprise of the merchant are directed to the conveyance of the raw or manufactured productions of this country to distant lands; bartering them for the precious metals, or for such foreign articles as may be useful at home or for exportation to other countries. The harmonious concord of these great interests is, however, disturbed by the operation of the present Corn-laws, which, if enacted with a view to favour the agricultural body, have not only entirely failed of their object, but have in turn produced injurious effects upon the manufacturing and commercial.

The fluctuating scale which regulates the importation of foreign corn acts on an average of years almost as a prohibition against its introduction. By its severe and fickle operation, we are discouraged from cultivating commercial intercourse on principles of reciprocal advantage with the corn-growing countries of Europe, and have moreover stimulated them to turn their attention to the establishment of manufactures. The hazardous results which are incidental to it prevent the more careful and prudent merchant from embarking his capital in the foreign corn-trade, and therefore it is left to individuals of a bolder and more daring spirit, or to persons more intimately acquainted with the details of the trade, who seek to realize gains commensurate with the risk they cannot avoid encountering. The foreign trade in corn, indeed, presents none of the regular features of ordinary commerce; it is a speculation in the widest sense of the word—a lottery, in which the gains are large if a supply be wanted, but the loss proportionably great in the opposite case. If those who engage in the trade fail to hit the market at a favorable moment, or be mistaken in their judgment of a supply being required, a severe loss on the adventure infallibly accrues by the operation of the duty, which, increasing in amount as the price of the corn falls, leaves to the importers no hope, under these adverse circumstances, of being relieved except by warehousing the grain, and keeping it in bond at an enormous charge until the return of another inclement season, when they may be enabled to retrieve their fortunes, and realize the capital embarked. Export would be unavailing to relieve them from the impending misfortune; for to say nothing of the heavy charges on removing an article so weighty as grain, it must not be forgotten that the price on the Continent had been influenced by a speculative demand for corn to meet an anticipated deficiency at home, and if the opinion of the existence of this deficiency were ill-founded, the price on the Continent would have fallen to its original point of depression. Besides, should the grain be re-exported before it is quite ascertained that it will not be required at home, the market-price of corn might rise again here, and the duty falling as the price rose, would again excite hopes of a successful result of the adventure, and point out the British ports as the most eligible for its deposit. The importers of corn have, therefore, no alternative under these adverse circumstances but to warehouse their grain, to take their chance of coming events, and wait patiently the course of seasons to relieve them from the difficulties and embarrassments which our system of Corn-laws entails on them. Should several following seasons yield an average crop, it is exceedingly probable that the expense of storing the corn imported may more than equal the first cost, and thus the whole capital originally embarked in the speculation may have been absorbed by unavoidable charges. I will bring facts under your notice to enable you to judge of the correctness of my statement. The quantity of foreign wheat and flour remaining in bond in January, 1833, was 670,000 quarters.* In the succeeding years the importation was exceedingly moderate until 1837, when there appears a considerable increase. In that year a considerable quantity of corn paid a high rate of duty, concerning which Mr. Tooke, in his excellent work on Prices,† remarks "that this entry of foreign

* See return to the House of Commons, No. 90. Session 1839.
† History of Prices.

wheat at so high a duty was not because the importation could afford that duty, but because the holders having been disappointed in their speculation on a much lower duty, were content to submit to a heavy loss in the alternative of having the wheat wholly shut out from a market for an indefinite length of time."

The following quantities of foreign corn paid duty for home consumption in the undermentioned years:

1833................	1,330 quarters.
1834................	390 ,,
1835................	125 ,,
1836................	1,945 ,,
1837................	210,900* ,,

Owing to the failure of the grain crop in America, there was a considerable export to the United States in the year 1837, and also to our colonial possessions, by which the quantity of corn in bond was reduced. The quantity remaining in bond on the 5th of January, 1838, was 585,000 quarters, and including wheat-meal and flour, 630,000 quarters.† The lowest expense of keeping wheat in bond is about 5s. per quarter per annum. If to this be added interest of money, deficiency in measurement, and

* The duty paid on this wheat was nearly £300,000.

† 392 lbs. of meal or flour are computed as a quarter.

perhaps accidental deterioration for the long period during which the corn remained in bond with the duty at a prohibitory rate, a loss equal to the original cost was probably sustained by the importers of foreign corn. Too many of our merchants can unfortunately corroborate the truth of this statement, if any doubt of its perfect accuracy were entertained.

Some alleviation might be afforded, if the suggested permission to grind foreign corn in bond were granted; for once made into flour, it assumes a marketable shape, by being rendered useful for such of our shipping as are engaged in distant voyages, who are permitted to supply themselves with foreign provisions, or the flour might be exported to such parts of our colonial possessions as are annually supplied with that article from the United States or Continental Europe. This permission would offer some chance of escaping from the total loss which of late years has overtaken those who have had the misfortune of engaging in the foreign corn-trade, or, in other words, who have attempted to supply the supposed deficiency of an unproductive harvest.

If the evil extended no further—if the Corn-laws only entailed loss or even ruin upon the speculator or importer, it might be deemed of minor importance, but it may be easily imagined that such untoward circumstances do not occur without involving other classes in the failure. Being unwilling to receive supplies of foreign corn, except at the moment when famine prices threaten us, we deny ourselves the opportunity of exchanging with our continental neighbours what might be advantageous either for their or our consumption. Unable, therefore, to cultivate commercial relations with those countries upon any regular or settled principles as to the interchange of commodities, we are compelled, in seasons of dearth, to make good the deficiency of an unproductive harvest by purchasing supplies of foreign corn with an export of the precious metals instead of the manufactured productions of this country.

Assuming, therefore, that the failure of the harvest be considered a national calamity, we increase the difficulty attendant upon this untoward state of things by the export of bullion, and hence the quantity of money required for the ordinary wants and convenience of the country is diminished. By exporting the precious metals the circulation becomes contracted, and money is rendered scarce, and the evil of an increase in the price of the necessaries of life is aggravated by a deficiency of means of purchasing them. The monetary pressure at home occasioned by the export of bullion is much heightened by the competition of buyers of corn in foreign countries, all anxious to purchase at the *nearest* market to enable them with more certainty to catch the favorable moment for its introduction *at the lowest rate of duty*. In consequence of this competition amongst the purchasers of corn, the price is raïsed against ourselves in the foreign markets, and this increase in price must of course require a larger sum of money to pay for the corn which our necessities may demand. A greater quantity of the precious metals will, therefore, necessarily be withdrawn from the circulation of the country, and a difficulty of procuring money for ordinary commercial transactions is added to the inconvenience arising from the augmentation in the price of the most important article of human consumption.

The commercial disadvantages to which we are subject by the Corn Laws arise from our being unable to meet the foreigner upon the ordinary principles of reciprocal interchange. We have little intercourse with the continental Corn-grower except when the fear of scarcity compels us to resort to his country to purchase the necessaries of life. It is not reasonable to suppose, when hunger drives us to his granaries, that we can bargain about the conditions upon which we are to receive our supplies. At that moment we cannot reject his corn, if he does not take our manufactures in exchange. How can we propose or insist on such conditions? Corn being a necessary of life, and under regulations nearly amounting in ordinary seasons to a prohibition, the foreigner knows why we come to his market; he is aware that we would not apply so urgently to him unless we were threatened by scarcity. He will, therefore, not sell, except on his own terms. We cannot expect him to act otherwise. His granaries would not have been resorted to by us except to provide for our pressing necessities. Why should he offer his corn cheap, or exchange it for British manufactures? Having no regular communication with us, he has no taste for our productions, but procures for himself what he requires for his clothing or convenience through such channels, whether foreign or domestic, as offer him the more ready and frequent opportunity of providing for his wants on the principle of constant and regular intercourse.

It is, therefore, most unreasonable to suppose that when we attempt to trade with the foreigner at times "few and far between," he can sell us his corn unless we pay him in the material which shall be of the most useful and current description. It is probable that the foreign corn-grower may on these occasions feel inclined to receive a small portion of British manufactured articles, but the quantity of goods that he will thus take can bear but a very small proportion to the amount in money that we must necessarily pay him for the corn that we require. Can it be expected that he should buy our manufactured goods, consisting either of cotton, linen, or woollen, whether they be articles of necessity or luxury, when the productions of his country are depreciated by our policy, and himself compelled to wear the cheapest and commonest fabrics of domestic make, and thus prevented from acquiring a taste for goods of British origin? It has been said that, if even the Corn-laws were altered, the foreigner would not buy our manufactured goods—be it so. If he will not buy what we desire to dispose of, we shall be the less able to purchase what he has to sell, and those countries who are unwilling to cultivate friendly relations on the great principle of mutual intercourse, will be shut out from the advantage of sending us their surplus grain unless they will receive British merchandize in payment for it. If better principles had prevailed, as large a quantity of corn as our necessities required might have been bought at considerably less cost, by which we should have at least moderated the export of the precious metals, and warded off some of the distress and difficulty which has fallen with such severity upon the commercial and trading classes. Some amendment, therefore, seems imperatively required in a law which has a tendency to increase the price of grain and promote the exportation of bullion in large masses, and which compels us to buy corn at the dearest instead of the cheapest market.

Although I am unwilling to divide attention by intermixing the question of currency with that of the Corn-laws, a passing observation on the effect produced on the circulation by the large importation of corn during the last year, and the export of bullion to those countries from whence our supply of grain has been derived, cannot be considered irrelevant. The apprehension that the Bank of England might be unable to stand the drain of specie, the efforts to reduce its circulation, the extraordinary rise in the rate of interest, and the sufferings which these measures have occasioned, are sufficiently notorious. The suggestions made to relieve the pressure on the trading interests by an issue of small notes, although prohibited by Act of Parliament, prove the severity of the distress, as well as the difficulty of providing a suitable remedy for the existing emergency. The only means of preventing a recurrence of similar evils appears to be by making such a change in the Corn-laws as may bring grain within the same regulations as are provided for other articles of commerce. It is not my intention to raise the question whether any, or what portion of blame, attaches to the Bank of England for not having endeavoured earlier to counteract the export of bullion by such restrictive proceedings as would have been more gradual in their operation, and therefore less oppressive to the community. You may, however, be assured that the pressure on the commercial interest could not have been avoided, nor the scarcity of money prevented, even if the circulation had been regulated on the principles contended for by those who assert that the paper currency should fluctuate in an exact ratio with the increase or diminution of the precious metals. Assuming, therefore, that the circulation had varied in the same manner as if the currency had been entirely composed of the precious metals, instead of consisting of a portion only of bullion and the rest paper, can it be supposed that if the country were compelled in the course of a few months, by sudden demand, to pay a large part of its currency for the purchase of foreign corn, the pressure of this drain will not be most seriously felt? A greater exercise of foresight on the part of the Bank Direction might probably have alleviated, but it never could have entirely prevented the inconvenience resulting from the diminution of the stock of bullion necessary for maintaining the circulation in a healthy state. The Bank would certainly have been in an easier position had it adopted restrictive measures earlier, but the commercial interests of the country would have been equally exposed to severe privations.

If the present shifting scale of duty was intended to protect the farmer, keep the prices of corn steady, ensure a supply to the consumer at a moderate price, and benefit the revenue whenever an importation was required, it has signally failed.

During the continuance of the Corn-laws the farmers have suffered the severest privations. The variations in price have been extreme, and when a supply of foreign corn has been required for the consumption of the country, it has not reached the consumer except at a very high price, whilst but little advantage has accrued to the revenue. Instead of the descending scale of duty promoting a supply in proportion to the rise in the price, experience has demonstrated the contrary. The risks which persons must incur by bringing corn from abroad are inevitably great; for should it afterwards appear that the home supply was sufficient for the wants of the country, and no advance of price consequently took place sufficient to compensate the importer, his loss would be considerable. Whenever, therefore, a demand for foreign corn takes place, his gain must bear some proportion to the risk he has incurred. It is evident that the fall in the duty operates as a *bounty* in favor of the speculator, tempting him to keep his corn out of the market as long as possible. For this object, whenever circumstances indicate that a foreign supply will be required, and an advance in the market takes place, the speculators, without any other combination than that arising from self-interest, withhold making sales, notwithstanding the rise of price may afford them a fair profit on their corn. Their gain is calculated not only on the *advance in the price of the corn*, but also on the *fall in the scale of the duty*, and as the duty *falls* in a greater ratio than the price of the corn *rises*, the duty operates as a *bounty* to withhold sales until it reaches its *highest protecting point*, when the *duty is also at the lowest.* It is by this means that the revenue received from grain admitted for home consumption is inconsiderable, for corn is seldom taken out of bond until the lowest rate of duty is attained. Then, again, should there be a large supply of corn taken out of bond and entered for home consumption, the average *price is sure to fall*, and *the duty to rise*, for the speculator, having made his profit by the reduction of the duty, is less concerned about selling a few shillings per quarter higher or lower. His profit is secured by the operation of the duty, as may be seen by the following description. Let it be supposed an opinion prevailed that a supply of foreign corn would be required for the consumption of the country, and that with this impression a purchase of corn had been made on the Continent deliverable in London at 40s. per quarter, and that it arrives here when the average price is at 66s. per quarter. The duty on wheat at 66s. being 20s. 8d.* a moderate profit might be made by selling the corn, duty paid, at that price. But the impression that the supply will be required induces the speculator to hold back in the confidence that should the averages reach 70s. he not only would gain 4s. *by the rise in the market, but* 10s. *more by the diminution in the duty*, making an *increase* of profit of 14s. Should the averages reach 71s., *he gains another profit of* 4s. *in the duty* with only an increase of 1s. in the price, making an addition of 5s., or an increase of profit of 19s. Should the averages advance to 72s., *another gain of* 5s. *is secured*, being a rise of 1s. in price, and a diminution of 4s. in duty, making his profit 24s. When the averages are at 73s., the extreme limit is attained, the duty being only 1s. per quarter; so that if an importation were made that might be sold at or about 66s., paying a duty of 20s. 8d., by withholding the supply until the extreme limit of 73s. be reached, a *gain* of 7s. not only would be made by the *rise* in the averages, but also a *profit* of 19s. 8d. by the *reduction* of the duty, making a *total*

* See the scale at page 12.

increased profit of 26s. 8d. Can we wonder that in seasons of apprehended dearth the price of corn reaches the utmost limit provided by the Act, when the tendency of the fluctuating scale is, not to promote, but to withhold the supply, not to keep corn from fluctuation, but to offer a *bounty* for raising it to that extreme point when the merely nominal duty is imposed? And, again, can the depression in the market occasion surprise? The corn importer, having succeeded in getting his corn admitted at a low duty, has no longer any object in keeping back the supply, and presses it forward for sale, which, *reducing* the price, *raises* the duty. Thus, by the operation of the double action of a rise in price and diminution in the duty, he protects himself from the admission of any corn on the same advantageous terms that he has secured for himself. If a state of things, such as above described, be conceived occurring just before harvest-time, an accumulated quantity of foreign corn being admitted for home consumption, you may easily suppose that the price will be affected by the supply thrown into the market, to the great injury of the British grower, who, in fact, would have to contend with a mass of foreign corn *duty free*, instead of having that fair protection which a better system would undoubtedly afford.

A very interesting account, to which your attention is particularly directed, is here given, extracted from the returns presented to Parliament, shewing the weekly averages from the commencement of the year 1838, to Jan. 5th, 1839, and from that date to July last, the importation of foreign corn during that period, and the quantity that paid duty in each month. It appears from this return that the price of corn in January, 1838, was moderate, viz., 53s., and the duty 33s. 8d. per quarter. The prices of grain were rising gradually from that date during the whole year.* The importation of foreign wheat from the 5th January to the 5th June, 1838, did not exceed 30,605 quarters. At this date the prices of wheat had advanced to 61s. 3d., and the duty had fallen to 25s. 8d.

The opinion gaining ground that the stock of wheat in the country would probably bc insufficient for its consumption, the importations increased considerably,† but *notwithstanding these importations and the stock remaining in granary* amounting to 585,000 quarters,‡ which had probably been in bond for some years, only the most trifling quantities were

* Vide Appendix. † See Appendix.

‡ Including meal, to 630,000 quarters.

entered at the current rates of duty for home consumption, viz.:

From January to June	......	2,570
,,	July	2,983
,,	August	11,394
	Total	16,947

In the month of September, the price having advanced to 73s., and the duty fallen to 1s., the whole of the quantity *imported during the year, and also that which had remained in bond from former importations,* amounting altogether to upwards of 1,440,000 quarters, paid the lowest rates of duty, and was admitted for home consumption, viz.:—

		Quarters.		s.	d.
Sept. 6	......	28,524	paid a duty of	2	8
Sept. 13	......	1,261,894	,,	1	0
Sept. 20	......	102,652	,,	2	8
Sept. 27	......	47,639	,,	10	8
		1,440,709*			

The averages then declined to 64s. 3d., and the duty advanced to 22s. 8d. The importation of foreign corn continued, and, with little exception, it was placed in bond until December, when the averages again reaching 73s., and the duty 1s., another quan-

* The total quantity, including flour, is 1,513,113 quarters.

tity of 260,000 quarters was admitted at the lowest duty, viz.:—

		Quarters.		s.	d.
Dec. 13	....	110,068	paid a duty of	1	0
Dec. 20	....	61,094	,,	1	0
Dec. 27	....	57,190	,,	1	0
Jan. 3, 1839	....	30,193	,,	1	0
		258,545			

It being then ascertained that last year's harvest was very deficient in quantity, and that a supply of foreign corn would be necessary, the price maintained itself at or above 73s., and the duty at 1s. Large supplies continued to arrive during the winter months, which were regularly entered for home consumption at the low duty of 1s., and the corn-market kept up until the latter end of the month of April. During this period 828,963 quarters were admitted at the lowest rates of duty. The price of corn then declined slightly, and the duty rose to 10s. 8d., when a large proportion of the wheat imported was placed in bond, until the duty falling to 6s. 8d., in the month of June, nearly the whole quantity was entered for home consumption, leaving on the 5th of July last but 40,000 quarters remaining in bond.

The following are the quantities of wheat

imported into Great Britain in the year ending January 5, 1839, specifying the countries from whence it came:—

	Wheat and Wheat Flour. Quarters.
Prussia	586,003
Germany	350,138
Denmark	133,565
Holland	82,010
France	60,830
Russia	41,408
Italy	31,006
Guernsey, Jersey, foreign	24,176
Belgium	18,436
British North American Colonies	11,647
Malta	11,355
United States of America	6,141
East Indies	5,403
Ionian Islands	5,370
Turkey	3,150
Egypt	811
Spain	421
Gibraltar	57
Portugal and Madeira	15
	1,372,332 *

By this statement it will be seen that the quantity of foreign corn imported into the United

* Of this quantity only 40,000 quarters of corn had been imported up to the month of May.

Kingdom from Jan. to June, 1838, was very inconsiderable. The large importation then commenced, nearly the whole of which was bonded, and remained in granary until the lowest point of duty was attained, when the immense amount of upwards of 1,440,000 quarters was admitted at once. After this the average price fell, and the duty rose to 22s. 8d. per quarter. The subsequent importations were again bonded until the price again rose to upwards of 73s., and the duty fell to 1s., when upwards of 260,000 quarters more were admitted; shewing that of 1,728,452 quarters of wheat admitted for home consumption in a few months of 1838, upwards of 1,700,000 quarters were taken out of bond at the lowest rate of duty. The returns for the half year, from last January to the 5th of July, shew that 1,600,000 quarters of wheat were admitted for home consumption, the greatest portion of which paid the lowest rates of duty.*

Having pointed out some of the evils of a fluctuating scale of duties for regulating the importation of corn, I come now to consider the advantages

* About 800,000 quarters have been admitted since July, *of which quantity nearly* 770,000 quarters were admitted in the month ending 10th of October.

which a fixed duty seems to present. It would be immaterial to the cultivator of the soil how protection is afforded so long as native produce is not depreciated by the growth of cheaper and less taxed countries. A fixed duty would be more uniform in its operation, and, in my opinion, equally beneficial for the protection of the farmer. The principle of protection being conceded, it seems material that the duty should be sufficient to prevent the British market from being inundated by the lower-priced corn of other countries. I cannot doubt that a rate of duty may be established, which shall be amply sufficient to protect the corn-grower from undue competition, and to ensure to the consumer a supply of corn in all seasons at a moderate price. The interests of the producers and consumers of corn might by this means be more closely identified. To regulate importation by a fixed duty would remedy the inconvenience arising from the little temptation offered to the commercial body to purchase a supply of corn when grain is cheap upon the continent. If our more opulent merchants were enabled to embark in the foreign Corn-trade, which, from the risks they must incur, they are unwilling to enter into under the existing regulations, they would doubtless go to the more distant market, and avail themselves of the favorable moment when corn might be purchased on the most advantageous terms. By this means an ample supply would be secured from the foreigner with the smallest outlay of money; whereas at present the hazards attending the importation of corn, and the details of management necessary to its success, limit the number of persons inclined to engage in the trade. It consequently remains in comparatively few hands, who are thereby better able to act in concert for the purpose of controlling the markets. This affords facilities for withholding the supply of corn until they are enabled to dispose of it for the consumption of the country at the extreme rate when a mere nominal duty is payable.

The corn countries of Europe are also subjected to the extremes of high and low prices arising from the fluctuations in this country. In ordinary seasons they grow more corn than they can consume, and having no ready demand for exportation in consequence of our high duty on foreign grain, the price becomes greatly depreciated in the country of its growth, impoverishing the grower, and depriving ourselves of the benefits resulting from active intercourse with them, except when under the alarm of scarcity. We are then driven to seek for subsistence at such prices as the foreign grower may demand. The advocates for the permanence of the present Corn-laws have laid much stress on the great variations in the prices of grain on the Continent, but it seems to have been lost sight of by them that those changes are produced by speculations entered into whenever a foreign supply is necessary for this country. If it were to my purpose, I could furnish evidence of the gambling that takes place in the continental ports whenever there is a prospect of the duty falling so low as to allow an importation of grain here on favourable terms. The rise in price caused by an influx of orders from this country, and the reaction occasioned by the prohibitory principle of our Corn-laws being again brought into operation, are reflected in the European markets, thereby shewing that all the Corn countries are .subject to violent fluctuations promoted by our moveable scale of duties. The very low rates which have tended so to increase the alarm of the British agriculturists at the prospect of home-grown corn being depreciated in price by the cheap commodity which might be imported, can be traced to the operation of our

Corn-laws. But the supposition of extreme cheapness must in some measure be erroneous. Although it be admitted that corn is grown cheaper abroad than in this country, it cannot be cultivated anywhere without considerable labour, and moreover the expense of bringing it to market must everywhere be incurred. Its specific gravity and the chances of its deterioration by vermin and other accidental causes are nearly equal in all countries. Whatever may be the cost of its production even in the cheapest country, heavy charges must always be incurred before it can be brought in a marketable state to our shores.

It is difficult to believe that, proceeding upon the best evidence that can be obtained of the cost at which corn can be imported from the several grain-ports of Europe and America, we could not suggest a permanent duty that should afford adequate protection to the English grower. Encouraged by the uniformity of a fixed duty, the merchant would purchase corn in the cheapest country on the same principle as any other commodity. He would import and warehouse it here until the state of the market would induce him to pay the duty upon its admission for home consumption. In this case, he would only run the ordinary risk which he must incur with any other species of merchandize. He would either gain or lose according as the market price of corn rose or fell, and would not encounter the superadded contingency of great gain or serious loss, produced solely by the fluctuation in the duty. A fixed duty would always ensure us a quantity of corn ready for immediate use the moment we required it. This supply would be brought *gradually* to market, and would probably find its way to this country as a remittance in exchange for merchandize or manufactures disposed of by us in the countries where the corn is produced. Whenever any portion of foreign corn was admitted for home consumption, the foreigner would have to dispose of his corn to the British consumer at a price *minus* the duty and profit to the importer, by which the farmer would enjoy a sure protection, and a revenue would also be obtained in aid of the taxes of the country. Under the present system the importer or speculator waits till the duty is either at the lowest point, or very near it, by which means foreign corn *free of duty* is actually consumed. Thus the revenue is injured without the least advantage either to the farmer or consumer, whilst a bounty is offered to the foreigner to come to this country and dispose of his corn at the highest price, instead of selling it to us at a low one.

If the principle of a fixed duty were adopted, the more distant markets would be equally available with those nearer home for supplying our wants, and the more extended the number of places at which we could obtain our supplies, the more moderate would be the price at which the corn might be procured. Instead, therefore, of every one rushing to the ports *nearest* to Great Britain for the purpose of securing a low rate of duty, we should have all the markets of the world open to our choice, and the ports where corn could be procured on the *cheapest* terms would be those most resorted to. If even we had to pay for our corn in bullion, which is extremely improbable with a constant trade, the more distant market would still be the more convenient. The prime cost of commodities is always lower at the point most distant from the place of demand, the difference in price between that and the nearer port being composed of increased freight and insurance, interest of money, and other charges incidental to the longer voyage, the prime cost of the corn being the chief disbursement made to the foreigner, whilst the freight and interest of money would probably be due to our own merchants.* Perhaps we may better explain this by the following:—Suppose corn be purchased at Hamburg at 40s. per quarter, free on board of a British ship, and that the freight and charges amount to 5s. per quarter more, the corn on arrival in London would cost 45s. The probable distribution of this cost would be, that the foreigner would receive 40s., and the British ship-owner 5s. per quarter. If a quarter of corn were purchased at one of the Mediterranean ports for 32s., the freight and charges would probably amount to 13s.; the cost price of wheat of the same quality as the Hamburg would, therefore, be also 45s. But the first cost of the wheat being in this latter case 32s., and in the other 40s., a saving of one-fourth of bullion would take place in buying our corn at the further instead of the nearer port. We are in this case assuming that the corn is similar in quality, and that British shipping is employed in both instances. But in consequence of the operation of our corn-laws, the distant ports are less resorted to, and the difference in the cost, instead of being only one-fourth, is often nearer double the price. It is, therefore, most important to us, when compelled

* It may be observed that the merchants of the Baltic ports, from whence such large quantities of corn are imported into this country, are also ship-owners, whereas British shipping is more largely employed to bring corn from the more southern ports of Europe.

to purchase our supplies with the precious metals, whether we buy our corn at 25s. or 50s. per quarter, —or whether we pay two and a half millions of pounds sterling for one million of quarters of wheat, or merely half that sum. With the present scale of duties, if the merchants went to the more distant countries, it is probable that before the arrival of the cargoes the price might have fallen considerably, and they would then be subjected to the loss, not only from any unfavorable turn in the market, but from the increase of duty also, which, had they gone to nearer ports, they might perchance have avoided.

If it be said that the more distant markets cannot afford the large quantity we require in the case of a deficient harvest, and that therefore the Baltic ports must always be resorted to as being the granaries of the corn-growing countries, I reply that we should be able to receive supplies both from near and distant ports, whilst at present we can in the first instance only go to the nearest. Amongst the countries nearest to us from whence supplies may be procured, Spain may be mentioned.* If order were restored there, and her resources developed, we might receive corn from her, in exchange for which she would be sure to require our manufactures. Amongst

* In the year 1831 we received a considerable supply from Spain.

the more distant countries may be included the United States of America, whose productive powers are very great, and where, no doubt, in case of a regular trade in corn, a constant supply could be procured. But the observation with regard to the more distant markets is intended to apply to price as well as to quantity, as affording a wider range for procuring supplies, and consequently at lower rates.

The following are the countries from whence we have received supplies from the 5th January to the 5th of July in the present year, shewing that when it was ascertained that the prices of corn would be maintained, the more distant ports were resorted to.*

Prussia	247,480
Italy	240,944
Germany . . .	218,794
France †	179,929
Holland	97,502
Denmark . . .	90,440
Russia	79,710
Turkey	33,471
Portugal	19,753
Carried up	1,208,023
Brought up	1,208,023
Malta	15,671
Belgium	13,052
Ionian Islands . .	8,424
Spain	8,833
Gibraltar	3,931
America	729
Other countries	4,466
Total	1,260,030‡

* I have been unable to obtain a correct return of the countries from whence foreign wheat has been imported into the United Kingdom during the first six months of the present year, but I have been favoured with the quantities received at London, Liverpool, Hull, and Newcastle.

† Chiefly from the Mediterranean ports.

‡ The total quantity of wheat admitted during the first six months was 1,618,744 ; of wheat meal 448,274, making a total of upwards of 1,746,000.

Great pains have been taken to propagate the opinion that grain would fall to a very low rate in case of any alteration of the present Corn-law. This notion appears to me erroneous. I cannot believe that the average price of corn would be materially lowered in this country if a fixed duty were established. It is more likely that we should raise the price of the produce of the poorer country, whose grain is now depressed from the absence of demand, than that our markets should be regulated by the quantity of corn they could send to us. Prices abroad will, therefore, assuredly rise instead of our markets falling. The principle of a fixed duty would entirely equalize the price of corn between Great Britain and the corn-growing countries of the world in every respect, with the exception of that amount of duty and profit to the importer. The rate of living here and on the continent, as respects corn, would be equalized, and as all the continental powers of Europe encourage the manufacture of goods of the same description as are made in this country, any advance in the price of corn on the continent must prove advantageous to the English artizan. The effect of the present Corn-law is to depress agriculture on the continent, reduce the rate of living there, and consequently the price of labour. This reduction in the wages of labour is an injury to ourselves, for manufactured goods can be made cheaper abroad than in this country, in consequence of the difference in the price of corn, which influences the wages of labour. The rapid mode of communication which is afforded by the means of steam conveyance has a tendency to equalize the prices of merchandise in all the markets of the world, and commercial capital, which a few years ago was only to be found in abundance in this country, has been greatly accumulated on the continent also. By this rapidity of communication, the variations in the prices of merchandize in Great Britain become more speedily known, and are quickly followed in the foreign markets.* The prices abroad being influenced by those current in this country a rise takes place simultaneously with ours, in all the markets and ports of continental Europe and of America also. In discussing our corn-law legislation, we must not forget that the law of 1828, which has now been eleven years in operation, was framed to meet the circumstances of the landed interest at that time, and regulated according to the then prevalent opinions. Since that period many great and

* See Appendix.

important changes have taken place, amongst which may be included the improvement of our system of agriculture, by which soils of every quality are cultivated at less cost and yield an enlarged produce.

Fears have been expressed that a fixed duty never could be maintained when wheat was selling at a high rate. This is perhaps true; but it may be asked in reply whether we have any duty under the present system when the price of corn reaches its minimum rate of protection. If, therefore, the duty were remitted when the price of corn rose to a high value, we should not be in a worse condition than at present. But a fixed duty is recommended on the assumption that, if it were adopted, a supply would always be reaching our shores, or deposited in granary, ready to be brought to market with every rise in the price that would afford a profit; whilst, under the present system, the corn is kept back until the foreign speculator is able to pocket that sum, which, in a fixed rate of duty, would find its way into the revenue coffers and benefit the nation at large. By the present system the rapid rise in the price to which the market is subject falls heavily on the consumer, and the sudden reaction caused by the quantity of corn released out of bond and thrown on the market, materially injures the farmer also. Assuming even that corn can be grown and imported into this country on an average of seasons at 40s., which is denied by many, and a duty of 15s. were imposed, it could not be sold at less than 55s., including the duty. Suppose a bad harvest should occur here, and the price of corn were to advance, a corresponding rise of probably as many shillings would take place in the continental markets, as would be equivalent to the advance in the British market. It must be remembered likewise that under a fixed duty no temptation is held out to persons to keep their corn any length of time out of the market; the prospect of a rise of a few shillings in price will not tempt them to do it, for the charges on keeping corn in granary are heavy. The object of the importer would rather be to turn his capital often by means of quick sales, than incur the risk of losing interest of money, and adding to the cost of his corn by bonding and keeping it in store, when he might secure a profit on his adventure by bringing it to market. The present Corn-laws, on the contrary, offer an inducement to withhold the supplies in the hope of making a large profit not only by the rise in the market value of the corn, but by means of reduction in the rate of duty. If that temptation were removed, the principles that regulate every other trade would be brought into action, and the corn importer will be as ready as other merchants to realize his proceeds, and to embark his capital again in new adventures. Moderate profits and quick returns would then become the ruling motto in the corn, as in every other trade.

It is feared by many that if the import of corn were regulated by a fixed duty instead of the present fluctuating one, capital would be withdrawn from the cultivation of land, and the agricultural interests greatly injured. Such fears, I feel assured, are entirely unfounded; on the contrary, I confidently believe that the value of land would be favourably affected by such alteration. The controversy respecting the withdrawal of the protection given by the present Corn-laws, and the substitution of some other mode, is prejudicial to the landed interest. So long as a large portion of our population are exhibiting symptoms of discontent and dissatisfaction with our present Corn-laws, and threatening their abolition, agriculture cannot be considered in a healthy condition. The belief so industriously circulated that the land requires protection inconsistent with the welfare of other great interests equally worthy of legislative encouragement, cannot be favourable to the capital invested in agricultural pursuits. The fear of this protection being suddenly withdrawn must be prejudicial. To this must be added the demand so frequently made for legislative interference which may be traced to our corn-laws. These stimulate prices in unfavourable seasons, by which enlarged cultivation is promoted. They at the same time give facilities to the corn speculator to hold back an accumulated stock of foreign wheat until the lowest point of duty is reached, which being then thrown on the market in an overwhelming mass, tends to bring on a violent reaction of prices to the injury of the farmer, and agricultural distress ensues. If the Corn-laws were once arranged on a definite principle of protection by means of a fixed and moderate duty, all controversy would cease, and nothing would prevent the flow of capital towards the cultivation of the land. The farmer would also feel assured that his trade would then be less liable to variation, that his best exertions must be applied to the cultivation of the land to increase its productive power according to the most approved systems, and to maintain the lead for British produce against any competition with which he may be threatened by the foreign corn-grower.

Another objection to a change in the Corn-laws arises from the belief that inferior land will be driven out of cultivation. I do not believe that the poorer lands would be seriously affected by such an alteration. The present fluctuations in the price of corn affect unfavourably the poorer soils. The cropping of them is often undertaken *out of course*, when the price of corn has been artificially raised. If the market should have afterwards fallen so as not to allow the farmer to realise the price upon which he had calculated, a heavy loss must be sustained by him through variations promoted by the Corn-laws, which were intended to favour the poorer land by encouraging the hope of high prices. The increasing dearness of hay, sheep, and other live-stock during the last few years, shews that there are many other means of cultivating the poorer soils profitably, whilst the too frequent growth of wheat, exhausting the soil, requires such an outlay of capital as cannot be compensated unless by continued high average prices, whereas if a more judicious course of rotations were steadily adopted in all seasons, a more profitable result might be anticipated.

Having shewn the disadvantages attending the present fluctuating scale of duties, and the advantages to be derived by adopting the principle of a fixed duty, a difficulty of some magnitude presents itself. This difficulty is the amount of the duty; for if it were fixed very high, it would prove equal to a prohibition, and would therefore be inoperative for any useful purpose; if it were very low, the opposition it would encounter from the landed interest would render the attempt to settle this question on equitable principles entirely nugatory. In advocating a new system for regulating the trade in Corn, it would be desirable to obtain the confidence and support of the agricultural body, who are so greatly interested in the proposed change. I am desirous that those who have invested their capital in land, and who have been induced to make expensive improvements to increase its fertility on the faith of the system of protection being adhered to, shall feel confident that they will not be injured. The average prices of corn in the several more important grain-ports of Europe and America have been examined with a view of suggesting a rate of duty which shall conciliate the corn-grower by securing him a fair price for his produce, and also protect the consumer from the high prices which the speculators have been enabled to realize whenever the wants of the country have required a foreign supply. Some persons are of opinion that a very moderate duty, added to the charges that must necessarily be incurred by bringing the corn from foreign countries, would be sufficient for the farmer, and that a duty of 6s. or 7s. would be an equitable protection. This sum appears to me inadequate, for without discussing whether the farmer and landlord pay any, and how much, more rates and taxes than other classes, it is desirable to *offer encouragement to the production of the necessaries of life at home*, and therefore a higher rate of protection should be afforded. Others are inclined to concede a duty of 10s. which they think would be ample; I am inclined, however, to believe that this amount would also prove unsatisfactory. On an examination of the prices at which corn may be imported into this country from New York, Rotterdam, Hamburgh, and Dantzic, it would appear that on an average of seasons corn could not be brought here below rates averaging from 35s. to 40s. per quarter. If to this be added a duty of 15s.

on all corn imported from places in Europe outside the Straits of Gibraltar, and 12s. from all other parts of the world, which is the amount I propose, it would bring the price from 50s. to 55s. per quarter, and this may be considered a remunerating price to the British grower. In ordinary seasons, therefore, this protecting duty would save the farmer from foreign competition. He would be as well protected by this duty as by the Corn-law now in force, for until the price of wheat shall have advanced to upwards of 50s., he would be safe from the competition of the foreign corn-grower, whilst the interests of other classes would be equally secured. Should the price rise above this limit, foreign corn would partake of the advantage that the British market might offer. But the importer of foreign grain would, under no circumstances, desire to undersell the British corn-grower. He would have an equal interest with him in endeavouring to get as much for his corn as the market would afford. The aim of every one is to get the most he can for his merchandise, and there is no reason to believe that a dealer in corn will act upon a different impulse to that of a dealer in any other article. If the corn-market of the last year be referred to, when foreign corn has constantly come into competition with that of home growth, it does not appear that the foreigner has attempted to undersell the English farmer by offering corn at less than its market value. On the contrary, in his endeavours to gain as much as possible, he deposits the corn in bond, and appears by no means inclined to sell it, except at the utmost price. It is, therefore, as unlikely that the foreigner will try to sell below the market price with a permanent duty, as that he should do so under the operation of the present Corn-laws. If, therefore, the farmer be insured from injurious competition by means of an ample fixed duty, which shall be high enough to secure him a fair remunerating price, his produce would be put on the same footing as that of any other branch of British industry, and he would obtain all the protection he ought to derive from any legislative enactment.

The object of a fixed duty being to correct violent fluctuations in price, and to secure a supply for the consumer in all seasons at a moderate rate, some method may be proposed to guard also the farmer's produce from being exposed to such a great depression as prevailed three years ago. As a portion of foreign corn will always be ready in the market to compete with that of British growth, thereby preventing its reaching a high price except under extraordinary circumstances, means may be suggested which shall also most effectually protect British corn from any extreme depression. This object may be attained, first, by imposing such an increased duty as will be a sufficient security against the admission of corn while prices are low. I propose, therefore, that when the average price of corn is below 50s. the duty shall be 25s. per quarter, which will be a security that so long as the price is below 50s. the farmer will be amply protected against foreign competition. Secondly, a further advantage might be secured to the farmer, *by giving to persons exporting British corn or meal the privilege to enter an equal quantity of foreign grain for home consumption duty free, within a period to be limited by Act of Parliament*, and under such restrictions as shall secure the revenue from any abuse. The permission to export British Corn with power of replacing an equal amount of foreign, would be the best guarantee to the farmer against any extreme depreciation of home-grown produce. This privilege would operate as a bounty, for when prices fell, a demand would surely spring up by speculators, who would make purchases of British corn for exportation in the hope of profiting by the importation of an equal quantity of foreign duty free, whenever, by a change of circumstances, the market price would admit of it. With such an advantage secured to the British Corn-grower, he need fear no competition with the cheapest countries, and if those high prices by which his imagination may have been dazzled in connection with the the present system, be considered remote, he may also bid defiance to that extreme depression which so recently threatened him with total ruin, notwithstanding the protection which the Corn-laws are supposed to afford.

If the principle of a fixed rate of protection is sufficient for other articles of British origin, no dissimilar one can be necessary for securing the prosperity of the cultivators of the soil. The argument put forth that the farmer's trade depends upon the state of the weather, is not sufficient to justify a deviation. His occupation cannot be considered a hazardous one; it is certainly influenced by the variations in the seasons; but thanks to Providence, these changes are not of such a nature as to involve him, in any year, in extraordinary losses or overwhelming misfortunes. If the weather be cold and moist, and therefore unfavorable for wheat the loss sustained thereby will in some measure be repaired by the superior growth of his spring-corn, grass, and vegetable crops. If, on the contrary, the season be hot and dry, an abundant harvest awaits the farmer to offer a fair return for his capital and labour. In one respect, his occupation differs from that of the trader; his property neither accumulates nor depreciates so rapidly; if he has not the prospect of such large gains, he is also out of the reach of misfortunes inseparable from commercial pursuits. If such protection therefore, be granted to him as shall secure him from being undersold in ordinary seasons in the home market, he has all the protection he ought to receive; and more, in justice to the rest of the community, he ought not to desire.

There appears to me a great objection in levying a duty on the average price of an article that varies so much in quality as grain. In seasons when the quality is uniformly good, although deficient in quantity, a high average price is maintained, whereas if much of the corn had been spoiled or damaged by the weather, a quantity of inferior corn must be brought into the market and sold at low rates, whilst corn of good quality would probably be in demand at comparatively high prices. The corn varying so much, a wide range of prices is established between the good and inferior qualities. This has a tendency to lower the average value of the whole crop in an unfavourable season, when much corn may have been injured, maintaining a high rate of duty, and shutting out supplies at a moment when an importation might be necessary. Are there not also, in such a season, great facilities for influencing the averages for private ends, and may not a combination be entered into by a few individuals in the several corn-markets from whence the averages are returned, to deal only in high or low qualities on the same day? Should they deal in corn of inferior quality, the averages are lowered; if, on the contrary, they deal in corn of superior description, the averages in as great a degree would be increased. When we reflect that a difference of twopence in the average returns may produce an increase or diminution of 4s. in the duty, can we wonder at individuals endeavouring to influence the averages, when the legislature has presented so great an inducement for the successful accomplishment of their purpose, and such comparatively easy means for carrying it into execution? It appears incredible that when the returns of the average prices of corn are stated to be at 71s. 1d. the duty should be 4s. per quarter *less* than when the averages are 70s. 11d., viz., that corn should be taxed to the extent of 4s. per quarter, although the average price has only varied twopence. I appeal to you, and ask whether such a system can work favourably for the agricultural interest, who must necessarily be sufferers by the artificial variations inherent in the present mode of fixing the duty. But this is one of the evils inseparable from a fluctuating scale, and it may be doubted whether the wisdom of the legislature can suggest any method that shall prevent combination by persons whose business it is to watch every variation of the market, for the purpose of profiting by the opportunities afforded, and to turn them to the best account. This explains the competition that takes place amongst speculators to procure the corn in the nearest foreign country when prices are rising, for the purpose of availing themselves of a low duty, for although it may be had cheaper in the more distant markets, yet,if the averages should have changedin the interval the importers could not avoid sustaining a heavy loss.

It appears by the returns presented to Parliament, that in the course of ten months ending in July last, 2,800,000 *quarters of foreign wheat* were imported into this country.* It is probable that the

* To October 10th, upwards of 750,000 quarters more.

average cost price of this corn was not less than 50s., and if that were the case, we shall have paid upwards of £7,000,000 to foreign countries for wheat only. If this wheat had been admitted under a system of a permanent duty, it is not only probable that it would have been brought in at less cost, but certain that the importation would have been more gradual. If we suppose that this corn may have been sold in Great Britain at the average price 65s. per quarter, 15s. of this would have gone to the of Exchequer in aid of the revenue and consequent abatement of the taxes of the country. With a better system a larger part of this corn would have been brought from distant ports, by which the shipping interest would have had a greater portion of profit arising from the longer instead of the shorter voyage. The fear of the British corn-grower being overwhelmed by a foreign supply in case of any change of the present system seems groundless. The freight and charges, in addition to the duty, should be to him a sufficient protection, whenever the corn-trade is regulated on the same principles as all others are. To the foreigner it would matter little what amount of duty may be imposed, so that it does not reach an absolute prohibition. A moderate duty securing the home-grower from the competition of the foreigner, no supplies will find their way to the British markets, unless they can be offered above the farmer's protecting price. Should foreign corn be imported into Great Britain, it would wait for a period of demand, with the certainty of its being disposed of with only the usual risk common to all mercantile adventures. Equally erroneous is the supposition that if the trade were regulated on ordinary commercial principles the foreigner will prevent the export of his corn. If unfortunately a general scarcity throughout Europe should happen in any particular season, it is very probable that the several governments may be influenced by a desire to retain the produce of the country for the supply of their own subjects; but if, by the encouragement of a general and certain trade, we promote intercourse in grain with the whole of Europe, and so rare a contingency should occur, it is less likely that it would seriously affect us. By whatever circumstances we might be threatened, it is certain that the same foresight which enables the merchant to maintain a supply of every article we can desire, will also, under the system of a fixed duty, induce him to provide us with a supply of corn sufficient for our wants whenever it may be necessary. The sudden fluctuations which take place abroad whenever we are overtaken by an unfavourable season would thereby be avoided. It may be supposed that this sudden demand, while it raises the price at the several ports where grain is to be purchased, produces also similar effects in a greater or less degree throughout all the countries of the world. The market prices of commodities in one country having a tendency to adjust themselves to the prices current in others, the influence of a bad season, which, perhaps, may only have affected ourselves, is therefore extended to other nations, and the price of grain is raised everywhere by the effect of a sudden demand arising merely from our own wants. If we admitted corn at all seasons, we should receive our supplies gradually at moderate prices, which would not interfere materially with the value of corn in other countries, although, as I have already stated, I feel convinced that the prices on the Continent would be raised instead of ours being lowered by the proposed alteration. It is, therefore, most improbable that a fixed duty would injure the home grower; it would only regulate the supply for the use of the community whenever an unfavourable harvest may have reduced the quantity necessary for the consumption of our population.

It may be proper to remark to you that in consequence of the contingencies attendant on our fluctuating scale, a depôt of corn is made in some of the Mediterranean ports nearest to Great Britain. Foreign nations are engaged in carrying corn between the ports of the Black Sea and Leghorn, Marseilles, and other places for the purpose of warehousing their supply to be ready for our use whenever the prospect of the duty is sufficiently low as to permit its introduction into this country on advantageous terms. Under a better system English shipping would doubtless go direct to those countries, by which the whole of the profit derivable from the voyage would be enjoyed by our own subjects instead of dividing it with others, whereby we receive only the minor profit to be obtained from merely bringing the corn from the intermediate port.

Some difficulty may, perhaps, arise as to the precise period at which the alteration of our system of Corn-laws should take place. It would be objected that a law should be proposed imposing a duty of 12s. or 15s. per quarter, whilst corn should be at or above 70s., and subject only to a duty of a few shillings. It may be true that when corn is at a price which, under the existing system, permits importation at a lower duty, it would be extremely impolitic to impose a higher sum. This difficulty would, however, soon vanish on the first appearance of a productive harvest. If it were thought expedient to change the present Corn-law, and to pass an Act imposing a fixed duty, such as I have proposed, it might be arranged that the duty should not take effect until the average prices of wheat reached the point at which a considerably higher duty than 15s. would become payable; or if such limitation should not be thought sufficient, power might be granted to her Majesty in Council, authorising Her Majesty, by Royal Proclamation, to declare the time when the fixed duty should become permanently payable. By this course every inconvenience attendant upon a change of the mode of levying the duty on foreign corn would be avoided.

In the foregoing observations I have been guided solely by the conviction that some important changes in the Corn-laws must shortly take place. In considering the alteration which the interests of the country seem to require, I have kept steadily in view the peculiar position of the British agriculturists. In the remedial measures that I have ventured to suggest, I have stated my own views only upon the maturest deliberation, and after consulting the safest guides and the best authorities. Personally interested in the welfare of the land, and living amongst those who are entirely dependent on agricultural pursuits, I can have no desire but that of seeing the cultivator of the land in a flourishing condition. The question I have put to myself is whether the condition of the farmer is best promoted by endeavouring to secure a permanent high price for his produce, or to prevent its depreciation. It is evident that we cannot ensure a high price for the class of producers, without committing an injustice against the class of consumers. Seeing the efforts that have been unsuccessfully made to accomplish the difficult task of maintaining a steady remunerating price for British corn, and the alternations to which it has been subject, I have directed my attention to the means that may save it from the recurrence of such an extreme depression as was experienced a few years since. In guarding the interests of the farmer, I have, however, not lost sight of what is due to the rest of my fellow-subjects, and have, therefore, proposed nothing that shall give greater protection to agriculture than its admitted importance requires. The information I have been able to collect may, however, be useful if even the conclusions to which I have come be thought erroneous, or the views I have here put forth considered impracticable. It is exceedingly difficult to meet the objections that may be urged against any description of Corn-laws, and it is in this sense that my conclusions may not be acceptable to those who are reluctant to abandon the present system, or to others who are disinclined to any restriction whatever. Having already stated that my purpose in writing these pages was to communicate my opinions to the Members of the Association, I need not again disclaim having any views either of a party or political character.

I have also limited my observations to matters of a practical nature arising out of passing events, and supported by the best evidence that could be procured. I have not touched upon the question of rent or taxation as affecting the price of corn, for I do not think it necessary to introduce these intricate subjects, which have moreover occupied the attention of so many eminent individuals far more competent than myself to handle them. I am, however, inclined to believe that the public are greatly misinformed on the subject of the rent of arable land, which, I have reason to think, is exceedingly moderate in most of the districts of England. I have also limited my remarks to wheat only, because that is the description of grain which affects the largest class of the population, whether buyers or sellers of corn. The same principle, however, is equally applicable to any other description of grain.

In conclusion, I venture to offer my opinion that the landed interests are justified in opposing any alteration of the Corn-laws by which the principle of protection shall not be fully conceded. No satisfactory reason can be adduced to shew why corn should be taken out of the pale of protection to be competed with by those who are not subject to the payment of our rates and taxes. As to the proposition so industriously circulated that we ought to admit corn from cheaper countries without a protecting duty for the purpose of reducing the price of the necessaries of life at home to a level with those on the continent, I believe, if the measure were entertained, its ill effects would be most felt by the class of society to whom the advice is so liberally administered. If the price of corn and other necessaries were to be lowered by the means recommended, the first victims of such policy would be the labouring population in the rural districts. If, however, a moderate fixed duty were imposed, I am fully persuaded that prices abroad would reach a nearer level to ours, and that, consequently, our manufacturing population would be materially benefited without any injury being inflicted on the agricultural class.

Some regard is surely due to the rights of property, large investments in land having been made on the faith of the principle of protection not being violated. If, therefore, this principle is to be entirely abandoned, and the country placed on a level with the continent, inviting foreign agriculturists to cultivate their lands carefully and to manure them highly, for the purpose of supplanting the British farmer in his own market, the landowners would have a right to compensation for any loss they may sustain, and a re-adjustment of all the burdens of the country should be submitted to. With what propriety could the landowner have been called upon to commute the tithes into a rent-charge upon his property, if, immediately on that arrangement, a principle be introduced entirely unsettling the whole of the capital represented in the soil? With no more consistency can the property of the landowner be depreciated for the purpose of improving the condition of other classes of society, than can that of the manufacturer or fundholder. If the state of the country be such as to require an equitable adjustment, let it be boldly avowed. Let all the capital which constitutes the property of the country be taken into the account, and each individual contribute his just proportion to meet an existing or apprehended difficulty. But it is not fair to advance the specious argument, that because corn is a necessary of life, and is grown cheaper in foreign countries than at home, an alteration shall be introduced that may entirely unsettle the value of landed property. The country, however, is happily not yet reduced to the predicament of requiring sacrifices on the part of any of its great interests. The progressive condition of mankind requires the occasional revision of laws which regulate the affairs of civilized society. Experience demonstrates that the Corn-laws require amendment, but it is only when undertaken in a spirit of justice to all classes that any permanent improvement can be expected. My object in recommending a reconsideration of the Corn-laws is, therefore, neither to bring the landowner into disrepute, nor to advocate forcible changes in the value of his property. I have only ventured to shew that a better protection may be instituted, one that shall preserve the balance of justice for the corn-grower, while it offers equal advantages to the rest of the community.

APPENDIX.

APPENDIX I.

Prices of Wheat as inserted in the "Royal Gazette," for every Week from the Year 1834 to 1838 inclusive.

Weeks.	Wheat.		Weeks.	Wheat.		Weeks.	Wheat.		Weeks.	Wheat.		Weeks.	Wheat.	
1834.	s.	d.	1835.	s.	d.	1836.	s.	d.	1837.	s.	d.	1838.	s.	d.
3 Jan.	49	2	2 Jan.	40	1	1 Jan.	36	0	6 Jan.	59	0	5 Jan.	52	4
10 —	49	2	9 —	40	5	8 —	36	6	13 —	59	6	12 —	52	11
17 —	49	1	16 —	40	7	15 —	37	0	20 —	59	1	19 —	53	7
24 —	48	10	23 —	41	3	22 —	37	10	27 —	58	9	26 —	54	10
31 —	48	7	30 —	41	7	29 —	39	3	3 Feb.	57	5	2 Feb.	55	4
7 Feb.	48	11	6 Feb.	41	5	5 Feb.	39	7	10 —	56	5	9 —	55	4
14 —	48	9	13 —	40	10	12 —	39	7	17 —	56	2	16 —	55	8
21 —	48	8	20 —	40	4	19 —	40	7	24 —	55	9	23 —	55	2
28 —	48	4	27 —	40	4	26 —	42	6	3 March	55	11	2 March	55	8
7 March	48	0	6 March	39	10	4 March	44	7	10 —	56	7	9 —	55	4
14 —	47	8	13 —	39	8	11 —	45	0	17 —	56	9	16 —	56	8
21 —	47	2	20 —	39	11	18 —	44	2	24 —	53	8	23 —	56	10
28 —	47	4	27 —	40	0	25 —	44	7	31 —	56	2	30 —	57	9
4 April	47	3	3 April	39	9	1 April	46	5	7 April	55	11	6 April	58	8
11 —	47	2	10 —	39	3	8 —	47	7	14 —	55	5	13 —	58	10
18 —	47	6	17 —	38	10	15 —	48	8	21 —	55	6	20 —	58	9
25 —	48	3	24 —	38	7	22 —	48	10	28 —	55	9	27 —	59	0
2 May	48	4	1 May	38	6	29 —	48	8	5 May	55	10	4 May	60	0
9 —	48	7	8 —	38	9	6 May	47	11	12 —	54	7	11 —	60	10
16 —	47	11	15 —	39	8	13 —	49	8	19 —	53	4	18 —	62	2
23 —	47	2	22 —	40	0	20 —	50	4	26 —	54	4	25 —	62	4
30 —	46	8	29 —	39	10	27 —	49	10	2 June	56	2	1 June	63	1
6 June	46	1[illegible]	5 June	39	8	3 June	49	5	9 —	56	4	8 —	64	3
13 —	47	10	12 —	40	1	10 —	51	0	16 —	56	5	15 —	64	11
20 —	48	10	19 —	40	4	17 —	51	1	23 —	56	11	22 —	65	6
27 —	49	6	26 —	40	0	24 —	50	6	30 —	57	0	29 —	67	3
4 July	48	11	3 July	40	5	1 July	50	8	7 July	56	4	6 July	68	0
11 —	48	4	10 —	41	6	8 —	50	7	14 —	56	1	13 —	68	0
18 —	48	1	17 —	42	1	15 —	49	4	21 —	56	11	20 —	68	2
25 —	48	5	24 —	48	6	22 —	49	2	28 —	59	2	27 —	69	1
1 Aug.	48	4	31 —	44	0	29 —	49	6	4 Aug.	60	1	3 Aug.	69	11
8 —	48	6	7 Aug.	43	2	5 Aug.	50	8	11 —	59	5	10 —	71	8
15 —	49	6	14 —	42	6	12 —	50	4	18 —	59	6	17 —	75	7
22 —	48	9	21 —	41	1	19 —	48	10	25 —	58	2	24 —	77	0
29 —	46	5	28 —	40	4	26 —	46	11	[illegible] Sept.	56	5	31 —	74	5
5 Sept.	44	3	4 Sept.	39	5	2 Sept.	48	1	8 —	56	6	7 Sept.	70	2
12 —	43	4	11 —	38	10	9 —	47	9	15 —	57	8	14 —	64	2
19 —	43	2	18 —	38	0	16 —	47	10	22 —	56	7	21 —	61	10
26 —	43	7	25 —	37	7	23 —	48	5	29 —	56	6	28 —	62	11
3 Oct.	42	9	2 Oct.	37	1	30 —	48	2	6 Oct.	55	9	5 Oct.	64	9
10 —	41	10	9 —	37	0	7 Oct.	47	2	13 —	53	6	12 —	66	0
17 —	41	1	16 —	37	11	14 —	47	0	20 —	51	8	19 —	65	7
24 —	40	8	23 —	37	0	21 —	47	7	27 —	51	0	26 —	66	4
31 —	41	6	30 —	36	5	28 —	49	7	3 Nov.	51	7	2 Nov.	69	5
7 Nov.	42	4	6 Nov.	36	7	4 Nov.	51	8	10 —	52	11	9 —	72	11
14 —	42	6	13 —	36	7	11 —	55	6	17 —	54	4	16 —	73	10
21 —	42	4	20 —	36	10	18 —	60	4	24 —	53	7	23 —	73	4
28 —	41	11	27 —	36	11	25 —	61	9	1 Dec.	52	6	30 —	73	1
5 Dec.	41	11	4 Dec.	36	9	2 Dec.	59	7	8 —	52	8	7 Dec.	73	6
12 —	41	1	11 —	36	8	9 —	60	4	15 —	53	5	14 —	78	4
19 —	40	11	18 —	36	6	16 —	60	6	22 —	53	2	21 —	78	4
26 —	40	6	25 —	36	0	23 —	59	2	29 —	52	9	28 —	78	2
						30 —	58	9						
Avge. of the year	46	2	Avge. of the year	39	4	Avge. of the year	48	6	Avge. of the year	55	10	Avge of the year	64	7

APPENDIX II.

1838.

Quantities of Corn imported and admitted for Home Consumption from the 5th Jan. 1638, to 5th Jan. 1839.

Months ending	Imported. Qrs.	Bus.	Paid duty. Qrs.	Bus.	Average Prices per Quarter, by which the I)uties were regulated. In the Weeks following the Certificates dated as under mentioned.	s.	d.	Rates of duty Pwqr. Foreign. s.	d.
					1838.				
					4 January -	53	0	33	8
					11 —.	5 2	10	34	8
February 5, 1838	1,791	0	370	7					
					18 — .	52	11	34	8
					25 — -	53	0	33	8
March 5 —	984	6	758	7					
					1 February	53	3	33	8
					8 — -	53	8	33	8
April 5 -----	25	1	1,081	0					
					15 —	54	1	32	8
					22 — -	51	7	32	8
					C 1 March •	M	il	32	8
					\ 8 — .	55	2	31	8
May 5 —	1,308	5	1,519	1	v 15 — -	55	3	31	8
					#22 — -	55	5	31	8
					V.29 — -	55	8	31	8
					5 April -	56	4	j 30	8
					12 — .	56	8	30	8
June 5 -----	26,495	5	732	0					
					19 — -	57	3	29	8
					•26 — -	57	10	29	8
July 5 -----	57,839	0	453	6	C 3 May -	58	3	28	8
					\ 10 —	58	10	28	8
					< 17 — -	59	4	i 27	8
					/24 — -	59	il	27	8
August 5 -----	91,237	5	5,976	7	(.31 — -	60	6	26′	8
					7 June -	61	3	25	8
					14 — .	62	2	21	8
September 5 —	241,237	7	12,145	1					
					21 — -	62	11	*24	8
					28 — .	63	9	23	8
					C 5 Julv -	61	7	22	8
					j 12 — .	65	6	21	8
October 10 -----	533,771	6	1,440,459	5	S 10 — -	66	4	20	8
					(26 — -	67	o	18	8
					C 2 Ausiist -	67	8	18	8
					U - -	68	5	16	8
November 5 —	18,101	6	11,233	7	n 16 —j .	#9	2	13	8
					/ 23 — .	70	5	10	8
					O) — -	71	11	6	8
					C 6 *September*	72	11	2	8
					) 13 — -	73	2	1	0
December 5 -----	43,464	0	489	7	V-0 — .	72	2	2	8
					(.27 — -	70	7	10	8
					4 October -	68	7	16	8
					11 — -	66	5	20	8
Jaunary 5, 1839	222,203	0	200,619	6					
					18 — -	(i5	o	21	8
					25 — -	<ii	3	22	8
Total in the year) ending 5 Jan.> **18J9.**)	1,211,160	1	1,736,206	6	C 1 November	I	7	22	8
					\ 8 — •	65	10	21	8
					< 15 — -	67	6	IS	8
					/22 — -	69	0	13	8
					V.29 — -	70	3	10	8
					f 6 December	7 1	6	6	8
					113 — -	73	0	1	0
					V20 — -	74	6	1	0
					(.27 — -	75	5	1	0

APPENDIX III.

1839.

Quantities of Corn imported and admitted for Home Consumption from the 5th Jan. to July 1839.

Months ending	Imported. Qrs.	Bus.	Paid duty. Qrs.	Bus.	Average Prices per Quarter, by which the Duties were regulated. In the Weeks following the Certificates dated as under mentioned. 1839.	s.	d.	Rates of duty per qr. Foreign. s.	d.
February 5, 1839	147,934	3	150,012	1	3 January	76	1	1	0
					10 —	77	8	1	0
					17 —	78	8	1	0
					24 —	79	8	1	0
					31 —	79	9	1	0
March 5 —	211,119	2	210,375	1	7 February	79	7	1	0
					14 —	78	11	1	0
					21 —	77	5	1	0
					28 —	75	10	1	0
April 5 —	460,068	6	468,576	1	7 March	74	5	1	0
					14 —	73	6	1	0
					21 —	73	0	1	0
					28 —	72	6	2	8
May 5 —	212,817	3	176,423	4	4 April	72	1	2	8
					11 —	71	7	6	8
					18 —	70	10	10	8
					25 —	70	4	10	8
June 5 —	301,515	1	91,890	1	2 May	70	1	10	8
					9 —	70	1	10	8
					16 —	70	4	10	8
					23 —	70	9	10	8
					30 —	71	2	6	8
July 5 —	285,289	6	491,195	2	6 June	71	1	6	8
					13 —	70	7	10	8
					20 —	70	3	10	8
					27 —	69	10	13	8
Total in the half year ending 5 July 1839.	1,618,741	5	1,591,472	2					

Yearly average prices of Wheat at Dantzig, Hamburgh, and Rotterdam, taken from the Third Report of the Select Committee on Agricultural Distress:—

	Dantzig.			Hamburgh.			Rotterdam.		
	s.	d.		s.	d.		s.	d.	
1826	21	8	......	20	0	......	25	6	
1827	22	3	......	26	0	......	39	1	
1828	40	2	......	35	0	......	38	6	Years of Demand for England.
1829	43	10	......	40	0	......	43	11	
1830	39	3	......	35	0	......	43	9	
1831	45	6	......	41	0	......	52	9	
1832	38	0	......	35	0	......	40	7	
1833	30	0	......	26	0	......	32	7	
1834	25	0	......	22	6	......	31	9	
1835	22	9	......	21	6	......	29	11	

The following were the prices current in the year 1838:

	Dantzig.			Hamburgh.			Rotterdam.	
January ..	27	30	......	27	33	......	35	37
February ..	30	33	......	30	34	......	35	40
March	30	34	......	30	33	......	32	40
April	34	38	......	32	35	......	36	42
May......	32	37	......	33	38	......	42	50
June	37	45	......	40	45	......	44	50
July	42	48	......	40	45	......	48	56
August....	44	49	......	48	50	......	55	60
September	48	52	......	40	48	......	50	58
October ..	47	52	......	46	52	......	56	62
November	52	59	......	55	60	......	60	68
December	58	62	......	56	8	......	60	70

THE PRICE OF WHEAT AT NEW YORK.

During the years 1837 and 1838 wheat ranged as high as two dollars per bushel. The lowest price of late years has been one dollar; but this is considered to be a very low rate. The present price is about one-and-a-quarter dollar per bushel.

An Account of Foreign Wheat and Flour brought into consumption in Great Britain in each year from 1815 to 1832 inclusive:—

	Wheat. Qrs.	Wheat, Meal, or Flour. Cwt.
1815	105,822*	39,960
1816	201,970	81,512
1817	694,260	1,059,909
1818	1,372,082	595,347
1819	107,786	17,685
1820	1,005	....
1821	....	....
1822	....	....
1823	....	....
1824	....	....
1825	372,403	88.477
1826	268,233	64,531
1827	510,279	17,928
1828	789,829	109,712
1829	1,259,951	332,100
1830	1,493,009	515,788
1831	1,084,931	926,895
1832	165,544	56,832

* The fractional parts are omitted.

Thomas Jevons (1791–1855)[1]

Thomas Jevons, the father of the economist William Stanley Jevons (1835–82), was the son of William Jevons (1760–1852) of Staffordshire who moved to Liverpool in 1798 to act as an agent for his Staffordshire employers in the sale of nails and iron. After some years in Liverpool William Jevons began his own iron business with financial help of the Unitarian minister of his chapel at Paradise Street, the Revd John Yates.[2] Thomas Jevons served his apprenticeship in the iron business in the firm of John Yates' son, Richard Vaughan Yates, before joining his father's firm as a partner, the firm being renamed Jevons & Son.

Thomas Jevons, a friend of Stephenson, had a flair for invention. In 1815 he launched on the Mersey a small iron pleasure boat, built to his design, the first iron boat, he claimed, to sail on seawater. He also designed a ribless iron lifeboat, a movable iron landing stage for steamers, and an iron coaster.

In addition to his interest in free trade, Thomas Jevons wrote on the reform of criminals, an interest he shared with his father-in-law William Roscoe (1753–1831), and was strongly in favour of decimal coinage. He married in 1825 Mary Anne Roscoe (1795–1845) who bore him eleven children.

In January 1848, following the railway boom crisis of 1847, the firm of Jevons & Sons went bankrupt. Thomas moved to a smaller house closer to the centre of Liverpool, and he became the manager of the Liverpool branch of the Dowlais Iron Company of Sir John Guest of South Wales. According to Keynes Thomas and William Roscoe's (in 1816) bankruptcies provided 'good hereditary cause' why Stanley Jevons did not 'overlook the phenomenon of business fluctuations'.

[1] Based on R. D. Collison Black and Rosamond Konekamp (eds), *Papers and Correspondence of William Stanley Jevons, Volume I. Biography and Personal Journal*, London: Macmillan in association with the Royal Economic Society, 1972, and J. M. Keynes, 'William Stanley Jevons 1835–1882' (1936), in J. M. Keynes, *Essays and Sketches in Biography*, New York: Meridian Books, 1956.

[2] In 1832 James Martineau became co-pastor, and in 1835 sole pastor of the Paradise Street chapel, an office he kept until 1857.

THE

PROSPERITY

OF THE

LANDHOLDERS

NOT DEPENDANT

ON THE

CORN LAWS.

BY

THOMAS JEVONS.

LONDON:

LONGMANS AND CO., PATERNOSTER-ROW;

AND

T. BEAN, 21, CASTLE-STREET, LIVERPOOL.

1840.

PREFACE.

Wherever the word *Corn* occurs in this work, it is used in a wide sense, to denote not only the four principal descriptions of Grain, namely, Wheat, Barley, Oats, and Rye, but also Peas and Beans.

With respect to all the calculations and estimates that are given in the following pages, the author wishes it to be understood, that he does not claim for them the credit of perfect exactness, which the nature of the subject renders impossible. If they are admitted as only approximations to the truth, that will be sufficient for the establishment of his conclusions.

Liverpool, 1st *January*, 1840.

THE PROSPERITY OF THE LANDOWNERS NOT DEPENDANT ON THE CORN LAWS.

Division 1.—The Object of this Work—The Means of Promoting the Prosperity of Agriculture by the Increase of Consumption.

THE object of the following pages is to point out the best means of promoting the prosperity of the landed and agricultural interests of the kingdom, and of guarding those interests from any evil effects that may be apprehended to arise from any modified duty on the importation of foreign corn, or of other agricultural products.

These means may be stated to consist simply in increasing, to the utmost, the consumption of our agricultural productions; and, also, their exportation abroad. But, obvious as this course appears, our agricultural societies and great landed proprietors appear, hitherto, not only to have entirely neglected it, but to have proceeded in an exactly opposite direction. They have stimulated the exertions of the whole body to cause an excessive increase of the productions of the earth; and this not only by improvements on lands already under cultivation, but by the inclosure and cultivation of large tracts previously lying in a comparatively barren state. Their conduct has been like that of a manufacturer who should go on manufacturing his articles to an extent greater than could be consumed, or of a merchant who should go on importing, in a like manner, without any attention on the part of either to the means of extending the use of their several articles of traffic.

How far the quantity of our agricultural productions can be pronounced excessive, or otherwise, is only to be determined by comparing it with the means of our population to purchase at remunerating prices to the growers; for the consumption of agricultural productions by our population and in our manufactories may be increased to an almost unlimited extent, provided there be no impediment in the way to repress it. Nor do we consider as an impediment, any fair range of prices which may be necessary as a remuneration to the farmers at all times, as well in seasons of scarcity as in those of abundance.

Division 2.—Proposed Repeal of certain Taxes that check Consumption.

In particularizing the measures which we consider it essential to adopt, let us commence with those which will afford a direct and palpable relief, and which, provided we are agreed, are entirely under our control, and upon the beneficial results of which there can be no doubt. These are the removal of all taxes which operate as a direct check on the consumption of farm produce, and the first of these which we shall mention is the Tax upon Horses.

For every horse which we prevent being kept from any cause, we thereby deprive the agricultural interest of the sale of produce which would require a breadth of land equal to five acres to raise,* to say nothing of what may be required to rear the stock. We, therefore, propose, at once, the repeal of the Duty or Tax on Riding Horses, Carriage Horses, and the Post-horse and Stage-coach Duty, in fact, on horses of every description; by which means we shall, certainly, ensure the keeping of an additional number of horses to no inconsiderable extent throughout the whole kingdom.

But, in addition to the Tax on Horses, that imposed on Carriages of every description ought, also, to be repealed, which would, undoubtedly, make a further and important addition to the number of horses which would be kept.

Another tax which we propose to be repealed, as one bearing unfavourably on the agricultural interest,

* London, in page 1012, paragraphs 6754 and 6755, states, that it requires five acres, on the average, to support one horse.

is the Tax on Male Servants. Remove this tax, as well as that on horses and carriages, and we immediately create a demand for an additional number of footmen, coachmen, grooms, post-boys, horse-keepers, &c. &c., which will surely require a further quantity of produce for their sustenance. And, beyond all this, the extra number of horses and carriages and of servants cannot be kept without causing the additional employment, and, consequently, the increased means of consumption, of numerous trades-people, artists, and artisans of almost every description, so that the entire good effects cannot easily be estimated. By pursuing this policy, it is probable that we may occasion a demand for an increased supply of farm produce that would require several hundred thousand acres of land to raise, and which could not fail to enhance the value of both land and produce.

It may be objected by some, that the Tax on Male Servants is a tax on luxuries, and, therefore, it ought not to be repealed. But it may with as much justice be called a tax on the industrial classes, in so far as it deprives them of one of their most valuable means of obtaining a livelihood. The tax on horses and carriages may also be considered in the same light; and, with regard to the motives which lead people in general to incur the expense of keeping either male servants or horses and carriages, it may be doubted whether the greater number are kept for the luxurious enjoyment of the rich and great, or for the accommodation of business affairs, and the necessities of the infirm and aged.

Division 3.—The Consumption of Food by the People may be increased.

The next proposition we have to submit is, that we should use all the means in our power to prevent the emigration of our population, as well those of the class called paupers as of any superior class. "*Every man*," says Loudon, in his Encyclopædia of Agriculture, page 1123, "*being a consumer, may be considered a promoter of the art* of agriculture, *by causin ag demand for its productions*." It has been thought, no doubt, that, by transporting our pauper population to distant lands, we have been doing the state some service by ridding it of an oppressive burden. But it should not be overlooked, that, if, by any means, we can provide employment for these people so that they may be enabled to maintain themselves at home, we shall have equally removed the pauperism, and at the same time retained a valuable set of customers. Of course, it is much more to be deplored, when such a state of things exists as induces our artisans and superior class of citizens to emigrate, and our most strenuous efforts should be directed to discover, and when discovered, to uphold that policy which shall retain such as these by their self-interests amongst ourselves. Every family of five persons that is allowed to emigrate, deprives us of a customer capable of consuming, by direct and indirect means, the produce of *ten* acres of land annually; but still further, every such customer whom we send from our shores to distant and foreign lands, becomes not only a customer to our opponents, but is actually put into a position for raising a greatly increased quantity of the products of the earth, which comes into serious competition with us under circumstances totally beyond our control.

It is to be feared, that the advantage to be derived by the agricultural interest from the general employment and prosperity of the population is not sufficiently estimated; nevertheless, it is to this source that we must look for one of the most important means of bettering the condition of our farmers. The consumption of agricultural products by the higher classes differs little, if any, in times of general depression from what it is in prosperous times; but the consumption of those products by the vast body of the people differs very greatly, and it is the power of this population to become purchasers that, for the most part, governs the price which the farmers are to get for their produce. This is a market capable of being enlarged to an almost unlimited extent. Some idea of its capability for increased consumption may, however, be formed from the following calculations.

The article Milk is one which may be considered almost indispensable; and yet its consumption falls very far short of what it might be. A family in good circumstances, consisting of five grown persons and five children, can readily consume four quarts of milk a day, or 1460 quarts per annum; and, should the population of London consume this article in the same ratio, it would require a supply of 1825 millions of quarts; but the actual consumption of the Metropolis is calculated at only 29 millions of quarts, showing a difference of no less than 1796 millions of quarts, which is equal to the produce of 561,250 cows; and as that number of cows would require a breadth of land equal to 1,683,750 acres for their sustenance, it follows, that the landed interest is deprived of its full measure of profit in a corresponding degree. We do not, however, mean to contend, that this ratio of consumption can ever be realized. We have intentionally put an extreme case, and the point we mean to establish by it is this, that there is an immense field of consumption, of this one article alone, lying totally neglected, to which the attention of agriculturists may be directed, and which, if improved, will yield abundant returns.

Again, in the article Butcher's Meat, it cannot be supposed, that anything like the quantity that might be consumed is actually consumed by the population of the United Kingdom, since it is a notorious fact, that the mass of the labouring and manufacturing body do not taste flesh meat oftener than one day in a week, and how many multitudes of them are in a still worse condition. If the lower classes of our countrymen could be enabled to consume only one ounce of butcher's meat per day each, in addition to what they now do, to supply that quantity would require the appropriation of an additional breadth of land to the extent of no less than *two millions of acres.*

The articles Butter and Cheese may be considered as luxuries to large classes of the people, and the middling classes also consume them very sparingly. It is probable, that the consumption of these articles may be increased to a large extent, and if we were to calculate, that each individual of the industrial classes was to consume, between the two articles, only three quarters of a pound a week, in addition to what is now consumed, it would require upwards of one million of acres of land to be appropriated for the production of the necessary supply over and above what is now occupied for that purpose.

It may be objected, that any very great increase in the consumption of the articles we have enumerated would be injurious to agriculture, since it would cause a large portion of tillage land to be thrown out of cultivation to be occupied as grazing land only. If this were the whole truth, which it is not, it might be answered, that, as far as milk and fresh Butter are concerned, and we may, perhaps, add, butcher's meat also, the landed interest enjoys a more thorough monopoly of their supply than it does, or ever can do, of any other farm produce, which circumstance might reconcile it, in some degree, to such a change. But, in fact, the objection is only true in part, for the articles butter, and cheese, and milk, and butcher's meat are, for the most part, consumed along with a portion of bread or pulse of some kind, and, therefore, an increased consumption of these articles will be advantageous to the tillage farmer, at the same time that it will greatly benefit the holder of meadow lands.

But, recurring to our estimate of what may be the amount of benefit to be derived from the full employment and consequent prosperity of the people, there is a compendious method of ascertaining it in the gross, which is this: if, by any means that may be within our reach, we can add from one to two shillings a-week to the wages of the industrial classes, that would give them the power of spending five or six millions of pounds per annum more than they now do, and, as the larger portion of what they spend goes for the purchase of food, we may calculate, that they would consume an extra quantity of produce, which would require from two to three millions of acres of land to raise, and it follows, of course, that the rent of land and profits of the farmer would be increased in a proportionate degree.

Division 4.—The close Connexion between Agriculture and Manufactures pointed out.

The question now occurs, how are we to attain this great good? To which it must be answered, that there seems only one way that directly leads to this desirable end, and that is, by promoting the prosperity of the manufacturing and labouring population; and, if we can show distinctly, that the interests of the landlord and farmer are intimately united with the prosperity of the manufacturers, so much so as to be very far beyond what is generally conceived, we shall have their willing co-operation to effect the object in view.

In order to prove, that the intimate connexion which we have alluded to, does really exist, let us investigate the nature of the operations that are gone through in carrying on the Woollen Manufacture.

First. There is a payment to the landed interest for the stock which is to produce the wool.

Second. There is a payment of rent to the landlord for the land on which the sheep are to subsist.

Third. There is a payment to the farmer for his trouble and profit in the management of his flock, and in bringing his wool to market.

Fourth. There is a fourth payment in cases where a woolstapler intervenes between the farmer and manufacturer; for the woolstapler obtains a profit on the transfer, a large part of which is expended for food, and, of the remainder, a considerable portion finds its way indirectly into the same channel.

Fifth. There is a payment to the owner of the spinning-mill, being the amount of the wages of his work-people and his own remuneration. The work-people of the mill expend their wages, and the mill-owner part of his profits, in purchasing food, which goes directly to the landed interest.

Sixth. There is a payment to the weavers, the fullers, the dyers, the dressers, &c. &c. The wages and profits obtained in these different processes are principally expended in meat and drink, which also tends directly to benefit the farmers and landowners.

Seventh. There is the profit of the master-clothier, merchant, or exporter, a considerable portion of which is expended for the benefit of the agriculturists in the purchase of farm produce.

Eighth. There are payments to carriers for cost of carriage, backwards and forwards, by carts and by canals; there are railway, canal, and turnpike tolls; and there is the benefit derived by the landed interest from the sale of produce to the parties who carry on all these operations.

Ninth. There is, lastly, the benefit derived by the landed interest from the sale of food to a vast number of different trades-people and artisans, who are employed in making and repairing the different buildings, machinery, tools, and materials requisite for carrying on the woollen manufacture in all its branches and ramifications.

From this statement, which is purposely drawn out at some length, it must appear manifest, that the agricultural body is deeply interested in the prosperity of the woollen trade and manufacture, and that it is well worth the notice of agricultural societies to assist in all feasible ways to extend this trade. The estimated value of woollen fabrics, according to M'Culloch, is £21,000,000, the half of which, at the least, finds its way into the pockets of the farmers and landholders. Of the above large amount it is generally stated, that about two-thirds depend upon home demand and the remaining third on the demand for exportation: it is certain, however, that, if we were to lose the export portion of the woollen trade, that loss would occasion a very great reduction of the home demand, and, in fact, there are no means by which we can judge what is the relative value of our foreign and domestic trade in wool and woollen goods.

But, it may be said by some, that the woollen manufacture is already sufficiently extended, for that we cannot now produce all the raw material for carrying it on, but must import a large quantity from abroad, and that the competition of this foreign wool in our market is injurious to the farmer and landlord. If the farmers were compelled to keep a certain number of sheep, whether they would or not, it might be admitted, that there was some hardship in the unrestricted importation of raw wool; but, since they are not so compelled, and since the fleece is not the only part of this kind of stock which yields a profit, there is no real hardship, and they have only to regulate their supply according as the general prices of the markets may yield them remunerative returns. Supposing, however, for argument sake, that the competition which home grown wool meets with from the sales of imported wool does keep down the price, notwithstanding any inherent difference there may be in the staple, and that the gains of the landed interest on this article are seriously reduced in consequence, if we were to stop the importation of wool altogether and give the farmers an entire monopoly of the market, their gains, on the whole, instead of being increased, would be very much more reduced, because a large part of the population which is now employed in the woollen manufacture, and whose payments to the landed interest are from ten to fifteen millions a year, must be thrown out of employment, and would, in all probability, transfer their industry to some rival country.

The proof, that the landed interest would be losers by a successful attempt to monopolize the supply of raw wool, and thereby pare down the trade to such dimensions as would be within their means of supply, may be seen on referring back to the sketch of operations which we have given of the woollen manufacture. It will there be found, that, although, in the case of imported wool, the landed interest of our own country would be no participators, in a direct manner, in the payments founded on three of the operations which we have particularized, namely, the first, the second, and the third, yet that, on the remaining six, it would be quite as much a gainer as if the wool had been entirely of home growth. The agricultural interest would not, however, be without some advantage from the first three operations, even though they were not to furnish one ounce of the raw material themselves. The wool we import from abroad cannot be obtained without being paid for, which can be effected in no other way than by a previous export of our own manufactures of like value. They have, therefore, actually derived no slight advantage from the first three items also, by means of operations carried on in some previous manufacture.

We have stated, in a former paragraph, that there are no means by which we can judge what is the relative value, to the agricultural interests, of our foreign, as compared with our domestic, trade in woollen goods; we may, however, venture this opinion, that, if there be any difference at all, the preference must be given to the export demand, for the following reason. Whatever portion of their income our population may spend in the purchase of woollen goods, they will, necessarily, have the less to spend in food or in drink; and if a man, for the sake of appearances or of comfort, will be niggardly and sparing at his board, the landed interest is the one that will suffer the most. On the other hand, for every pound sterling of woollen goods exported abroad, there is no direct abstraction of a like amount from the pockets of our countrymen. They are left with their whole income in hand, to spend it as they like. The individual who exports the goods is the only exception; and we may safely trust to him to get back his pound sterling from the foreign nation to which he has exported his merchandise, with a good profit into the bargain.

The conclusion we must necessarily draw from the whole of this investigation is, that it is the interest of the agriculturists to encourage, to the utmost of their power, the woollen manufacture of our country, as well that portion which depends on foreign trade as that which is confined to our domestic consumption, for they are equally interested in the success of both: and we cannot fail to draw this conclusion also, that, if we were to prohibit the importation of wool, or impose a duty on the importation so high as to depress the manufacture of woollen goods, we should sustain a loss where we expected to ensure a gain. Nevertheless, it is right that some duty should be payable on the importation of wool, because we believe that it will bear it; and, if it be imposed on some sound principle, it will be beneficial to the country generally, and, at the same time, not injurious to the woollen trade.

Let us now examine in what manner and how closely the landed and agricultural interest is linked with the prosperity of another of our great staple manufactures, that of iron, and we shall find that it is quite as much concerned in the interests of this branch of manufacture as it is in that of wool, if not more so, because almost the whole amount of the money that is created by the smelting and manufacturing of iron, and that is now becoming very enormous, is expended for their benefit.

The cost of a ton of malleable iron, of the value of ten pounds, at the iron work where it is made, may be analyzed as follows:

	£.	s.	d.
Royalty or rent paid to the landlord for liberty to get the mines	0	10	0
Wages to miners, colliers, limestone getters, furnace men, refiners, puddlers, rollers, engineers, labourers, clerks, &c..	6	0	0
Cost of materials consumed in the mines and works, principally timber, bricks, and iron implements, the greater portion of which goes for the benefit of the landed interest	2	0	0
Interest of capital, rent of land, and profit of the iron master, from the expenditure of which the landed interest receives its portion of benefit...	1	10	0
	£10	0	0

This account sufficiently explains itself, and, therefore, needs no comment: we may, however, remark, that, considering the very small sum that is paid for the raw materials of which iron is made, only ten shillings, at the most, for the quantity that is required to make one ton of iron, and the enormous proportion of the whole cost that is expended in wages, we might, not inappropriately, designate an iron work as a MILL FOR THE CONVERSION OF PROVISIONS INTO IRON.

But the above account does not exhibit the whole of the link that connects the landed interest with the iron manufacture; it only shows the beginning. The greater part of the iron that is made is afterwards wrought into a thousand different articles, all of which are enhanced in value by the wages of the artificers employed, until some of them become of more value than their weight in gold, which may be instanced in the case of the hair balance spring of a watch.

The entire value of the Iron Manufacture of the country it is impossible to ascertain; but the amount of iron and ironmongery exported abroad, computed from the Parliamentary Return of the quantity exported in the year 1838, was upwards of £4,000,000, which, as far as concerns the landed and agricultural interests, is nearly the same as if they enjoyed an export trade in corn to the extent of 1,500,000 quarters, or of the produce of 400,000 acres of land.*

* Perhaps, after iron, the article Glass is that by which we create the greatest amount of wealth out of the least valuable materials, and by

The Cotton Manufacture is of too vast importance not to be noticed here, although it is not necessary to go into any minute details showing its connexion with the landed interest. We trust we have sufficiently traced the steps, or processes, which link the interests of agriculture and manufacture together, and that, in referring to the Cotton Manufacture in general terms only, we shall not have to encounter that jealousy which has been fostered, in later years, by the low and false antithesis, intended to create and prolong an enmity between Land-lords and Cotton-lords.

There is nothing in the Cotton Manufacture that causes its relations with the landed interest to differ from that of woollen, but this one thing, that, whereas in the latter we produce a certain portion of the raw material on our own soil, in the former we import the whole. But, since our climate will not grow cotton to perfection, this circumstance precludes the idea of any clashing of interests in that particular. We have shown whence the particular benefit is derivable by the landed interest

the extension of this manufacture great numbers of our people may find more profitable employment than they now do. The chief ingredient in the composition of glass is sand, to which are added, in much smaller proportions, soda, or salt, alkali or kelp, and red lead; and a large quantity of coals are consumed in the melting process. Many women, for whom suitable employment is very much wanted, may find it in different departments of the glass manufacture; and, on all accounts, the duty ought to be totally repealed without delay.

from the woollen manufacture, in case the whole of our wool should be imported, and none whatever raised at home; and the same reasoning applies to the Cotton Manufacture. There are, however, a few additional processes to which many descriptions of cotton goods are submitted, such as, sizing and glazing, which unite the two interests more directly together. The consumption of flour by each loom is estimated at 4 lbs. per week, which makes the total quantity annually consumed in this way to amount to 220,000 barrels, and the land required to raise it, from 35 to 40,000 acres.

The extent of the Cotton Manufacture is so vast, and the population entirely dependant upon it for daily food is so great, that any lengthened depression in that trade must make itself felt by the farmers. On a rough calculation, we should say, that the Cotton Manufacture, throughout all its branches and necessary adjuncts, affords subsistence to a population of one and a half million of souls, and occasions the consumption of farm produce to the extent of five millions of acres annually.

Now, if, from any preposterous jealousy that may exist of the wealth of the cotton lords, we uphold a policy that has a tendency to depress this manufacture in any permanent way, we should very soon have such a surplus of agricultural produce as would greatly reduce the rent of land, not only at the principal seat of manufacture, but throughout all

England; whilst, on the contrary, if we can forward any policy that will extend this great trade, we shall have an extra consumption, which will raise the price of corn and of provisions generally; and, in proportion thereto, the profits of the farmer and the rents of the landlord will also rise.

We trust enough has now been said to convince the most sceptical, that a connexion of the most intimate kind exists between the landed and the manufacturing interests; that the one cannot flourish without the other; and that they must rise or fall together.

Division 5.—The Exportation of Agricultural Produce may be Extended.

We now come to a subject more immediately connected with the landed interest, and which affords a direct means of bettering its condition,—this is, by promoting, to the utmost extent, the exportation of our agricultural productions in a more palpable form than that which we have hitherto had under consideration; and to this point the agricultural societies of the kingdom would do well to devote some attention, and not to expend their whole efforts to increase the productions of the country without any regard to distribution.

There are three ways in which the products of our soil may be exported: first, in their natural and original state; second, in the form of some manufacture into which they have been converted, either forming the whole fabric or substance of the article, or only a part of it; and, third, by the exportation of such articles as have occasioned the consumption or destruction of the produce of our soil in making them. We exclude, however, from this head, the provisions consumed by the people employed to make the articles, that having been already under consideration: we only mean to include the produce that has been consumed or destroyed in the mode of manufacture.

First. Of the first of these divisions little can be said, as our agriculturists have not turned their attention in any degree to a foreign market, although there is no doubt that it might be made of great importance.

Any portion of our supplies of produce that may be taken to our home market serves, for a while, to stay the demand, and we must wait the consumption of that before we can dispose of a further quantity; but any portion that may be abstracted from our stock, and exported abroad, does not abate, in the least degree, the home demand. On the contrary, the creation, or the enlargement, of an export trade, in farm produce, will have a double effect on the prosperity of our landed interest, for, whilst the abstraction of that portion which is exported abroad will enhance the value of what remains to be disposed of in the home market, it will, at the same time, cheapen all those foreign commodities that are received in exchange.

The principal articles of agricultural produce exported abroad, chiefly to our colonies, are flour, potatoes, butter, and cheese, and, *perhaps*, hay. Holland exports large quantities of the latter article. To the above we may also add, that, if we establish a moderate fixed duty on corn, and a pretty free importation be encouraged, it is not unlikely that considerable quantities of our own superior grain may be sold, for seed-corn, at a much higher price than what we pay for imported corn, and be exported abroad as part payment. It is to be regretted, that the statistical returns of the export of farm produce are so few, since it is a knowledge which may be highly useful, particularly to the agricultural body.

Second. Under the second head, there is a much wider field for the operation of the trading department of agriculture; and it is necessary to mention a few only of the articles, to show how we may command a market to any extent we choose, provided we afford sufficient inducements, by facilitating the exchange of commodities in return. The principal articles are as follows:

In the shape of beer, ale, and porter we export malt and hops.

In the shape of whisky, gin, and alcohol we export malt, hops, and potatoes.

In the shape of cyder and perry we export apples and pears.

In the shape of linen, sacking, and twine we export flax and hemp.

Even if it depended on the mere gratification of tastes, this alone would be sufficient to create and maintain a not inconsiderable trade, did not our fiscal regulations present almost insurmountable obstacles both to the exportation of these articles abroad and the importation of a sufficiency of value in exchange. As an illustration of the above position, it is said, that a bottle of champagne and a bottle of London porter have been sold in St. Petersburgh at the same price. They may be really equal in value: we would not assert to the contrary; but they are not, generally, placed on an equality in this country. But the fact serves to show, that, if people were allowed freely, and at a moderate cost, to gratify their tastes, there would be no calculating what would be the interchange of commodities. We ourselves, although the makers of a most excellent spirit, called gin, yet import the same description of spirit, and pay an enormous duty upon it, merely because Dutch gin is somewhat different from our own.

Third. Under the third head, the different kinds of produce that are consumed in the manufactures of the country, the following is but a very limited and imperfect account, but it is sufficient to show, that this vent for our agricultural produce is deserving the attention of those interested in the prosperity of agriculture, and particularly with the view of increasing the number of articles, since there are not a few which may be found capable of yielding a profit to our farmers more ample than any ordinary description of farm produce.

We enumerate the following articles under this head, namely, size, starch, woad, saffron, teasels, tow, weld, madder. And, were a statistical committee to be appointed by each agricultural society in the kingdom, to inquire into the above three modes of promoting the exportation of agricultural produce, and to attend also to the regulation of the duties payable on importation, so as to give the British farmer *fair* play, he would not require any *favour* to enable him to bear his head high above all opponents.

Division 6.—A broader Cultivation of Hemp and Flax Advantageous to the Landed Interest.

The articles Hemp and Flax, and the manufactures that are made from them, being more particularly connected with the pursuits of a rural population, and, also, with the agriculturists, than any other, require a separate consideration.

Hemp has been grown, from time immemorial, in the Isle of Axholm, and, for many centuries past, in the county of Suffolk. It is, or was, also grown in Sommersetshire and several other counties; and, as to its quality, Loudon, in his Encyclopædia of Agriculture, states, that English hemp, properly manufactured, stands "unrivalled in its strength." If, then, we can excel all other countries in the quality of this article, as produced from our own soil, and if we have already an important trade depending for existence on the growth of hemp, either at home or abroad, surely this is as strong a reason for encouraging the home growth of hemp as we can possibly have for any other agricultural product, not excepting corn. We should rather be induced to give a preference to the growth of hemp, when we consider, that we are dependant on one nation alone for our supply of this article; whereas, the whole world almost would stretch out their arms to us to be allowed to supply us with corn. But, if we can show, that there will be more profit to the agricultural body by the growth of hemp, under like circumstances, than there is by the growth of corn, it will be manifestly our duty, as well as our interest, not to favour the culture of the latter to the almost entire exclusion of the former.

If we were to put hemp and corn on the same footing with respect to duties, the following scale must be adopted, premising, that, for the purpose of this calculation, we take the produce of an acre sown with corn to be 3½ quarters, and that to grow one ton of hemp requires four acres of land.

Comparative Scale of Duties on Corn and Hemp, supposing each to pay a like duty, acre for acre, for the protection of the landed interest.

	s.	d.		s.	d.	
When corn pays	0	1½	per quarter, hemp should pay	1	8	per ton.
„ „ „	1	0	„ „ „ „	14	0	„
„ „ „	2	6	„ „ „ „	35	0	„
„ „ „	5	0	„ „ „ „	70	0	„
„ „ „	6	8	„ „ „ „	93	4	„
„ „ „	10	0	„ „ „ „	140	0	„
„ „ „	20	0	„ „ „ „	210	0	„
„ „ „	25	0	„ „ „ „	280	0	„
„ „ „	30	0	„ „ „ „	350	0	„
„ „ „	40	0	„ „ „ „	560	0	„
„ „ „	50	0	„ „ „ „	700	0	„

The first line of the above table shows the present duty on the importation of hemp, which is 1d. per cwt., or 1s. 8d. per ton, and the duty of 1½d. per quarter set opposite to it shows what would be an equivalent duty on corn. The fifth line shows what was the late duty on hemp, say £4. 13s. 4d. per ton, and its equivalent duty of 6s. 8d. per quarter on corn is shown on the opposite side.

It has been said, "that the culture of hemp, in this country, is not, generally, profitable, and that, except where grown for local manufacture, it is a crop of only secondary consideration:" a single glance at the above table will explain the cause of this. The highest duty that has been payable on the importation of foreign hemp, for the last ten years, is £4. 13s. 4d. per ton, which is equivalent to a protective duty of £1. 13s. 4d per acre per annum on land, whilst the highest duty payable on corn, during that period, and which was actually paid on some small quantities in March, 1836, was 54s. per quarter, which is equal to a protective duty of £9. 9s. per acre per annum on the land.

Our landholders, however, can neither realize £9. 9s. nor even £1. 13s. 4d. per acre for the whole of their land; and this, of itself, is a proof how really inoperative protective laws are.

But the saying which we have quoted above, and which has been confirmed by many eminent agriculturists, demands more than a passing notice. It amounts to the admission, that the cultivation of this kind of produce *is* of *prime* consideration, and *is profitable*, in certain localities, even without the aid of any protective duties to help it, nay, even in spite of the blighting influence of those laws. This admission is decisive of the question at issue; and the truth of it establishes the fact, that protective duties are not absolutely necessary for the success of the agricultural interest; but, on the contrary, that there are ways and means of promoting its success totally independent of protection.

The whole of the reasoning that applies to the culture of hemp applies equally to the culture of flax; but this latter article, being still more of a

British staple than hemp, to be outstripped in the culture of it is what we should not allow. Formerly, it was the policy of the country to encourage the growth of flax; but it does not appear, that its home growth was ever stimulated by any such stringent means as those which have been resorted to to force the growth of corn. The present duty on imported flax is merely nominal, being the same as on hemp, only 1d. per cwt.

To grow one ton of flax requires a breadth of land of about three acres; and, therefore, to encourage the growth of this article, in a similar way to that which we adopt with corn, would require the following scale of duties:

Comparative Scale of Duties on Corn and Flax, supposing each to pay a like duty, acre for acre, for the protection of the landed interest.

			s.	d.					s.	d.	
When corn	pays		0	2	per quarter, flax	should		pay	1	8	per ton.
"	"	"	2	6	"	"	"	"	26	3	"
"	"	"	5	0	"	"	"	"	52	6	"
"	"	"	10	0	"	"	"	"	105	0	"
"	"	"	15	0	"	"	"	"	157	6	"
"	"	"	20	0	"	"	"	"	210	0	"
"	"	"	30	0	"	"	"	"	315	0	"
"	"	"	40	0	"	"	"	"	420	0	"
"	"	"	50	0	"	"	"	"	525	0	"

The quantity of flax imported amounts to about 45,000 tons per annum, which will require about 135,000 acres of land to raise. The quantity of hemp imported is about 30,000 tons per annum, requiring about 120,000 acres for its growth. Together, 255,000 acres. And, solely because of a fancied superiority of the growth of corn above that of hemp and flax, we blindly force ourselves to the extreme growth of one article, and abandon the other, for the benefit of foreigners, without a just consideration of its value in other respects. The preparation and manufacture of these two articles used, formerly, to be a source of employment, to a very great extent, for our rural population; and, as the retention of them on the soil is the highest possible interest of the landlord, the cultivation of these articles ought to be encouraged, for that very reason alone, instead of being neglected for that *ignis fatuus*, and, positively, unattainable result, a maximum price for corn.

Division 7.—Present Duty on Corn False in Principle and Deceptive in Operation.

We now come to the consideration of the last, but by far the most important, of the means which we have to propose for the benefit of the landed interest, the adoption of which is, we believe, the only way to secure its permanent prosperity: this is a modification of the Corn Laws.

It is attempted by our present system to ensure remunerative prices to the farmers by the imposition of a scale of duties on foreign corn, founded on the principle of a maximum or minimum price, as the case may be. Now, this is a false principle of action, and, therefore, its aim and end never can, under any circumstances, be realized. To secure a maximum price for corn, or to prevent its going below a minimum price, we must effect the following necessary conditions. First, we must control all the growers of corn, that they may not grow too much; second, we must control all the consumers, that they may not consume too little; and, third, we must control the pecuniary means of the consumers, that they may be enabled to pay for what they consume: not one of which conditions is within our power.

Nor, indeed, can *protection*, as a principle, be made permanently available: protect one interest by too high a duty, and two counteracting influences are immediately brought into operation: on the one hand, increased efforts to produce more of the article so protected, and, on the other, a decreased consumption, this latter being brought about either by abstinence altogether, or by the use of some substitute not similarly protected; and by these means the business generally settles down to a worse state than that in which it was before protection was attempted.

We can show, by a very simple illustration, one of the ways by which our present protective system, as applied to corn, is rendered abortive. In the north of Ireland, our linen manufacture is carried on to a considerable extent. To supply the raw material for that manufacture, by what is thought to be the most favourable means, we allow the importation of flax and of flaxseed, at a nominal duty. The quantity that is imported, in consequence of this exemption from duty, sets at liberty so much land as would otherwise have been appropriated to its growth in the neighbourhood, and the land thus liberated is naturally applied to the growth of that article, which, in consequence of our fiscal regulations, holds out the temptation of the best and most secure returns, namely, corn. Now corn, being allowed to be exported from Ireland to England duty free, comes into immediate collision with the interests of the English farmer, and nullifies, to a certain extent, his fancied protection against the introduction of foreign corn.

We have made this illustration, not with the view of creating any jealousy between the farming interests of Ireland and of England: very far, indeed, be it from us to think of such a purpose; nor will it be found, on reflection, really calculated to produce such a result, as both England and Ireland are, at the same time, equally losers by this circuitous process. We have put the question thus, because, as the immense supplies of corn from Ireland have tended greatly to keep down prices in the markets of England, to the loss of both the English and Irish farmer, it is more likely to command the attentive consideration of those more immediately interested in the results.

But, in examining the working of the above operation a little further, it will be found, that, besides the clashing of interests produced by its concealed effects, there is a manifest and positive loss to the country, which might be saved by the direct import into England of any certain quantity of corn, duty free, from abroad, and the growth at home, instead of the import, of a corresponding breadth of Flax or Flax Seed. By importing Flax Seed from abroad the Irish farmer has to pay the freights and charges necessarily incurred upon it from its place of growth to the foreign port of shipment, and thence until it arrives at his own doors, and, at the same time, he has, also, to bear the freights and charges for conveying to the English markets the corn which he is, in a manner, forced to grow, in preference to the flax seed which he would otherwise naturally raise ; thus there are two sets of freights and charges to be borne by this circuitous operation, where one would suffice.

Now, supposing the duty on the import of flax seed to be put on an equality with that on corn, acre for acre, the Irish farmer will certainly grow less of corn, which he has, for the most part, to send to a distant market for sale, and more of the required flax seed, which would be all consumed in his own neighbourhood. This will be true, however, only in the event of the duty to be imposed being a moderate one, such as will not depress the linen manufacture by raising too much the cost of the fibre of flax. If the just point of duty could be hit upon, so as, on the one hand, not to injure the linen trade, nor, on the other, the farmer, then the linen manufacture would flourish more than ever, and a still greater consumption of Irish corn on Irish soil be the consequence, which would still further relieve both the English and Irish markets.

We are open to the objection, that it is not profitable to sow any kind of land with seed that has been grown upon that same land, and to repeat that operation year after year, but that it is necessary to go to a distance for fresh seed. All the change that it is necessary to make, may, in general, be effected without going beyond the bounds of some neighbouring parish. It cannot, certainly, be more necessary for us to go to foreign countries for seed, than it is for foreigners to come to us: and, therefore, as respects foreign seed, the objection cuts two ways. Any exchange of this kind that may be effected with advantage, and without the constraint of law, is conformable with the policy we would advocate.

We do not overlook the fact, that the policy of admitting various kinds of seed, of foreign production, at a very low duty, has been acted upon, of late, with great advantage to our farmers, notwithstanding its apparent interference with their interests. It has been furnished to them from abroad at a lower price than that at which they could themselves grow it at home, estimated according to the fancied price they can obtain for home grown corn, although, perhaps, not really so low, if all things were duly taken into account. This imported seed performs for them the service of a staple from which they produce their crops, on the same principle as the manufacturers of cotton and woollen goods elaborate their respective fabrics from the raw materials. Such seeds as are imported for sowing should, therefore, be admitted for home consumption at a corresponding rate of duty to that which is imposed on other raw materials imported for the purpose of being manufactured.

But corn is also a seed, and although it differs from other seed, and from most other raw materials also, in this respect, that it is, at the same time, both seed and substance, still, the same principle of taxation might be justly applied to it, for, if it be imported as seed only, and as such used by the farmers in the light of their raw material, wherewith they are to work for the increase of their substance, then it should be charged with duty the same as any other raw material. If, on the other hand, it be imported for its substance only, and be used as bread for the people, it might, without any very forced analogy, be considered in the light of a raw material for our labouring classes, by which they, also, are to work for the increase of their worldly substance, and be admitted for their benefit on as easy terms as the raw material used by the farmer and master manufacturer.

This point leads us to the consideration of another very important principle which the same illustration will enable us to develope. The articles, flax in the fibre, and flax seed, are both admitted for home consumption at a nominal duty; nevertheless, the duty on flax seed is above double that which is paid on flax in the fibre, acre for acre. From this circumstance, it might naturally be concluded, that the linen manufacturers of the north of Ireland would import the whole of their flax, or the greater portion of it, at least, from abroad; and that it could not possibly answer for the farmers, in the same neighbourhood, to import their seed from, probably, the same distant country, to pay double the duty upon it that the fibre is subject to; and, after that, to sow the said seed, and mature the crop, for the purpose of supplying those very manufacturers with the staple which they are perfectly free to import from all the world. Yet, it is a fact, that the linen manufacturers do not import any of their raw material from abroad; whilst, on the other hand, the farmers of Ireland do avail themselves of the foreign seed, pay duty upon it, and, with its produce, furnish the manufacturers with the whole of the staple they require, and, it is to be presumed, at a lower price than that at which they could import a similar quality from abroad.

Now, what is the explanation of this anomalous circumstance? It is this: that the cost incurred by the transport of the foreign fibre from the place of its growth to the place of its manufacture, the loss of interest, the insurances from sea risks, and other losses and damages incurred on the transit, would amount to so much more than it would do upon the seed necessary to produce a corresponding quantity of fibre; and the difference thereon being taken into account, along with the cost of carrying the surplus corn to the English market, both together are quite sufficient to afford the Irish farmer a fair profit, and, at the same time, to secure to himself the entire monopoly of his own market. And this is a proof, beyond all dispute, that the protection which is afforded to the farmer, by time, place, and circumstance, is one that cannot be contravened.

The following table will illustrate the position which we have been endeavouring to establish.

Table showing the comparative Cost of Carriage incurred on Importing sundry articles from abroad into the United Kingdom:

	s.	d.
The seed sufficient to sow one acre of Flax, about	0	9
The produce of one acre, in Butter, about...........................	0	9
The produce of one acre, in Cheese, about...........................	1	6
The produce of one acre of Flax Seed, about.........................	7	0
The produce of one acre of Flax, in the fibre, and of Hemp, from.. 10 0 to	15	0
The produce of one acre of Corn, from .... 15 0 to	20	0

The drift of all this reasoning points to the great fact, that we must adjust our duties on corn, and on other agricultural products, so that one article shall not be overloaded with duty, or clogged with restrictions, whilst another is admitted duty free. We have shown, that the policy of admitting one article duty free, for the advantage of one particular trade, carried on in particular districts of our country, has a tendency to derange the just balance of our markets in general, and produces a positive loss, without increasing the profits of the favoured trade. We have endeavoured to show, that any attempt to protect any particular trade, by loading the imports with heavy duties, will only temporarily affect prices, and afterwards produce counteracting effects, so that no permanent benefit can result from it. There is, therefore, no other course left but a middle one, that of nicely adjusting each interest, so that no one shall feel that another is more or less favoured than itself; and this is consonant with the only true principle on which all duties ought to be levied, namely, for revenue, and not for what is falsely called protection.

We have a certain amount of revenue to raise which is absolutely necessary for the service of the state; and, whether we raise the whole of that revenue from one article only, or from a hundred or a thousand different articles, still each individual of the state contributes his quota in exact proportion to his expenditure; for, however we may vary the mode of raising the revenue, the burden is distributed over every article in the land that can be the subject of bargain and sale between man and man.

But, although it is of no consequence to each individual, as far as concerns the *quota* he is called upon to contribute towards the general burden of the state, in what way that burden may be imposed, it is of great consequence to different classes of individuals in the aggregate, and of vast moment as regards the prosperity of the people at large. By a judicious system of collection, our burden, heavy as it is, may be lightened, so as not to be felt sorely by any class; whilst, on the contrary, if we forsake the true principle of seeking how this load may be safely and most easily borne, and endeavour to use it as an instrument to prop up one or other separate interest or class, although with the very best intent and guided by talent and foresight all but superhuman, yet, we shall assuredly create such a disarrangement of what would otherwise be naturally adjusted powers, as will cause the machine of state to drag as with an immensely heavier load. The resolution of this is simply as follows:—If we attempt to levy more duty on any one article than that article can bear, we depress the interests of every party having any connexion with that article, and, in exact proportion to the injury we inflict, we, at the same time, injure all the other interests of the kingdom that reaped any benefit whatever from the prosperity of such depressed interest.

That foreign corn has not, hitherto, yielded a revenue to any great amount is not to be wondered at, since the duties imposed are so fitful and uncertain, and, moreover, have not been levied for the sake of revenue. The law at present in force has neither been successful in raising any considerable amount of revenue nor in protecting the landed interest: it has had no other effect than that of "keeping the word of promise to the ear and breaking it to the sense:" it has soothed the agriculturists into the sweet delusion, that all was, at least, safe as far as their interests were concerned, it being forgotten that there are two parties to every bargain, and that, whilst they trusted to the law to secure their expected harvest of profits, their opponents, in the shape of speculators, both foreign and domestic, ever watchful to secure that harvest to themselves, of bankers, merchants, and manufacturers, who, impressed with fears of impending evils, when corn rises, draw in their operations to check trade and commerce, and of a vast population which, by the use of inferior food, show their inability to pay high prices or their determination to resist what they esteem a forced exaction of their means: all these combine to render of none effect the fallacious principle on which the present corn duties are based.

Accordingly, we find, that the duty raised on foreign corn, from the passing of the act up to the present year, a period of ten and a half years, has not exceeded 6s. 4d. per quarter on the average, the quantity of imported grain, of all kinds, averaging, for the same period, 1,100,000 quarters, to which we may add 60,000 quarters for meal and flour, and the revenue about £380,000 annually.

The following table exhibits the particulars of the above; and the account may be taken as the actual measure of the quantity of foreign corn which this country is able to pay for under the existing laws, and the utmost amount of duty which, under the same circumstances, can be exacted.

RETURN TO AN ORDER OF THE HONOURABLE THE HOUSE OF COMMONS,

Dated the 27th of February, 1839, for

An Account of the Total Imperial Quarters of Foreign Wheat entered for Home Consumption in the United Kingdom from the time the Act 9 Geo. IV., cap. 60, came into operation, to the 5th day of January, 1839; the Total Amount of Duty received thereon; and showing what that Duty was equal to per Imperial Quarter on the aggregate average of all this period.

The same Account for all other kinds of Foreign Corn, Grain, Meal, or Flour.

	FOREIGN CORN, MEAL, AND FLOUR.			CORN, MEAL, AND FLOUR, the Produce of, and Imported from, British Possessions out of Europe.		
	Quantities charged with duty for home consumption, under Act 9 Geo. 4, cap. 60, from the passing of the Act (15th July, 1828) to the 5th Jan., 1839.	Amount of Duty received thereon	Rates of Duty taken on the Average of the whole period.	Quantities charged with duty for home consumption, under Act 9 Geo. 4, cap. 60, from the passing of the Act (15th July, 1828) to the 5th Jan., 1839.	Amount of Duty received thereon.	Rates of Duty taken on the Average of the whole period.
	Quarters.	£.	*per Qr.*	*Quarters.*	£.	*per Qr.*
Wheat	6,777,620	2,039,115	6 0	519,530	98,121	3 9
Barley	1,389,982	414,921	6 0	314	23	1 6
Oats	2,138,584	766,429	7 2	8,977	295	0 8
Rye	164,885	35,516	4 4	—	—	—
Peas	475,922	176,920	7 5	6,592	635	1 11
Beans.........	550,616	265,776	9 8	—	—	—
Indian Corn	102,713	19,271	3 9	5,482	384	1 5
Buck Wheat	37,361	11,906	6 4	—	—	—
	Cwts.		*per Cwt.*	*Cwts.*		*per Cwt.*
Wheatmeal and Flour	2,215,037	191,978	1 9	595,745	41,622	1 5
Oatmeal	177	52	5 11	1,843	78	0 10

WILLIAM IRVING,
Inspector-General of Imports and Exports.

Inspector-General's Office, Custom-house, London,
26th March, 1839.

Division 8.—Duty on Corn, proposed for the purpose of Revenue.

Turn we now to the modification of duties which we propose should be made on the import of corn, and of other agricultural productions, and to the reasoning and calculations necessary to show what will be the result.

We propose, that a fixed duty of 10s. per quarter be imposed on grain generally, which is equivalent to what might be called a protecting duty of £1. 15s. per acre per annum, on such land as will yield 3½ quarters of corn to the acre. For the same reason that we would impose a duty on corn, we would impose an equal duty on every agricultural product, according to the average produce of an acre of land, modifying the scale, however, so as to find out the point at which each article will yield the greatest amount of revenue, without distressing, or, if possible, injuring, in the slightest degree, the interests of the classes that are to consume each article. By a comparatively equal scale of duties, imposed on this principle, we shall have each description of land applied to the growth of that kind of produce for which its quality of soil, general aspect, locality as to markets, or other advantages most fit it to be applied. By this means only shall we obtain the largest, and, at the same time, the most profitable, returns to the farmer, to the landlord, and to the country at large. By the regularity and economy with which the foreign trade in corn can be carried on, under a fixed duty; by the wider range of markets which, through the same means, will be open to us; by the adjustment of the duties on other farm productions; by the repeal of the taxes we have pointed out, as checks to consumption; and by the increased means of the people to consume a much larger quantity of food than they now do, consequent on the fair opening which this better state of things holds out, there will be an absolute necessity for a greatly increased import of corn, or other farm produce.

We estimate, therefore, that it will be possible to import annually about three millions of quarters of corn, or about two and a half times the average quantity hitherto imported. And that this is not impossible we may confidently assert, because we have actually imported a larger quantity within one year. It appears, that, in the year 1831, there were imported 3,451,809 quarters.

The import we have assumed will be an increase of about one and three quarter millions of quarters, which would be the produce of about 500,000 acres of land; and, since the breadth of our cultivated land is estimated at 35 millions of acres, this assumed increased import would, if grown at home, be the product of only about one-seventieth part; and, taking into account the increased consumption which we have alluded to, we would ask, if it is possible that this small proportional increase of crop can have that very great influence on the rent of land which is generally dreaded?

But it may be objected, that this is not a safe view of the question, since this particular import ought to be placed in contrast with our own production of *corn only*, and not with the whole produce of our cultivable land; that, in this view of the case, the import of one and three quarter millions of quarters of corn, which is about the one thirty-fifth part of our consumption of corn, could not fail to have a very serious effect on the price of corn in our markets, and that such increased import ought not, therefore, to be permitted.

If any weight be allowed to this objection, then, we may ask, on what grounds the protective laws can be supported, which must increase the production of corn in so much greater a degree? If, by relying on protection from the importation of foreign corn, the farmers, generally, sow only one-tenth more breadth of grain than, under other circumstances, they would have done, that would yield an increase amounting to 5,000,000 quarters; if they cultivate one-fifth more, that would yield an increase of 10,000,000 quarters; if one-third more, that would give us an accession of 17,000,000 quarters over the unconstrained production of grain.

As we already import, on an average of years, 1,160,000 quarters of corn, the increased import, on the assumption which we have made, would amount to no more than 1,840,000 quarters, which, it will be admitted, is very much below what the farmers themselves may easily be led to produce. Protection, then, in this view of the case, has done, and may again do, much more mischief to the agricultural interest, as far as the production and price of corn are concerned, than the utmost import of foreign corn that could possibly take place under any moderate and fair scale of duty imposed for the sake of revenue.

If the above reasoning be correct, and the assumed increased import of foreign corn, with the duty added, can have so very little effect on the price of corn as we have alleged, what need is there, it may be asked, to make any change at all; and why should the manufacturing interests press a change so strongly? The answer to this question gives us one method of estimating the value of the foreign corn trade, and a most important one.

Every 100,000 quarters of corn that we grow at home is the work of about 1,700 to 1,800 people to produce, whilst every 100,000 quarters that may be imported from abroad gives employment to some five or six thousand people to acquire, and, therefore, the greater the scope that may be allowed for the increase of the foreign corn trade, the more employment there will be for the mass of the people, and the profits of trade, and manufactures, and, consequently, of agriculture, will increase accordingly.

The merchants, traders, manufacturers, and operatives have, therefore, a strong interest in the foreign corn trade, independently, altogether, of its effects on the price of corn. It matters not to them what the price of corn may be, provided their own employments are in a flourishing condition so as to enable them readily to pay that price. Nor are the agriculturists, in the least degree, less interested in the increase of the foreign corn trade, and, paradoxical as it may appear, for the very same reason. The greater the quantity of corn that the industry and skill of our manufacturing population enables them to import and to pay for, the higher will be the price that they must necessarily give, because every addition to the quantity must, undoubtedly, enhance the cost of production abroad in the same way that it does at home, and the cost of carriage also must increase; and, since our own corn stands first in the market, it must necessarily first feel the influence. But, further than this, the condition of the mass of our manufacturing population being very much improved by the wider scope allowed for the exercise of their talents and industry, they will certainly be enabled to consume a greater quantity of other farm products, and to pay a better price for them also, and thus will a natural and fairly acquired increase in the foreign corn trade be attended with prosperity, even though it should be followed by a general advance of the prices of agricultural products.

But it may be remarked, that, in the comparison we have instituted of the value of home and of foreign corn, as the production or acquirement of the one or the other respectively affect the condition of the population at large, we have not done justice to home-grown corn, having neglected to take into account the rent of land, which goes to the landlord, and is spent by him to the benefit of the state; that we have forgot the cost of the seed, the tithes, &c. There is, however, an equivalent to be set against all these, in the wages and profits obtained on the previous operation of acquiring the raw material on which the manufacturer must work to enable him to pay for the imported corn. The operation will commence and be pursued as follows.

Suppose we see a prospect before us of extending any particular branch of trade, the cotton trade, for instance, and we determine to pursue it; and, suppose we start from the present time, and say, that we can and will increase the cotton trade to the extent of £1,000,000 per annum. To begin this operation will require, in the first instance, an import of, we will say, about £300,000 worth of cotton wool, in addition to what we now import. Now, in order to import this extra quantity of cotton wool, we must export the *produce* of England or its *manufactures*, to a like amount, or nearly so; and to acquire this extra quantity of produce or manufactures, a stimulus will be given to our farmers and graziers, our woollen, and linen, and iron workers, &c.; for unless, by the efforts of one or all of these, we can create an extra quantity of products with which to pay for the required extra quantity of cotton wool, it cannot be imported, and, therefore, the very first step towards this increase of trade could not otherwise be taken. It will be perceived, then, that the landlord has had his rent, and the farmer his profits, out of the previous stimulus of the people and previous export of products, in the very first step towards an increase of the cotton trade.

Having exported £300,000 worth of our productions, we then get in return a corresponding quantity in value of raw cotton, upon which the carriers, the spinners, the weavers, the dyers, the printers, and others, without number, are set to work; and, by means of the expenditure of wages, and the consequent consumption of provisions, with something added for interest and profits, they make that £300,000 worth of raw cotton into £1,000,000 worth of cotton goods. It is no matter what we do with those cotton stuffs, whether we wear them on our own persons, or export them abroad, to purchase, by their means, more of the necessaries or luxuries of life. The argument is, that we have created, and have at our disposal cotton manufactures to the extent of £1,000,000 in value; or, if the value be disputed, to the extent, say of 10,000,000 pounds in weight; and, upon the provisions expended in the manufacture of these particular goods, the landlord, the farmer, and the clergy will also have received their dues, which proves that their interests cannot be sacrificed in any way.

But supposing, for argument sake, that the cotton lords have wrung the extra quantity of work expended upon the £300,000 worth of cotton out of the bones, and sinews, and nights' rest of the poor people in the factories, without the employment of a single additional hand, and without the payment to the people employed of an additional penny in wages, however we might deplore such a circumstance, still it is not an unmitigated evil. The factory people, pressed, we may suppose, by hard necessity, have submitted to the task imposed upon them: they have not been coerced by unjust or illegal means, but have given their free consent. Moreover, other persons have been employed besides those in the factories, and a considerable increased consumption of materials has taken place, such as flour and starch, dye stuffs, oil, coals for steam-engines, and for different heating and boiling processes, to say nothing of wear and tear of machinery, tolls on canals, turnpike-roads, and railways, employment of extra horses, and a thousand other things, which it is impossible to enumerate. The cotton lords cannot obtain all these things without giving a full equivalent; and, therefore, in the regular progress of the case we have under consideration, they cannot fail to contribute to the prosperity of large classes of people, however much they may be supposed to grind down their own work people. It is in vain, however, to deny, that this conversion of £300,000 worth of raw cotton into manufactured cotton goods will cause an increased expenditure of wages in every department of the cotton manufacture, not excepting those earned in the factories, and which will occasion, of course, an increased consumption of farming and other products.

It will, however, be contended by some, that it is a fallacy to suppose, that such a greatly increased quantity of cotton stuffs as we have instanced can be thrown into the market without bringing the price down to a ruinous rate, and that, although we have imported and paid for £300,000 worth more of raw cotton and turned the same into cotton fabrics, still the sum total that the whole of our manufactured stuffs, including this increased quantity, would realize, would not be increased. Even if this were true, our own population would be able to furnish themselves with more and better garments, for the same money, than they previously could do. But this result could, by possibility, be true only in two ways: either by our closing our ports against all the markets of the world, or else all the world closing their ports against us; in neither of which positions are we ever likely to be placed. We have, however, presupposed, that there was a fair opening in view for disposing of this extra quantity of cotton goods before the manufacturers were supposed to commence the proceeding; but, as the more immediate results of any extension of our manufacturing industry would, if unprofitable, be visited upon the master manufacturers themselves, we might fairly trust to them for the due consideration of this point, and leave the consequences in their hands: we shall, nevertheless, follow out the process to its ultimate limits.

The power of extension of our commerce, and the success with which it may be crowned, do, indeed, depend upon our willingness and ability to take the products of our customers in return, for, if we will not take from other nations the products that they have to part with, or only a limited supply of them, and that at uncertain and distant periods, those nations cannot possibly become regular and profitable customers to us. The whole question of the prosperity of our entire people, including landlords and farmers, merchants and manufacturers, centres itself here, can we, or can we not, become purchasers of foreign products to any larger amount than we are now? If we can, then those foreigners will become purchasers from us of our products and commodities to a like extent: then our whole population will be employed, and profitably employed too, and new life and vigour shoot throughout the whole frame of society.

Before affording any facilities for the regular import of corn, it may be objected, by some, that we should, first of all, make the most of our own lands; that there are thousands upon thousands of acres still lying waste, particularly in Ireland, which country, it is said, can produce and spare for England more than double the quantity of corn that it now does. If this be true, which we do not doubt, and our fiscal regulations remain in their present state, it will be so much the worse for the farmers themselves. Ireland has already increased her exports of grain to England from 461,371 quarters, in 1802, to 3,474,302 quarters, in 1838; and, should Ireland go on to double this latter quantity, the sooner we alter our present policy the better, in order that we may be able to dispose of the surplus which that great increase, added to what England and Scotland may also effect in the same way, would assuredly occasion, particularly if we persist in upholding, in the mean time, our present selfish system. For, although a great and speedy increase of our agricultural productions might relieve us from some of our present difficulties, it would bring on others of a different kind, not the least of which would be a severance of the little hold we yet have of our continental relations, and, thereby, render us still more liable to be the sport of the vicissitudes that attend all human affairs.

There is only one objection more which we think it necessary to notice. This has been put, in the form of a taunt, to the manufacturers, in the following question. Since you are so strenuous to have corn admitted, duty free, would you be willing to admit manufactured goods, duty free, also? Some individuals amongst the manufacturers have been bold enough to answer this question in the affirmative, without due consideration, for, assuredly, this could not be done without causing immense injury, for a time, to all parties.

We have shown, that, in all descriptions of wares made of iron, the wages of labour expended upon them, and rents and profits which they yield, form almost the sole cost; and it will be admitted how large a portion of the earnings of wages is expended in agricultural produce. The effect, then, of an import of manufactured iron wares, duty free, would be tantamount to an importation of provisions to a certain extent, duty free. We have shown, also, in the woollen manufacture, and the same statement applies equally well to the linen and cotton manufactures, how great a portion of the cost of the different processes goes to purchase food, in fact, goes into the pockets of the farmers. To admit, therefore, these productions, duty free, would be extremely detrimental to the landed interest. It would be no less detrimental to the revenue also, to say nothing of the still more important consideration, which is too frequently lost sight of in the discussion, that it would throw multitudes of our population out of employment, who, in the consumption of the necessaries of life, do now actually pay that share of duty which each article they manufacture can bear.

As respects the admission of foreign manufactures to entry for home consumption, the fair thing between the two interests would be this: to ascertain, as nearly as may be, how many acres of farm produce were consumed in the fabrication of the different descriptions of goods, and then to fix the duties at the equivalent rate, acre for acre, as on corn: this would be holding the balance even as between agriculture and manufactures. The colonial interest might, however, put in a claim for consideration; but their policy would be for a reduction of duty, which may be effected when the corn duties are put on a solid foundation, and which would give greater comfort to our people, whilst, at the same time, it would increase the amount of revenue and the profits of the colonial interest.

The effect of a duty on the importation of manufactured goods, regulated by the measure of the duty on corn, would be this: that, if foreigners could beat us in the manufacture of some particular article, that article would be imported, and pay duty accordingly. The state would, in this case, reap the benefit of the duty, which would be its object, and the only just and wise reason for imposing one; and the consumers of the article, manufacturers as well as agriculturists, would have the benefit of a cheaper and better article than could be manufactured at home. The individuals engaged in the manufacture of that particular article would be the only sufferers: it may be supposed, that they would be very few in number, and the injury would only continue until they could turn their talents to account in some new direction. But even supposing the worst, who shall say that individual interests shall be set in opposition to the general weal?

The conclusion at which we would arrive is this, that the farmers, and, consequently, the landed interest, cannot be injured by an unrestricted import of corn, at a fair fixed duty, and this, we think, will be amply proved by the following considerations:

First. Under a fixed duty, and supposing the demand for grain in our own markets to be no way increased, we need never fear the importation of so large a quantity of grain, in any one year, as we have already imported under the present law; because, if we impose a fixed duty of 10s. per quarter, which is 9s. per quarter advance upon our present minimum rate, there cannot possibly be given such an excessive impulse to importation as is given when both high prices at market and low duty combine.

The utmost quantity of foreign corn admitted to home consumption in any one year since the present law was enacted, was in the year 1838, when the duty was paid on 1,948,477 quarters within the year. If, under a fixed duty of 10s. per quarter, we ever import a larger quantity than this, or even a larger quantity than the average annual import, it must necessarily be occasioned, not by fortuitous circumstances alone, but by the demands of our people, arising from their increased prosperity and consequent ability to find the means of payment.

Second. In the event of a fixed duty on corn, we can never have the price go so high as to force both importation and home growth to an inordinate extent, nor so low as to repress the home growth as well as the importation, in an extraordinary degree; for be it strongly impressed on our minds, that the very same cause that operates to force an excess of import at one time more than at another, operates also to force an excessive home growth, and the opposite effect takes place after great abundance and extremely low prices.

A better regulated price for corn at all seasons must necessarily be the positive result of a fixed duty, because, the farmer would in this case have one settled point on which to found the calculations for his returns. Under the present order of things, when he has to decide what seed he shall sow, he has no ground on which to judge what may be the state of things as to the admission of foreign corn when he shall reap his harvest; the only accurate idea he can have is this, that, if there should be a general bad harvest, foreign corn will be admitted duty free or nearly so; if there should be a general good harvest, then he may rest assured, that the duty will be high enough, but, at the same time, he will feel, that its being so will be of no earthly consequence to him.

But, further than this, if, when the farmer is about to decide what kind of seed he shall sow, the price of wheat be high, it is more than probable, that, in a doubtful mood, whether wheat or some other grain would best suit the land, for the rotation of crops may certainly be varied to some extent, the high price would bias his judgment, and he would give the preference to wheat; at the same time, all the other farmers in the kingdom who may be similarly placed would be considering and deciding in the same way, and, therefore, when the harvest came, we should have a superabundance of wheat, and, consequently, a scarcity of some other grain.

Our farmers have only one period of the year, the seed time; in which they can vary their crops, but corn-merchants and speculators can vary their operations all the year round, and when the farmer has decided irrevocably what sorts of grain he must bring to market, under all circumstances, such decision, too, having, of necessity, been made for months and months before he can bring his grain to market, they can, at any time, during the same period, alter their imports as their knowledge of the growing crops shall point out.

If, then, from the combined causes we have alluded to, the farmer has sowed too large a proportion of wheat, he must sell his superabundant crop at what he can get for it, foreign wheat being, under such circumstances, entirely out of the question; but other descriptions of grain, which were neglected, in a measure, at seed time, by this very means have become scarce; then prices rise, and importation becomes absolutely necessary, and the foreigner, besides reaping the benefit of the high prices, is allowed to introduce these particular sorts at the lowest duty.

There being five species of grain that are usually imported in considerable quantities, it may be said, that the chances are five to one that some one of them may be admitted within the year at the lowest duty. These odds are decidedly against the landed interest of this country, and in favour of the foreign landholder; and we may, therefore, be justified in declaring, that, as to all practical results to the agricultural interest, the lowest duty on grain is actually in operation, and has been so since the present law was enacted.

The following table exhibits, not the lowest duty chargeable within the respective year, but the lowest average duty of the whole year actually paid on the several articles noted. It is taken from the Appendix to the Second Agricultural Report of 1836, page 232, as quoted by M'Culloch, and sufficiently justifies the above remark:

TABLE.

Year						s.	d.	
1824	Duty paid	on	Oats,	average of the	whole year,	4	9¾	per Imp. Qr.
1825	"	"	Do.	"	"	4	0	"
1826	"	"	Do.	"	"	2	3	"
1827	"	"	Barley	"	"	4	0	"
1828	"	"	Wheat	"	"	1	9¼	"
1829	"	"	Rye	"	"	2	1¼	"
1830	"	"	Oats	"	"	4	2¾	"
1831	"	"	Barley	"	"	1	7	"
1832	"	"	Oats	"	"	2	6½	"
1833	"	"	Wheat	"	"	5	6	"
1834	"	"	Do.	"	"	5	7	"
1835	"	"	Do.	"	"	5	8	"
			General average of the above			3	5	"

Third. By imposing a fixed rate of duty on corn of 10s. per quarter, in lieu of the present scale, we really advance the duty on corn, on the average, since the actual duty paid on the whole of our imports, for the last ten years, does not average more than 6s. 4d. per quarter: the difference, therefore, would be 3s. 8d. per quarter, in favour of British and Irish, and against the foreign farmers.

This being admitted, it may be said, that this change would depress the importation of foreign corn in a ratio corresponding with the actual increased rate of duty levied, say about 58 per cent. advance on the present available duty; and that, in this view of the case, we have proved too much, and contravened the argument urged in a former part of this work, namely, that any increase of duty must necessarily depress imports; that, if we depress the import of corn, we depress the export of manufactures, and, by depressing the manufacturing interest, we depress agriculture, and, consequently, lose, in one way, what we gain in another.

This would be true, provided the duty of 6s. 4d. per quarter, which has been the actual average, duty paid, on foreign corn, for the last ten years, had been the result of a fixed duty and a regular importation, and in lieu thereof we were now to impose a fixed duty of 10s. per quarter. But, owing to the extremely disadvantageous way in which foreign corn has been imported and admitted to home consumption, during the above period, the depression of the importation for the past must have been, upon the whole, very much greater than the proposed actual advance of duty could, by possibility, be supposed to occasion for the future. And, moreover, the country must have suffered greatly, in a pecuniary way, from extra prices paid to foreign farmers and merchants, who, of course, advance their price on the prospect of this market being open to them, from extra freights, from loss of interest of capital, from rents and other charges, and from the terrible effects of adverse exchanges, brought about by the extreme irregularity of the foreign trade in corn.

The proposed additional increase of operative duty, particularly if followed out by corresponding duties on other descriptions of farm produce, will have no other depressing effect than that of giving the farmer a more determinate command of the different productions which our soil and climate and surpassing skill are capable of bringing to perfection. By the present fallacious scale, the farmer has no such determinate control, on the contrary, it affords to the merchant and speculator and foreign farmer the means of operating against his interests, with the odds in their favour; but, by the substitution of a fixed duty, he would have a real control over the imports, because, as he can calculate what is the general average cost of corn, whether grown at home or abroad, and add the duty thereto at once, so he can determine what particular portion of his lands will yield him a crop that shall ensure to him, at the least, a return of his rent and outlay, the remaining portion of his land being applied to the production of other kinds of produce. In this case, it does not necessarily follow, that there will be a greater breadth of produce imported, but only a substitution of one kind for another, our own farmers having the choice of growing what they think will best suit their lands, without the fear of a deluge of imports, at a nominal duty of 1s.

per quarter, to interfere with their fair and just expectations of a profitable return; for, be it remembered, that, in the case of a deficient harvest, which is the general cause of high prices, the duty, if considered only in the light of a protective one to the farmer, should actually be increased, rather than diminished, in order to afford him an adequate return.

Fourth. But a fourth reason why corn, and, consequently, land, cannot, on the whole, sustain any fall in their value by the proposed substitution of duties is this, that, by imposing a duty on corn for the purpose of revenue only, we can afford, without injury to the revenue, to remit the whole of the duties on horses and carriages and male servants, and, by these means, considerably increase the consumption of farm produce.

The number of horses, carriages, and male servants now subjected to duty in the United Kingdom, with an allowance for stagecoach and post horses, and classing the whole together in one enumeration for brevity, amounts to between six and seven hundred thousand, and the total amount of duty levied amounts to about £1,800,000. Now, by the remission of the whole of this duty, it is not unreasonable to calculate, that the number would be increased by 10 to 15 per cent., say by about 80,000 in the aggregate; and, making a round estimate for the consumption of the extra number of servants and of horses, and for the extra employment of other people occasioned by the keeping of so many additional carriages, we cannot be far wrong in stating, that the whole, together, would require the produce of about 400,000 acres of land to subsist. We should, therefore, have a positive increased demand for corn, and grass, and hay, and provisions, created by this very change of duty which is so greatly dreaded, but which is thus capable of being made subservient to an advance in the price of farm produce rather than a decline.

It may be objected, that so great an increase in the number of servants, and of horses and carriages to be kept in consequence of the proposed remission of the duty, cannot possibly take place; for, that the amount of the tax to those that are able to keep these luxuries is a matter of very little consideration. It is impossible to believe, that a reduction of duty, amounting to £1,800,000 per annum, can be made without causing a very considerable increase in the number usually kept; but, when we consider the difficulties that the present taxes, and the regulations attending their collection occasion, particularly to persons who are not conversant with business affairs generally, and, least of all, with that very intricate affair, the schedules A B and C of a Government assessed tax paper, we allude to livery-stablekeepers, coach-builders, publicans, and others letting out horses and carriages to hire, there cannot be a doubt that a very large increase would take place.

The usual hire of a horse for a ride of a few miles only, if hired from any large town, is at present 10s., and of a horse and gig 15s.; these would be reduced probably to one-half, and the number kept for hire in this way would be more than doubled. The rate of posting, which is now 1s. per mile, for a one-horse vehicle, and 1s. 6d. per mile for a chaise and pair, would, if the post-horse duty were repealed, be reduced some 30 to 50 per cent.; consequently, there would be a great increase of posting, and there would be scarcely a roadside inn of any description that would not furnish its one-horse chaise for the benefit of the wayworn traveller.

Fifthly. There would be no fall in the price of corn, and, consequently, of the rent of land, because, in order to pay for the increased quantity of produce that we should necessarily import, under the improved order of things we have pointed out, our people would be more fully employed and better paid than they now are. That would enable them to consume more butter, and cheese, and milk, and butchers' meat than they now do, and from which would arise the necessity of a still further import. There would necessarily follow a greater resort to our markets by foreigners desirous of supplying our increased wants; and be it particularly borne in mind, that some countries, Denmark, for instance, have nothing whatever to sell us but such farm produce as we ourselves grow; and some ports have nothing whatever to sell but one single article, wheat. There would, therefore, arise a still further demand for our manufactures, so that we cannot place any positive bounds to the prospect. Nevertheless, no jealousy ought to arise in the breasts of our agriculturists at this extended view: the landlord cannot get *two* rents from his land in *one* year. The utmost that both landlord and tenant ought to look for, and the utmost they can, under any circumstances, realize, is such an increase in the value of the products of the land as the general employment of the people will enable them to pay: the prosperity of the people, then, is their best, their only stay.

Sixthly, and lastly. There can be no permanent reduction in the prices of corn and, consequently, in the rent of land, but, on the contrary, there must necessarily be a continual increase in their value, because we have a population which is increasing at the rate of *one thousand human beings a day*, provided only that we afford that population full scope for the exercise of their industry, by which alone they can acquire those necessaries and luxuries which they would desire to enjoy.

This great rolling tide of population has not only outstripped in its consumption all the efforts of our agriculturists to produce the greatest quantity of food which they have been able to produce from the breadth of land which was formerly under cultivation, but also all that which they have been able to raise from the immense extent of common lands redeemed within the present generation, but it has, also, in the face of the most distressing fiscal regulations that affect the price of corn, forced us to inport the produce of 2,000,000 of acres of land annually from foreign parts. This irresistible power will require a progressively increasing supply of food, which can only be raised by the cultivation of many hundred thousand acres of land every year, in addition to the quantity that has been under cultivation each preceding year; and, on this increasing demand alone, supposing they do not paralyze it, our landholders have a far better security for their interests than can be afforded by any system of protective duties which can be devised by the art of man.

T. BEAN, PRINTER, 21, CASTLE-STREET, LIVERPOOL.

LORD BROUGHAM'S

SPEECH

IN THE HOUSE OF LORDS,

ON

TUESDAY, FEBRUARY 19, 1839,

ON MOVING

FOR A COMMITTEE OF THE WHOLE HOUSE

ON

THE CORN LAWS.

SECOND EDITION.

LONDON:

RIDGWAY, PICCADILLY.

1839.

Henry Peter Brougham, Baron Brougham and Vaux (1778–1868)

On 29 December 1838 Joseph Parkes (1786–1865) who had acted as a go-between the radicals and the Whigs wrote to Cobden about the prospects of recruiting Lord Brougham for the free trade campaign:

Tomorrow I & a leading friend of his will try our best to launch him. But it is just as the humour takes him. ... you never know whether you have him or not. The truth is (& his apology for his inconsistencies) that he is an insane man, tho' I never knew him in a more sane or democratic humour than just now. It is just the *natural* opportunity and a *proper* subject for him for a new public pedestal. He led the niggers' orchestra last Session, & if he will head the Corn Law revolt he will do more popular good. Besides it is Political Economy & in his line.[1]

Similarly Arthur Aspinall in *Lord Brougham and the Whig Party* summarized Lord Brougham's positions on politics and economic policy as erratic.

At one time he was the chief organiser of the campaign against the income tax; at another he voted for that 'odious imposition'. At one moment he urged the repeal of the obsolete navigation laws, whilst at a later moment he strongly condemned an attempt to repeal them. In 1815 he supported the corn laws; in 1830 he demanded their drastic modification; in December 1845 he was preparing to lead the protectionists against Peel; and a few months later he declared himself boldly for free trade.
. . . Brougham's speeches on economic subjects were primarily intended to serve personal and party ends. They afforded him excellent opportunities of advertising his cleverness and industry, and he turned them to political account by making them the vehicle of attacks on the Government.[2]

Thus his speech may be regarded as fairly representative of Whig free trade rhetoric rather than the idiosyncratic theories of an individual thinker. His advocacy of free trade was largely due to opportunism rather than an independently arrived at policy, an impression strengthened by his later quarrel with the League's leadership.

[1] Quoted in McCord, *The Anti Corn Law League*, p. 39

[2] Arthur Aspinall, *Lord Brougham and the Whig Party*, Manchester: University Press, 1927, p. 229.

SPEECH.

Lord Brougham—In rising to address your Lordships on this very important subject, which occupies the minds of all men out of doors, and which, I think I may add, attracts no small share of attention within this House, I confess that I feel considerable uneasiness in performing the task which I have undertaken, sensible that I appear before you opposed in no common measure to strong feelings on your part, proceeding, I say it, with all possible respect, from very great, and I am sure very groundless prejudice and misapprehension. It has often been my lot when standing at that bar or sitting on that bench, in the discharge of my professional duties, or when delivering, as a peer of the realm, my own private opinions—it has often been my lot to advance doctrines which were distasteful to this House—when I knew that your sentiments differed widely from my own. I have sometimes gone against strong, conscientious, and deep-rooted convictions grounded upon principle; I have sometimes been compelled by a sense of duty, imperative upon me and unyielding, to run counter to what you may have deemed your interests; but on the present occasion I feel that both these antagonist feelings and principles are working against me, for many of you think that you have an interest in opposing me upon this subject, and that if you failed to do so, you would likewise be failing in the discharge of your duty. Little, therefore, should I hope of being able to discharge mine, if I did not know that here in this House, in this the highest Court of Judicature, the gravest and most dispassionate senate in the country, there is a body of the most enlightened men that adorn and fortify the constitution, who never will rashly decide on any proposition without first hearing it thoroughly discussed, and who, much less, would decide against it without giving those who have propounded it the most ample, impartial, and calm hearing upon its merits. That you should reject a proposition only to hear—that you should say "no" to a prayer only preferred that you should consider and examine—that you, this High Court of Judicature, this grave senate, this body of accomplished, learned, and deliberative men, should turn a deaf ear upon the prayers of the people, and when evidence is tendered at your bar in support of those prayers, you should turn away and refuse to hear it—that you should say, "True, the subject is one of the greatest importance in its principles, and most perilous in its possible results, but we will not hear one tittle of what you are prepared to prove upon oath."—I will not believe it, my Lords—I will reject the idea as utterly impossible—I will not believe any thing so monstrous, on any authority but your own, nor until you shall tell me that this monstrous impossibility is true.

My Lords, I derive great consolation from another source. I am here to war against no particular interests—I am here to oppose no portion of the community, nor any body in the state. Whoso expects to hear one word pass these lips disrespectful to any class of the Queen's subjects, as a class, will be disappointed. Whoso expects to hear one word fall from me in disparagement of the landed interests, or in depreciation of its extensive and by me ever to be acknowledged importance, will go hence disappointed. Whoso expects that I shall utter one word betokening a wish that any preference should be given to the masses of numbers over the rights of property, will likewise go away disappointed. I stand here, the advocate of the cause of the country—the landed and professional interests—the producers and the consumers—the workers-up and the exchangers of every commodity. All those classes are comprised in the great view I take of this question, and I shall be "out of court," that I may use a professional term, if I stand upon any other than those comprehensive, universal, and Catholic grounds, embracing at once the interests of each, and the interests and the rights of all. But I hope not to sit down without satisfying you, that you may grant the prayer of these petitioners without shaking the interests of the landed community, which at first sight might have appeared to be endangered by it. What, my Lords, is their prayer? You will observe, that I am not here to argue the Corn Law upon its merits—I am not here to ask that you grant the prayer for repealing the Corn Laws either wholly or in part. I am only here to ask your Lordships to tarry and to hear the case before you decide upon it; to look at the facts, to examine and investigate the details, in which I am ready to give you all the assistance in my power. All I shall do further now is, to state so much of the facts of the case which the petitioners are prepared to prove at the bar upon oath, as may be necessary to drive those of you who oppose the prayer of the petitioners into this dilemma, either that you admit my propositions of fact to be true, and therefore say they require no proof—or that they are so manifestly false that no proof can demonstrate them—or that the matter is in itself so utterly unimportant, that whether the facts be true or false can be of no moment. It may save the time of your Lordships if I state the different matters of fact in due order, thus aiding the inquiry by somewhat of arrangement, by giving order and method to the subject; and then it will be for you to say whether or not I tender statements which are in themselves impossible to be proved, or statements which are utterly immaterial which ever way the proof may turn out, or statements which must at once be admitted to be true; for those are the only three conceivable grounds on which this question can be rejected.

Let me, then, come to consider what the present Corn Law actually is, and then what it does; your Lordships always bearing in mind that every assertion I make is meant, not as a statement which I call upon you to believe or admit or decide upon either way, or even to consider with a view to its truth or falsehood, but as a statement of what I am prepared to prove upon oath at your bar. I am now opening the evidence to your Lordships.

The former encouragement given to the agricultural interest of this country by the Bill of 1804, commonly called Mr. Western's Bill, from the name of my noble friend now a member of this House but then of the other, was by opening the ports for the importation of foreign grain only while the price, taking the average of a certain number of districts—of, I believe, twelve different districts—continued to fall below a certain amount. When corn was high the ports were open, but when it reached a certain low price the ports were closed, so that at the higher prices the trade in foreign corn was free; it was only stopped at the lower price; and I am prepared to offer proof that all the objections which were urged against that plan, and they are neither few in number nor light in weight, apply without any exception to the present system, falsely supposed an improvement on the other. Instead of the opening of the ports when the price of grain came to one level, and the shutting the ports when the grain was lower, which was an absolute rule, we have now contrived and fashioned a certain scale, taken on an average, not of twelve maritime districts, but of a certain number of towns; and instead of taking the average once in eight weeks, we take it week by week, regulating the admission of foreign grain thus. There is no prohibition at all. It is not, like the bill of 1804, absolute prohibition or entire permission, but the very same thing is operated by means of a duty. When the price is 73*s.* there is a duty of 1*s.*; this allows all foreign grain to enter our ports. When the price is 70*s.* the duty is, I think, 10*s.* 8*d.*; when it is 65*s.*, the duty is 21*s.* 8*d.*; and when the price is 63*s.*, the duty is 23*s.* 8*d.* When the price is 60*s.* the duty rises to 26*s.* 8*d.*, and when the price is 50*s.* the duty is 36*s.* 8*d.*; so that as the price lowers, the duty is rising until you come to the price of 45*s.*, and then the duty is equal to the price, or, in other words, 45*s.*

My Lords, the proposition, and the first proposition which I have to maintain is, that there is no difference whatever between this system and the former as regards its consequences upon the corn trade; I shall show by the most incontrovertible testimony, that in principle and in practice there is no difference conceivable between the plan of 1804 and the present plan of a variable duty. Your Lordships will recollect that a certain price must be given for foreign wheat, to which, if you add the expense of transport and the other expenses of insurance, harbour dues, &c. it will be equal to the whole price at which the imported grain must be sold here; in other words, a price which is the lowest you can sell it for here. Then it follows that there is always a certain price, including the duty, at which foreign grain cannot be sold here, because the price will exceed the home price, and therefore the foreign grain be excluded. Suppose, for instance, the average price of wheat for a certain number of years at Dantzic to be 36*s.*, and I am prepared with persons to prove this the fact, and my Noble Friend has given me a vote on this occasion indirectly, in saying that he desiderates proof on the subject, [Lord Wynford had expressed doubts]; but, as I stated, 36*s.* was the average price for a certain number of years in Dantzic. I am also prepared to prove, that the cost of conveyance, the shipment at Dantzic, the bringing it over here, the harbour dues, the insurance, the landing, and the carrying this corn to the markets, amounted altogether to 10*s.* 6*d.* the quarter.

I am ready to prove this upon oath at your bar, and consequently 46*s.* is the price at which Dantzic wheat, or Polish wheat shipped at Dantzic, can be sold in our markets upon the average of those three years. I have stated these matters in more detail for this reason, because in a subsequent part of my statement I shall refer back to them to show that those who have an extreme fear of our markets being lowered by foreign grain, do not take into consideration that foreign grain must be bought at a price as well as English grain, and that the agricultural alarmists have greatly exaggerated the quantity and the cheapness of foreign grain, for I am ready to show that 46*s.* 6*d.* is the average price, below which Baltic wheat cannot be sold in our markets. Suppose, then, the price to be, by the operation of the present Corn Laws, 70*s.*, then foreign wheat has to pay a duty of 10*s.* 8*d.*, and 10*s.* 8*d.* added to 46*s.* makes very near 57*s.* This would open the ports, very likely, but I do not think that much grain would come over at that price. But suppose, my Lords, the price falls to 65*s.*, then the duty is 21*s.* 8*d.*—say in round numbers 22*s.* What, then, would be the price of foreign grain here? About 3*l.* 8*s.*; a price sufficient to shut the ports. It is quite clear that the price shuts the ports when it falls to 63*s.* and the duty is 24*s.*; therefore the price must be above 62*s.* to enable foreign corn to be sold in our markets; and then the grain comes over, but is excluded from our markets when it arrives, and must go into bond. All below 62*s.* is "Exclusion," just as much as by the bill of 1804. All above 70*s.* is "Open ports," just as much as by the bill of 1804; and, consequently, we have precisely the same state of things, the same to demonstration on principle and on the *rationale* of system, the consequences of which I now open to your Lordships, and which I will prove upon the oath of persons who have felt those consequences; aye, of persons who have been ruined and undone by them, whose suffering under them continues to this hour, and will for ever continue to oppress them, unless some miraculous interposition shall save them. They can hope nothing for themselves—but to save others from their fate, and warn you from persisting in the course to which they trace their own ruin, they will tell you upon oath their sad story. The consequences are the self-same with those, the dread of which and the experience of which drove you from the plan of 1804 to seek refuge in the new, and, as you supposed, improved plans of 1815 and 1828.

My Lords, I have now, I think, explained generally the nature of the plan; and may I solicit your attention to those consequences to which I referred? In answer, in far too triumphant answer, to the first of the three alternatives I stated, as the only conceivable grounds of refusing to hear evidence at the bar, the impossibility of tendering any at all of the existence of those dreadful consequences. I now state to your Lordships not only that they are highly probable, but that, instead of its being impossible, I shall show, by testimony upon oath, that they have happened, and that they are actually occurring daily, and therefore altogether certain and inevitable. First, I shall show by reasoning that they must occur whilst the present system continues, and I am able to show this by a very short consideration of this system as I have described it. I will assume for the present, that the corn trade is a traffic that deserves to be encouraged. I will assume that we look occasionally to a supply of foreign grain. I will assume that, for some reason or other, I could define it if I thought it necessary, but I will assume that we think it better not absolutely to be confined to the grain of our own country. And why do I assume all this in the way of argument, but as matter of fact? It is because the Bill assumes it, the Act of Parliament assumes it, the very Act of 1804 assumed it; for nobody would exclude grain altogether—nobody ever proposed an absolute prohibition, an inflexible and perpetual exclusion. It is admitted that when the price of grain is high here we cannot rely upon our own resources, but must look to foreign corn. We exclude it when the price of grain is low here, because then we can rely upon our own resources; but our allowing it to come in at any price at all, completely demonstrates that the Parliament of this country, at present and under the existing system, looks, and professes to look, and intends to look, and legislates and provides as if it looked, to the occasional necessity of foreign supply.

Having set my foot on that position, with which I am provided by the Act of Parliament, I next proceed to ask if it does not follow, as a matter of course, that the corn trade is an object of encouragement, and that we meant to encourage it under all the restrictions and limitations imposed on it? We thought that the former act discouraged it too much; and as our purpose was encouragement, we wished to effect that purpose by the change of the law in 1815 and 1828. Now I will demonstrate these things—I will first show by argument that it is very probable, and then I will tender evidence to prove that it is true in point of fact, that this system is fatal to the corn trade. I will not abate one jot of this proposition. I will not be satisfied with convincing your Lordships, that it is only hurtful. I will not be satisfied by proving it mischievous on the oaths of a cloud of witnesses, who are ready and anxious to come to your Lordships' bar, some of whom have been ruined themselves, and whose only hope is that their fate may prove a warning to others, and thus be the means of preventing their brothers in trade from meeting the same ruin. I will not be satisfied with proving upon oath, or by argument or by both, that the present system is pernicious to the corn trade. This is nothing, unless I demonstrate, first, by argument, that it is probable, and then, by evidence, that it is certain that the corn trade is destroyed by this system. I will suppose one case, and upon it turns the greater part of this question. Suppose certain merchants, when the price of grain is at 72*s*. or 73*s*., and the duty therefore down to a shilling, join in a venture for the purpose of supplying a certain number of quarters of grain, say forty or fifty thousand quarters. They ship it at Dantzic, where the price is 36*s*., or at Malta, where the price is 42*s*., or at Odessa, where the price is 24*s*.—suppose that from any or all of these ports they ship a hundred thousand pounds worth of corn. The venture is collected on the shores; it is embarked in the vessels; it sails from the different ports, crosses the sea, and arrives; and then, when the importers all expected that they might be permitted to land their corn, and when we, the consumers, well might hope that the markets would receive a benefit; and that the pressure of scarcity, which had raised the price of wheat to 70*s*. a dearth if not a famine price, would have been relieved by this importation of foreign grain—the merchant adventurers find instead of this, that the price has fallen from 70*s*. by the last week's average, when their ships were at sea, and when it was utterly impossible to stop the venture, when the purchase was made and was coming over, when it was in the middle of the Atlantic or of the North Sea,—they find all of a sudden during the last week by a change of the weather, or the speculations of the grain-dealers at home, that instead of the price being 70*s*., it has come down to 65*s*. or 62*s*., a prohibition price, because at that price, the duty is at 24*s*. and Malta wheat could not then be landed in the river under 80*s*. Wherefore the merchant finds that he cannot land one single ounce of this corn without ruin, They may land it if they choose to be ruined: [a Peer said, "They might bond it."] I know they may bond it. Does the Noble Lord suppose I did not know that? I am extremely ignorant of the subject, I dare say. I have often observed that it is tiresome and painful to argue it, and I have never discussed it half so much as some of your Lordships; but I happen to know that there are such things as bonded corn warehouses, and that the 100,000*l.* worth of corn might be bonded; which leads me to what I was going to state, namely, the consequence of bonding. It is a very easy word to use, my Lords, "Oh, bond it, and then you can be ready to get it out when the duty falling allows it to be sold." But what is the consequence of bonding? Why that it costs 6*s.* per year per quarter. That is the expense of a bonded warehouse. The grain must be turned, generally once a week; it must be stowed away; rent must be paid for the warehouse; interest on the purchase-money, at five per cent. at least, must be added; and the result of the calculation is what I have stated. If this statement is disputed, I have witnesses to show its truth. All I ask is, to be allowed to prove these things, and to demonstrate that 6*s.* is the amount of those expenses of warehousing. What is the consequence? You may tell these adventurers that when the price of corn gets up again they are allowed to fetch it out of the bonded warehouse, and bring it into the market; but I am sure they would say that they had much, very much, rather they had left it at Odessa, or Dantzic, or Malta, than have to pay the expenses of freight, insurance, and bonding.

But, unhappily, this is not all; it is a dream to fancy the profits of the adventurer are only deferred; a different account will be told in London, in Bristol, in Liverpool, in Newcastle—a place from which my Noble Friend (Lord Durham) presented a petition complaining of the law; and most naturally, for there is no place where its effects have been felt more, as I know professionally, than at Newcastle-upon-Tyne—this I know from my recollections of the Northern Circuit. What is the consequence? They cannot get their corn out till prices rise. They may wish for it; but let them sigh and weep ever so bitterly, the wind will not breathe the louder for their sighs, the rain will not fall to the measure of their tears. Their fate depends upon the weather, and until the price of wheat gets up to 70*s.* not one ounce of their venture comes out of bond. What is the consequence? It may have to wait in the warehouse two years. That is a loss of 12*s.* Then the whole of the profits twice told are absorbed. It may have to wait three years, or four years, and what will your Lordships say if it has to wait five years? What if six years? What if it must wait seven years? Why, not only the profits of the venture, but the whole of the capital is absorbed—42*s.* a quarter are absorbed. This, my Lords, no man can deny is the possible consequence of the system. No man can deny that it is a probable consequence. But I go farther, and, as I told your Lordships, when I put a case I do so not only as being probable, but as being able to prove it—what I have told your Lordships, and I implore your attention, and particularly the attention of the Noble Duke (Wellington), and of the Noble Earl (Stanhope) opposite—I have not put a possible or a probable case—I have put a case that has happened, that took place here, in this city where you now sit—it happened on the banks of the river that washes these walls! A merchant imported 100,000*l.* worth of grain from the Baltic in 1831. The price then allowed him to do so. He hoped to be able to land it, and he expected to make a reasonable profit. The ports were open, the duty being as low as a shilling, when he shipped the corn in the Baltic; the ports were closed when the vessel arrived in the river. He had recourse to a bonded warehouse. He was told in his distress, as I have been told in my argument this evening, "Oh, there are bonded warehouses." Yes, and into these bonded warehouses went this £100,000 worth of grain, and that £100,000 of the merchant's capital might as well have gone into the river upon whose banks those bonded warehouses stood. Seven long years was this merchant kept out of possession of his money; for seven long years prices kept so low that not one handful of this grain was sold in the markets of London; during these seven years, as I am fully prepared to prove, not only the profits, but the *corpus* of the adventurer's capital were consumed in charges. The house failed; it was a Newcastle house, and this is another reason why I said the petition was most justly presented from that place, for no place has suffered more; but this house, a most respectable one, failed, became bankrupt, and has not paid a shilling in the pound, and, if evidence is allowed to be produced at the bar of the House, I will prove upon oath that the commission-agent, who was neither merchant nor speculator, lost £21,000 by being such commission-agent, in consequence of the failure. That which has happened to these most respectable men may happen to any one man any one day on which he enters into a speculation of this sort. Others as well as they will find that the ports which were opened when the grain was ordered will be shut when it arrives here, and consequently they will have to share the ruin of these unfortunate individuals. The trade in corn is one which no prudent man enters into—a trade which is not fit for discreet merchants to embark in—a trade which is not fit to receive capital, from the nature of its channels, precarious, tortuous, endangered by shallows, and studded with rocks and quicksands which no soundings will enable to fathom, which have never been buoyed, nor ever laid down in map or chart, which cannot be depended upon for an instant, and which shifts like a rapid river's course with the winds and weather of the twenty-four preceding hours. Let fine weather come, let the harvest look well, let the ear of corn appear full, down goes the price, the ports are closed, and the merchant finds he has embarked in a trade the channels of which are the most unsafe and unfit for the reception of capital that he could select. As a gambling trade, a speculation for needy and hungry adventurers, for persons without capital, often without principle, it is well adapted; but for a regular trade, of a wholesome species, it is utterly unfit.

The next view of the subject which I am about to take, or rather the next head of the evidence which I am about to tender, relates to the immediate effect of this system in cramping the corn trade, and its pernicious effects upon prices. I am ready to admit that on this point there is a great deal of exaggeration on both sides. I think that the fears of the landed interest have exaggerated the mischief which is likely to be produced; and I think that the hopes of the manufacturing interest have also exaggerated the cheapness likely to be produced by the repeal. This is my opinion; it may give no satisfaction to the petitioners, who feel so strongly on the subject; but it is my opinion. Nevertheless, at all events, I think it most probable, and I am ready to prove it, that there will be some cheapening of the commodity, although not very considerable, in consequence of the repeal of the Corn Laws, and of having the trade in grain absolutely free. I think what I have already said respecting the price of wheat at Dantzic shows this: There the price on an average is 36*s.* to which the expense of freight, &c. namely, 10*s.* 6*d.* being added, the whole cost is a little under 50*s.*, the price at which foreign wheat can be sold in our markets, though without any profit; but when it is selling at 55*s.* or 60*s.* here, that, at all events, is 5*s.* or 10*s.* more than we can get it for from Dantzic. In Malta, upon an average of ten years, down to 1836, the the price was 42*s.*, to which add for expenses of freight, &c. 15*s.* 6*d.*, you will thus make 47*s.* 6*d.*, or under 48*s.* for Malta grain; whereas, during these same ten years we had an average of price at 48*s.*, though some years it was 58*s.*, I may assume therefore that the excessive fears about the 10*s.* difference are groundless. Odessa also is different from either of the other places. It has been represented, by way of alarming the agricultural interest, by a respectable witness called Saunders, that wheat was selling at Odessa for 10*s.* or 12*s.*, to which the expense of freight, &c., being added, say 10*s.* or 12*s.* more, made something under 30*s.* for the price of Ukraine wheat in our markets. This gentleman was at one time, as I have heard it said, an enemy to the Corn Laws; but when he made the statement I am alluding to he had become an enemy to their repeal, and a friend to the existing system; and, I suppose, under the influence of prejudice, or of zeal, which burns fiercely in converts, and blinds them to what is passing before their eyes, he omitted a very material circumstance, namely, that although during the time he mentioned the price was 10*s.* or 12*s.* at Odessa, yet during the same period the Dardanelles were shut, and in consequence wheat was a mere drug in the market; but it attained its usual and natural price when the channels of trade were open, and the 12*s* or 14*s.* became more nearly 30*s.*, which added to 15*s.*, the expense of transport, makes 45*s.* Now there is not any very material difference between this and the Baltic, for although the price in the Baltic is higher than that at Odessa, yet the expense of transport is a great deal less—only two-thirds of the expense of transport from Odessa and Malta.

The difference in the price of bread on the Continent and here is undeniable, and it is considerable. I think, moreover, that if the price of bread is permanently less there than here, we may assume it is partly owing to the Corn Laws; but we must be careful not to suppose the difference so great generally as at particular times it is found to be; for when in 1838 the 4lb. loaf on the other side of the Channel was 4*d.*, here it was 8*d.*; manifestly a temporary and not a permanent difference. I do not say, as is commonly said, that this is wholly attributable to the Corn Laws—far from it. I do not wish to make one in raising a clamour about cheap bread, because I am opposed to the present system. I began by stating that I do not expect any very great cheapening of bread; I said I did not believe that it would fall very much. This opinion may be wrong, or it may be right; but at all events it is arguing my case on the lowest ground and giving every advantage to my adversary. Yet it is very far from leaving my case weakened as against him; for suppose wheat to fall only 5*s.* by the repeal; suppose upon an average the price on the other side of the Channel to be permanently 5*s.* lower than here, when we consider that fifty-two million quarters of corn, all kinds included, are consumed in this country, or, at all events, that twelve or thirteen millions of quarters of wheat are consumed, only see what an enormous sum is thus levied through the operation of those laws. I will not dwell upon this, as it is not the view I chiefly take of the question. I have in view a much higher object than making bread cheap; not that I undervalue making cheap the staff of life, very far from it—not that I undervalue the effects of the present system, both on the comforts of the people, and on their general industry—not that I underrate these by any means; but I am afraid, from the nature of things, that very great cheapness is not likely to be constant; the landowners, under their terror, exaggerate their apprehension; whilst the manufacturers on the other hand, cherish exaggerated hopes, like persons enchanted with a fairy prospect on which they love to gaze. Both take a superficial view of their respective positions. But suppose there is only one shilling rise caused by these laws. Suppose, instead of seven shillings or five shillings being the difference, as I have just argued, and as you may at the very least expect; suppose it to be but one shilling—then I say that this one shilling a quarter is a tax levied upon the whole people for the benefit or the supposed benefit of one class; and I ask your Lordships to pause and reflect for a moment what that shilling means.

It means a tax—it means head-money—it means a capitation-tax, known by that hated, that justly execrated name, a poll-tax, which this country in civilized times never consented to—which in any age of our history was never viewed with other sentiments than those of abhorrence, and which is only the resource—the natural and fitting resource—of arbitrary governments—a tax from which there is no escape, for all eat and drink – a tax which falls upon all classes, the poor equally with the rich—upon men who can hardly support life by the sweat of their brows, and men wallowing in wealth with £100,000 a year—the family of the one paying 5*s*. a year, at the rate of 1*s*. each to this tax, which is as much as the man of £50,000 or £60,000 a year pays, having the same number of children. But there is a great deal more than this to be said. Bread forms much the larger proportion of the food of the lower classes than of your Lordships. You have your luxuries, whilst the poor man is taxed for every particle of food he consumes [a Peer on the opposition benches said, "so are we"]. I am aware of that. I know that there is a duty upon spices and wines as well as upon bread, but the poor man pays on his bread in his humble sphere, and out of his scanty means, as much as the wealthiest of your Lordships, while this forms nearly the whole of his subsistence. I think that fact enough to disincline any man from the tax, and to make us all refuse our assent, to any but the most ample and incontestable advantages—the most cogent arguments to justify so odious a taxation. I have already said that I care not if, having brought down the duty to 7*s.*, and from that to 5*s.*, and again from that to 1*s.*, and having paused to make this observation, I care not if even the shilling be taken away altogether. It is very possible, for ought I care, that it will not lower the price at all. My argument will not in its main branch be impaired. I am now to remind the landowner, in order to quiet his exaggerated alarms, that the opening our market permanently cannot leave prices abroad so low as they are there. In all the calculations of facts as to supply, suffer me to say that this most material circumstance has been totally left out. The alarmed farmers on the one hand, and the sanguine manufacturers on the other, have totally forgotten that the 36*s.* price at Dantzic, the 42*s.* at Malta, and the 24*s.* at Odessa, which some folks, for the purpose of their argument, made 12*s.*—are the present prices only ; but let the Corn Laws be repealed, let our markets be laid open, and let there be a steady demand for grain [cries of "hear, hear!" from the opposition benches]. Suppose there is a free importation of grain as of any other article, is it not perfectly clear that you increase the demand, and therefore the price, if the supply continues the same? The Noble Lord who has interrupted me is extremely quick. I was just coming to what he suggests, but I must go by steps in my statement, and I cannot take two steps at a time, as some other Noble Lords seem able to do.

Suppose the supply to be the same, if the demand increases in the English and Scotch markets, for Ireland may be left to herself, what would be the consequence? Why that at Odessa, in the Baltic, and at Malta, wheat would rise, and Polish wheat, for example, could not be sold at the comparatively low price of 36*s.* But it is said that the consequences of the additional demand will be to occasion a greater growth of corn, and open new tracts to its cultivation. That is very possible; but I am prepared with evidence to show the difficulty of such an alteration. How little land is there that is not covered with thick and almost impenetrable forests? How difficult is it to get hands to cultivate it, and how little of the land capable of cultivation lies near the sea, or navigable rivers, however plentiful it may be in the remote recesses of Volhynia and the Ukraine? I have evidence on oath to prove this; yes, both documentary and parole evidence, if your Lordships will give me leave to produce it. It is barely possible that in the course of years, as for many years it cannot happen—but it is barely possible that in the course of time an additional extension of agriculture may cause an additional supply of foreign grain, and the consequent effect would then be to reduce the price, which would in some degree counteract my statement. But admitting that the manufacturer will gain nothing at all in point of cheapness, and the agriculturist will lose nothing, I am now coming to what in my mind is an infinitely more important consideration for both than lowering the price of grain. I am now about, in the rest of my statement, to assume that there would be no cheapening of the price of food whatever, and I am about to show your Lordships, and, if permitted, to prove upon oath, what would be the inevitable consequences, and what must be the inevitable benefits of having a free trade in corn.

Now, first of all, it would give the best possible security against famine, and the present system, on the contrary, exposes us to the greatest possible risk, and to the greatest danger of encountering that last of public calamities. That is the first proposition which I am fully prepared to prove. I am prepared to show your Lordships this, by evidence which I can produce, but first I am by argument to prove that this is not improbable; in order that you may not say, "What is the use of producing evidence to that which cannot possibly occur?" In the first place, it is to be remembered, that in all calculations of chances, where the estimate is made upon but a few instances, the result becomes a matter of great uncertainty; and the fewer the instances the greater uncertainty must prevail. I pray your Lordships' attention to the course of reasoning which I am now pursuing, as though quite plain and easy in itself, it requires some little attention, accurately to comprehend it. Suppose a man should try to calculate what number of male or female children there would be from any given marriage, in any given country, that would be a calculation wholly impossible to make. But, suppose, upon the other hand, a person were to make a calculation as to the number of male and female children there would be in a parish, he could not be very certain in his calculation if he made it in a very small parish; but he would be the nearer the truth, the larger the parish, respecting which his calculation was made. But let him then extend his calculation over a larger portion of the community—over an entire country, or continent, and his calculation would amount almost to a certainty. Suppose, then, a calculation were made as to the changes of the weather; and this is coming very near to the present case, which is much affected by the seasons. Now, to tell what weather there would be upon any given day, in any given year, would be impossible. [Viscount Melbourne was understood to say the attempt at such calculation had been made.]

In the Noble Viscount's reading, in his various reading, he may have found that such a thing is not impossible. But, in my reading, I have not found it laid down that such a calculation can be attended with any certainty. Suppose the attempt was made to calculate that in any one given year there would be a good season, that would be a thing very difficult to determine. No man could undertake to determine it ; but suppose you were to take ten years—suppose twenty years, and say there would in those be certain variations of seasons—the calculation would be easier, it would be more certain ; and suppose you extend it to a century the calculation would amount to nearly a certainty ; as in such a long period of time, there is always found to be a balance of good and bad seasons. That then is exactly the case with the crops of a country in any given year. No man can attempt to say that in this district the grain will be abundant, and in that the crop will fail—no one can venture to predict this of a particular farm, of a particular county, or even of a particular country ; and yet it might be carried over the world and the prediction would be found to be good, that the crop would be abundant in one place, and would fail in another ; for it very seldom happens that there is an universal failure of the crops all over the world, because countries differ greatly from each other in climate, in soil, in productiveness, and in various other circumstances, that influence crops, and the weather differs in different parts of the world during the same months; so that you have nearly a moral, or rather a physical, certainty that, looking at the whole world, you will hardly find at the same time the season bad, and the failure universal, or the season every where favourable, and all the countries having good crops. What, then, does the Corn Law, in its exclusion from this country of foreign wheat? What does it affect by excluding the foreign supply? It strikes all other countries out of the calculation, and in a time of scarcity leaves the nation to the certainty of famine. It confines your chances against famine to one country—it confines your chances to one kind of weather. To avoid scarcity, you have but one chance, and you are left, more or less, depending upon the mercy of the fickle wind and the uncertain elements. But this could not be the case if the whole of Europe were open to supply you—your chances against famine would be still greater, if the East, if Africa, if America, as well as Europe, were open to you; for then you would be able to say, there cannot be a scarcity with us, without a scarcity every where, because you would be well off, if others were well off. There would be all the difference between dearth and famine—the dearth, the consequence of the bad season, you could not avoid ; but, if man did not interpose his luckless hand, that dearth never could be converted into a famine. Dearth there would be only ; but Corn Laws convert it into famine. I am ready, my Lords, to produce to you the evidence of persons who have been traders in all countries; I am ready to produce to you persons of large and long experience, who are prepared to show you that the good season in one country is generally, if not always, balanced by a bad season in another country. They will show you this so plainly, that you must concur with me in the inference to be drawn from their evidence, and from the facts which they will depose to, that if you have the grain trade universally free, famine is as little to be dreaded in this country as an earthquake or a volcano.

The first great evil, then, which is done by the Corn Laws, is their taking away our great security against famine, and the converting of dearth, when it does occur, into that extreme calamity. Next, it makes the price of grain fluctuating and unstable. I am the more anxious to press this view of the case, of which in all its details I here tender evidence upon oath, because I recollect, at the period of the discussion on the Corn Law Bill, when the enemies of the Bill said to the promoters of it, " All you want by your Bill is to make grain dear!" "O, no such thing!" it was replied, "nothing can be further from our intention than to raise the price of grain." Then it was said to them, "You want to keep corn up to a certain price." To this it was declared, "No, no—nothing of the kind; we do not seek that at all. That is no object of ours; it is a mistake altogether." This, indeed, appeared to be very odd: you, who are for a Corn Law, will not let in foreign grain at a low price; and yet you say you do not wish to keep up the price; and then, you are dealers in grain, and yet you do not wish it to be dear, nor do you actually wish it to be cheap; then what is it that you mean, or what is it that you do wish? "Oh!" it was answered, "we'll tell you what we want—steadiness of price; for steadiness is of more importance than cheapness to the consumer, of more value than high prices to the producer. What we want then is, not to make corn dear, we would rather have it cheap; what we dread is, not cheap corn, but a fluctuating price for corn; we shall make it cheap, but we will not have it unsteady." [An exclamation of "No, no!" from a few on the opposition benches.] I heard these arguments elsewhere—I imagined the same course of reasoning would be adopted here, and I supposed the same degree of rationality would be found here as elsewhere. It is, my Lords, a great object to have prices steady and to avoid fluctuation. I know that your Lordships concur in that proposition; and I entirely agree with you. I do object to fluctuating prices. Famine and want, the consequences of dearth, may by prudence be averted; but of all the curses that ever afflicted a country, that which must ensue upon the tampering with prices is the last of calamities, as it must be attended with the most pernicious, if not the most fatal, consequences. Who can look back upon the fatal history of our currency, from the ill-starred measure in 1797, which began its depreciation, down to the rapid and unreflecting restoration of its standard in 1819, and not be deeply sensible of the calamities which those revolutions in our monetary system inflicted upon the country. The restoration has indeed been almost as disastrous as the depreciation. I take blame to myself, on the retrospect, for not endeavouring to break the fall by some mitigation of that measure. Not that I was a member of the Bullion Committee in 1819; my name was proposed, and a factious vote kept me off, though a very large minority gave their support to the motion. When the Report was discussed, and the Bill introduced, I was labouring under severe illness, and could hardly bear any part in the debate. Had I been in full possession of health, I feel confident that I should have endeavoured strenuously to obtain such a modification as might prevent the country, as well as other debtors, from repaying with twenty shillings every sixteen or seventeen which had been borrowed. However, what little support I gave was to the Bill, and I have ever since deeply regretted it. For I was well aware, and I urged it at the time, that a far greater rise in the relative value of money and goods would take place than the mere difference between the market and mint price of gold. Such, however, having been the unspeakable mischiefs of a fluctuation in all prices, the pound varying from thirteen and fourteen shillings to eighteen and twenty, how much does it behove us to prevent the fluctuation in the price of grain by all the means in our power; of grain which, next to the precious metals, regulates the price of every thing else, by affecting most materially the price of all labour? In holding, then, that fluctuation is the greatest of evils, and steadiness of price the greatest good, I plant my foot on this position, and say that I cannot look but with alarm on the continued operation of the Corn Laws. Your attention is called to this point—whether the Corn Laws have or not obtained this object? I do not now stop to enquire whether they have made corn dearer; I say they do not prevent the fluctuation of prices. I am about to tender evidence that they do not prevent fluctuation; and then I mean to go a step further, and to shew you that they cause fluctuation. I shall not detain your Lordships many minutes, while I give you one or two very important and very obvious facts. I first take a period of seventeen years—from the year 1773 to 1790—and in that time the fluctuation was not more than 2*s*. the quarter; 4½ per cent. was the fluctuation in the price of grain for that period. I am taking the average by years—and on the average of that period the greatest fluctuation was not 4½ per cent. Taking, therefore, these seventeen years; you perceive that there was then a very steady price. I then stop at the year 1790. For very obvious reasons, I mean to omit the next fifteen years, and pass to the years 1804 and 1805. For there were the two years of scarcity in 1795 and 1796, and there were the still worse years 1800 and 1801. The fluctuation in 1801 was so much as 100 per cent. Where in any years many disturbing causes occurred to interfere with the prices, I pass those years over, because I have no right to argue upon them, and I have now to call your Lordships' attention to another period, from 1815 up to 1838; and what do we find? That in the year of the least fluctuation, the fluctuation was not 4½ as in the seventeen years already mentioned, but 11¾ per cent., and that under the influence of the steady operation, the equalising operation of the Corn Laws! and in the year after Sir Henry Parnell's Bill passed the House of Commons, it happened that under the steadying equipoise, or the regulating influence of the Corn Laws, the fluctuation was not 4½ per cent., as it had been before; it was not even 11¾ per cent., but it was 94¾ per cent.! Here, then, was a fluctuation in price of nearly cent. per cent. in the same commodity during a single year!

The Duke of WELLINGTON : What year?

Lord BROUGHAM : I believe it was a very remarkable year. It was the very first year after the improved Cor i Law. It was in the year 1816, that the fluctuation was 94¾ per cent. [a Noble Lord observed, "There was a depreciation of the currency—it was then beginning"]. Sir Robert Peel's Bill was in 1819, and there was not a farthing in the pound difference from January the 1st to the 31st day of December in that year. How, then, is that depreciation to be made the ground of fluctuation? It would be different if you could show that the pound was now not more than thirteen shillings, and then rose to twenty shillings.

Viscount MELBOURNE : The issues were very greatly contracted.

The Duke of WELLINGTON : There was, too, an alteration in the currency in 1816.

Lord BROUGHAM : Undoubtedly, if the ounce of gold rose from £3. 18*s*. 10½*d*., to £4. 10*s*., and then fell to £3. 18*s*. 10½*d*. ; if there were any such alteration between the Mint and the market price of bullion, you might account for the fluctuation in corn ; but I will venture to say that during the whole of the year 1816 no such thing occurred. There was a contracting of the issues of the Bank ; but could that alteration produce this effect on prices when it hardly produced any sensible effect on the market price of gold? Now, I engage to prove that never, from the beginning of the year to the end of it, was the difference so much charged as 3*s*. between the Mint and the market price of bullion.

The Duke of WELLINGTON: How much does that make?

Lord BROUGHAM: Instead of 95 it would not make 5 per cent.; a fluctuation in the market price of four shillings would be less than 5½ per cent, for it is on a sum of £3. 18*s*. 10½*d*.; and then we thus find under the influence of the Corn Laws, which were to make prices steady, that the fluctuation is not less than 90 per cent.! I am now going to read to you a list of those fluctuations. In 1817, it will be found that the fluctuation was 52 per cent.; in the next year it was 23 per cent.; then it was 36 per cent.; we then come to the year 1820, but it will be said that the fluctuation was here influenced by the return to cash payments. It is to be observed that the market price of gold has ever since Sir R. Peel's bill been £3. 18*s*. 10½*d*., which is the mint price. Now, then, mark the fluctuations since that time, and while the currency has not fluctuated a farthing. In 1821 the fluctuation in corn prices was 53 per cent.; in 1822 it was 32 per cent.; in 1823, not a year of particular scarcity, but one in which prices might be expected to be steady, the fluctuation of grain was 56¼ per cent.; in 1824 it was 25 per cent.; in 1825 it was 13 per cent.; in 1826 it was 13 per cent. This shows how little human calculations are to be depended upon. You have variations of 33 and 30 per cent. until you get to 1836, when it was 71 per cent., though in 1836 there was no scarcity, and the ports were shut. In such a year no fluctuation of prices was to be expected, and yet there was a fluctuation of 71 per cent. in the prices. Such, then, we find to be the working of the Law in that year. But if we take it from the year of the first Corn Law—from the time of Mr. Western's bill in 1804 and 1805, we find a fluctuation of 30 per cent.; and in the year 1806 we find a fluctuation of 46 per cent. I purposely avoid giving the years of great scarcity, and, at the same time, I must say that there never was so great a difference between the issues of Bank paper as to make these variations in the prices which I havestated, and which from the official returns I am ready to prove at your bar. I have stated these facts, and I am now ready to prove by witnesses that the Corn Laws, so far from preventing, have occasioned or exasperated the great evil of fluctuation.

My Lords, I am one who, above all other things, attach the highest importance to the steadiness of prices. It is not only of prime convenience, but of the utmost importance to all mankind, to know exactly the amount of their income; it is not only of the last importance to the merchant, to all individuals who are engaged in the speculations of trade, and to the manufacturers, and, above all, to those who are employing hundreds and thousands of hands, and who are paying hundreds and thousands a-year in wages to their men—not only to them is it of the highest importance, nay of the last necessity, that they should know what price they can securely and undoubtedly look for, instead of their being left to grope their way, without the smallest glimmering of light to afford them a chance of seeing when they enter on a speculation whether it will redound to their wealth or prove their ruin, or whether it would not be better for them to rest, according to the proverb, " when you see not your way before you, stand still ;" but for all and every person—for the industrious and the poor who live by the work of their hands, or for the capitalist who endeavours to realize profits from his stock ; to either, to all, even to the mere idle consumer who lives upon the land and has an income to spend, to him and to all classes it is of the last importance to have prices settled, that they may know what is exactly the cost of the commodities they deal in, whether as purchasers or as consumers, and may have a steady and unvarying income for their occasions. Now the price of grain is felt more or less in all commodities. When the price of grain is settled, then you have, in other words, settled the income of every man, and his resources are regulated. You have thus done the best service to the manufacturer, the agriculturist, the trader, and the consumer. If, on the other hand, you tell me that the price fluctuates, then it is plain that no man's income and no man's resources are within his own knowledge, and no man, under such circumstances, can prudently and economically manage his own affairs. I believe that a certainty of price, followed by a certainty of knowledge of a man's income, are, of all other elements, those most calculated to secure prudence of conduct; while, of all the elements likely to induce or to support an extravagant disposition, the very first and most potent is being uncertain of your resources, and finding that these vary from year to year. But to guard against extravagance, the parent of evil, and to promote economy, the nurse if not the mother of virtue, is the most sacred duty of all who assume, whether as rulers or as lawgivers, to administer a nation's affairs. Holding, therefore, that a constant fluctuation in prices is calculated to make every man a speculator and a gambler, I must hold that a fluctuation in the necessaries of life is that which every prudent lawgiver should guard against. It is for these reasons that I tender evidence to you, to expound to you at length the evils of the present system in this respect.

I now come to another and the next head—hardly inferior to that in interest, nor altogether disconnected with it. The fact is that the Poor Laws—

Earl Stanhope: The Corn Laws.

Lord Brougham: I beg the Noble Lord's pardon—I meant Corn Laws; but having him before my eyes, I naturally mentioned Poor Laws. It is more his fault than mine. I might, indeed, advert to the Poor Law, as by no means unconnected with this subject, since the burden of maintaining the poor must fall upon the land, and the great interest of landlords is to have cheap food; but by some strange fatality, those who possess the soil do not perceive that the high price for corn can be counterbalanced by the burden of the poor-rates, and that therefore it is not all gain for them, even if the system permanently kept up the price of grain. They forget that while they are the sole dealers in and sellers of corn, they are likewise the only supporters of the poor, whom corn must be purchased to maintain. The effect of fluctuation and of uncertainty must fall upon them; for if a number of hands, in consequence of the fluctuation, be thrown out of employment, they must come upon the poor-rates, and be supported from the land.

I am now about to open another very important head of the evidence I desire to submit to you. It is the inequality of price produced by the Corn Laws in different parts of the world. I offer to prove upon oath, that the consequence of the present system is not only to prevent grain from being cheap here, but to make it unnaturally cheap in other countries, wherever we are traders, consequently cheaper there than here. It not only makes corn unnaturally cheap for them, but it makes a greater difference than there naturally ought to be between the price of corn in England and elsewhere, and the consequence is, to make a greater difference between wages in England and elsewhere—consequently a greater difference than naturally ought to take place between the prime cost of the produce of all manufactured goods in England, and the prime cost of all manufactured goods elsewhere—consequently a greater difference than naturally ought to exist between our goods and theirs, by affording greater facilities in other markets to foreign manufacturers of goods, than to your own manufacturers--lastly, and another consequence, or rather the same consequence in other words, when you, under the pretence of giving protection to the productions of the soil, increase the burden upon the manufacturer, you thus increase the difficulties of the manufacturer, shut out your own productions from foreign markets and give in reality a premium to foreign manufacturers at the expense of your own. But this is not merely probable from reasoning. I tender to you the proofs upon oath, to demonstrate that it is as true in fact as probable in argument. I am ready to prove, by a host of witnesses, that this is the operation of your law, and that the consequence of its cessation would be felt by the foreign manufacturer. Mark! I am ready to prove this upon oath. But, if you say this is not to be proved here, then you admit it to be true, and then the resolutions which I propose will be adopted by you; for you must acknowledge the truth of that which you deny me the opportunity to prove, and I am not only ready to show you the effects which the Corn Laws have produced on our manufactures, but that they materially influence our exports of goods to foreign markets. In order to enable our merchants to send our goods to the foreign markets with profit, it is necessary that the means should exist for the foreign merchant to furnish in return goods for yours. Nominally the transaction is managed by money or bills; but that is only the medium and the sign of real exchange and barter of commodities; and unless you take his goods from the foreigner, he certainly will have nothing to give you for your own. What then is the effect of the Corn Laws? To the countries which have other articles to give you besides grain, you will find your merchants carrying on a considerable trade, and that your manufactures are very much exported thither. But how is it with countries which have only grain and timber to send in return—for the principle applies to timber as it does to corn—you having passed the same sort of law, to favour some of your Colonies which produce timber, and thus you have produced a further bad effect upon the Baltic trade. The good cheap timber of the Baltic must be excluded, and the people of this country deprived of the especial comforts of cheap houses, in order that the Canadian planters may sell again their inferior timber at a higher price after a long voyage, and thus it is that great countries which are more near to you than the Colonies, are prevented from dealing with you; and your own manufactures, excluded from those nearer home, are sent to a distance or abandoned.

Countries adjoining the Baltic, to which the voyage can be made in ten or twelve days or a fortnight, are so much better for you than those to which you must make a voyage four or five times exceeding that in duration. But timber and grain are all that the Baltic countries can offer you, and if you will not take their productions, they cannot purchase your manufactured goods. Thus, then, you are not content to raise the price of the commodity, and to lower the price to the foreigner by the Corn Laws—you not only give the foreign manufacturer a premium at the expense of the home manufacturer by these laws—but crippled and hampered as he is by the Corn Laws, you next shut him out altogether from those markets, where there is but one thing he can get, and which, if he deals in those markets, is the only thing that they can give in return, excepting timber, which, by another bad law, you have also excluded from our marts.

I am now going to show you that what is probable, is true. I am ready to prove it, for the reason I have given, by parties who know the facts, for I propose to prove my statement by strictly legal evidence given upon oath. The operation of this last evil is confined to Europe, and particularly to the North of Europe, to Germany and to the Baltic. We have, then, this test furnished to us, and it is a test which you cannot scruple to apply. Examine what has been the course of your exports to these countries I have just mentioned, and see whether they have declined—whether they have kept up, stood still, or increased. Then see what are your exports with another set of countries, which have other commodities to give you in exchange for your own goods—commodities which no bad law excludes. Go to Africa, to Asia, to the West Indies, to South America, to North America; to every country that has goods to give you in exchange, as Africa has its ivory, its woods, its gums, and America its cottons. Examine, then, the export to these latter countries, and see whether they have stood still, increased, or diminished; the result will be to show you how your trade is driven with those countries which the Corn Laws affect, and how with those which they do not affect. I am now to open the evidence, which I am ready to adduce upon oath. Go then first to the countries which are not affected by the Corn Laws. I am prepared to show you the difference between the exports thither in the years between 1816 and 1836; it was a great increase of commerce. I offer to prove at the bar, that in the course of twenty years, the American and African trade increased between 1816 to 1828, from 16,000,000*l.* to 28,000,000*l.* There was, therefore, in that period of time an increase of seventy per cent. in the exports to countries which the Corn Laws did not affect. This clearly shews no want of capital, no want of skill, no want of mercantile enterprise; and it must be truly satisfactory to observe that this great and progressive demand abundantly shows that your manufacturers are sure to find customers when those customers have the means of buying from them : that is to say, when you yourselves do not by your absurd laws cripple their means of taking your goods. In these branches of trade we find America supplying us with hides, tallow, cotton ; the West Indies with their various productions ; Africa with its gums, wood, teeth, and gold dust ; and where-ever the natives have had the means of buying, there we find an increase of our trade to the enormous amount of 70 per cent. in 20 years.

But how was it with those countries which our Corn Laws deprived of the means of purchasing? Taking the five years ending in 1820 as compared with the five years ending in 1836—there was a difference of 20 per cent. or a diminution of one-fifth in our European exportation. And was this from one or both of the two reasons which I have assigned—the unnatural depression of price of labour to our rivals occasioned by the Corn Laws, or the Corn Laws preventing us from taking the produce of other countries in exchange for our goods? The witnesses which I can produce will show what their experience has led them to believe, and what I believe, that it was not from the one or the other of these causes, but that it was from both the reasons to explain which I have already applied myself—I mean both the favour which the Corn Laws unnaturally gave foreign manufactures in competition with your own, by keeping down their price of production and raising yours ; and the exclusion, by shutting up the home market against foreign produce, of the only articles with which they could have paid for your manufactures.

I will enter a little into detail of evidence on this important point. Of these two kinds of causes I will adduce illustrations. I will furnish a test of the effect of the Corn Laws in depriving foreign nations of the means of purchase from different branches of our commerce and manufactures; and the manner in which the exports have decreased in some trades and increased in others, furnishes me likewise with a remarkable instance precisely of the same kind with respect to competition: because it shows the alarming circumstance of the growth of new branches of manufacture, unheard of in former times, in different parts of the Continent. I shall prove, by the evidence of witnesses who have gone to the spot, who have examined for themselves—persons of skill, of knowledge, of experience—by them I shall prove that the Corn Laws have forced the establishment, almost against nature, in different parts of the Continent, of those rival branches of manufacture. Now, looking at the kind of things of which the exportation has increased, and the kind of things of which the exportation has decreased, I find the matter very instructive. I find that the raw material has increased in the exports, while the manufactured material has decreased. Thus take bar and pig iron and cutlery—I find that the exportation of bar and pig iron has increased greatly, while cutlery has hardly at all advanced, and, in some places, has even fallen off. The exportation of manufactured woollen cloth has decidedly fallen; but that of wool has increased—the raw material; and yarn—raw material again—has increased also. Of woollen goods, the exportation to Russia was, in 1820, 346,000*l.* worth; while in 1836, sixteen years later, it was only two-fifths of that amount, or 123,000*l.* On the other hand, the wool exported during the three years ending 1821 was 178,000*l.*; while in the three years ending 1837 it amounted to 3,744,000*l.* In like manner the importation of yarn during the former period was only 154,000*l.*; while during the latter period it was 2,472,000*l.* So the trade in the raw material materially increased, while the trade in the manufactured article as clearly manifested a falling off. Again I offer to prove upon oath at your bar, that whereas in former periods the English purchaser governed the market, in later times the Germans and Belgians have governed it and regulated the prices. These are facts, of which I here tender evidence by witnesses.

I will illustrate further by a few facts, which also I am prepared to prove, the operation of all this. I will show you the establishment of manufactures abroad, and the places where they are established. We know that the great staple manufacture of Nottingham, from which my Noble Friend presented a petition to-night, has been for many years stocking hosiery. In 1815 there were in Saxony, the other great hosiery mart, 1000 stocking frames. In this country there were at the same period 16,300 stocking frames. But at the present moment in Saxony there are upwards of 16,000 stocking frames established. They have in that period arrived at an equality with us. This is one particular branch of trade. I could shew your Lordships that spinning machinery has been established in various parts of France and the Netherlands. But my great proof shall be more compendious, more satisfactory, more decisive than that. I will go to the fountain head, instead of tracing the minute rills. I will make for the root, and not count the leaves on the boughs. I will shew the seeds of whole manufactures, sown and sprouting under your Corn Laws. I looked round, and considered what kind of manufactures form the best test of the general increase of manufacturing establishments over the world; and it immediately occurred to me that the manufacture of machinery was the best; because, instead of going after the different streamlets, I at once reach the great source which supplies them all. I can shew you, then, a number of establishments for the manufacture of machines, and the component parts of machinery, wholesale; which demonstrates an incalculable increase in the establishments where such machinery is used. I can shew you that spinning-jennies, levers, cranes, tooth-wheels, axles, spindles, all the varieties of machinery, are made on the Continent, demonstrating the increase of manufactories as conclusively as if one should go round to those other manufactories and obtain a return from each. I am prepared to prove this by the evidence of persons of respectability, who went to France from no idle curiosity, but from alarm at finding themselves outdone in the foreign market, and who examined for themselves, and heard with their own ears, and saw with their own eyes, the things which I shall state, and which they offer to prove. And what were the results of that examination? At Dresden there is a great manufacture of machinery established—at Chemnitz, in Saxony, another—and both under the superintendence of English overlookers, and chiefly worked by English hands. At Prague there is another large establishment, which serves to supply Bohemia with machinery. At Vienna there is another of the same kind; and so encouraged and patronized has this been by a paternal government, by a judicious and politic government, that the establishment was planted and carried on in an imperial palace. There were actually two manufactories established in a r oyal castle. At Elberfeld and at Aix-la-Chapelle there were others—at each place a flourishing establishment of machinery. Now, I pray your Lordships to remember that when I say "a ma-"nufacture of machinery," it imports a vast number of manufactories of cotton and other goods; for a manufacture of machinery is, as it were, a manufacture of manufactories. Each one proves many manufactures of other kinds in those countries to be established.

But with respect to the amount of material wrought up, you may ask how much of business these manufactories do? I am prepared to prove at your Lordships' bar, that at Zurich, where there is a great manufactory of machinery—where spindles, wheels, cranes, spinning-jennics, and every sort of machinery is made—no less than five tons of pig-iron per day are melted and cast. This your Lordships will feel is a fair illustration of the extent of those concerns; but another may be given from the number of hands employed; and this also I am prepared by evidence to establish. At Liege there is a manufactory of machinery where four thousand hands are employed, under English auspices too, and worked by English capital. A Noble Lord presented a petition to-night, which I saw made an impression on the House. He said in commenting on the prayer and statements of that petition, that if the Corn Laws were repealed the English farmer would be reduced to the necessity of seeking his fortune in a distant land. I do not deny the importance of the observation. I am far from saying that you ought to shut your ears against those who solicit your opening them to that statement. *(Cries of Hear!)* Yes, I say you ought to hear, but to hear both sides. I say it is fit to hear what those petitioners only represent as a possibility—only state as an opinion of theirs—only give as the apprehension of their minds—naturally sensitive, yet perhaps not naturally the best informed on this subject, though naturally and inevitably deeply interested in it: I say to such as cry "hear!" that the apprehensions and anxieties of those not very well informed individuals should obtain hearing before you. But then, if you listen to their apprehensions of what may happen—how much more does it behove you to hear my statement of what has happened—of what is every hour happening—of what will continue to happen until it overwhelms your manufactures? For my statements will be proved on oath by persons who have seen what they state—who will not represent their vague conjectures, their apprehensions, their fancies, or their fears of what may be; but who will tell you on oath of what they know is, and has been, and will be, and must be, because it has already taken place, and experience has realised, and is every day realising, their worst apprehensions. I am told that farmers may emigrate, though they have not done so—though the emigration of farmers was never known—and though the emigration of the peasantry of a country is impossible. *(Cries of Hear!)* My prayer to your Lordships is to hear. I only desire you to hear. But I desire that you would not hear fears and fancies, and shut your ears to facts and truths; that you would not hear vague apprehensions of what may one day take place, and refuse me liberty to bring evidence before you of what has already happened, and is going on a degree or two to the southward of this Hall. The unnatural emigration of even a single farmer I lament; but let me ask your Lordships, is it natural or is it desirable that our English manufacturers should go abroad to a foreign country any more than our farmers? Your Lordships thought it a consummation much to be deprecated that a single English farmer should go abroad : yet if a single English farmer should go abroad, and become tenant to a foreign noble, instead of an English peer, we should indeed have to regret the loss of a most valuable member of society, and there the loss would end. But if an English manufacturer goes to Zurich we do not merely lose one citizen from Birmingham or Wolverhampton—we do not merely lose a good Justice of Peace at Quarter Sessions—the state is not merely diminished by a unit however respectable—but he goes to set up manufactures—to make machinery—to work iron into spindles, and wheels, and spinning jennies—to work up five tons of pig iron every day in the year, for the purpose of meeting the demand, of spinning-jennies to support the fatal competition with your own spinning-jennies in the markets of Europe. Another going to Liege does not merely take away a respectable member of society from this country, but establishes works where 4,000 men are employed in the manufacture of cotton-twist, or, still worse for this country, in the manufacture of twist-spinning machinery.

I now come to what is said by my noble friends opposite, those who are so anxious to hear, but so unwilling to listen, who are so anxious for one side being well heard, that they do not think of hearing the other at all; while my prayer is that you should indulge with an audience, not only the men who dread and apprehend, but also the men who can prove and swear. I now go from the case of the manufacturers to the landed interest, and all that I have said respecting fluctuations, all that I have said respecting steadiness of price, applies to the landed interest just as much—not more, but just as much as to the manufacturers. I say as much as the manufacturers. And I say that the agricultural any more than the other class has no interest, as many imagine, in retaining these Corn Laws; but, on the contrary, every interest in checking the downhill progress of our manufactures which those Corn Laws are unquestionably causing. But now I address myself to the landed interest, and state what distinctly applies to their case. And first I think it is something for my position, that some of the greatest agriculturists—greatest in skill, in experience, in the extent of their farming operations and in the amount of capital absorbed by them, but beneficially absorbed,—have been decidedly of opinion that they would be better without the Corn Laws than with them. I can produce strict legal evidence of this. I can bring testimony to show that this opinion has been held in the highest quarters; and indeed, if I were to name among all your Lordships any one who has a great stake in the country more than another —who has no possible interest in throwing impediments in the way of agriculture—who ought to be more wedded than another to that interest—whose means of subsistence and enjoyment are more especially derived from the land—I should name my noble and much-loved friend who is bringing forward this motion; for I am only endeavouring to lay a foundation by evidence for the case which he is afterwards to lead. The Noble Earl, I mean, who is connected with Yorkshire, with Ireland, and with Northamptonshire; with districts of this country where manufactures are wholly unknown—and with Irish districts where a manufacturer was never heard of, and where the strongest prejudices prevails against any alteration in the Corn Laws; yet that Noble Earl has a most unhesitating a most unflinching opinion that he is the worse for the Corn Laws. So, likewise, is it the opinion of a great—the greatest agriculturist connected with Norfolk (the Earl of Leicester) that the present system of Corn Laws is no benefit to the farmer. No matter what his peculiar opinions may be in detail. I do not inquire at present respecting the kind of alteration which should be made. A fixed duty is opposed to the present system, and those who are for the present system are against a fixed duty, while I am against any thing of the kind, and will neither have the present system, nor put a fixed duty in its place. Another who was always opposed to these laws, is one whose loss I must always deeply deplore; one of the dearest friends I ever had in life; a man whom to name is to honour—the late Earl of Thanet—he whose opinion on every subject is entitled to command respect, a person of the most vigorous understanding, and correct judgment that ever was bestowed upon man, and united with the most honourable, high, and chivalrous nature—but on this question especially is he an authority, for few men engaged more extensively in agricultural operations of various kinds, and no man more thoroughly understood farming in all its branches. It was his conviction that the maintenance of the Corn Laws did more harm than good to the farmer. But perchance he did not know how to form an opinion—perhaps he knew nothing of farming—perhaps he was ignorant of political and economic matter. No! He was intimately connected with land, and skilful in farming; his general knowledge kept pace with his skill as a farmer, and he was an enemy to the Corn Laws on the ground of interest, both as a farmer and as a landlord, as he was their enemy upon sound principle as a statesman. And, my Lords, I can also produce to your Lordships farmers, with deep interest as farmers—who will give exactly the seme testimony on oath at that bar.

One fact I may mention by way of blunting the edge of that feeling which I see over-powering in some quarters at the bare supposition that a repeal of the Corn Laws, or the opening of the ports, would be no detriment to the farming interest. The period of the closest and most complete monopoly of the home market to the home growers was from 1832 to 1838. Now, what was the price of wheat at that time? During the whole of these years, till the ports were open, the average price of grain was 36*s.* and a fraction (cries of "no, no!" A Noble Lord observed that that was the lowest price.) I am going into a comparative statement, and it is a matter of indifference whether I take the highest or the lowest average. It would signify if I spoke of the absolute price, but when I take a period when the ports were shut to compare with a period when the ports were open, it is quite indifferent—36*s.* 7*d.* was the lowest price; it was the average of December, 1835 (cries of "one month!") No doubt it is one month; I take the month of December, 1835. I have no average for a time when the ports were open, excepting the month of December, and, therefore, I take the same month when they were shut. The average of the same month of December in 1838, when the ports were open, was 77*s.* That is one fact, at least, to blunt the edge of the appetite for my destruction which I saw in Noble Friends around me.

Now, I may say there is this detriment, this very material detriment, to the landowners from the present state of the Corn Laws. I will for the present admit they are as wise as if framed by an angel. I will admit that all my arguments are vain—that all the evidence I tender against them proves nothing. I will admit all that their warmest eulogists are pleased to pronounce in their favour. At all events they are repealable, and at all events it must be conceded that fluctuation of prices has not been prevented under them. At all events it must be likewise granted that as long as these laws give rise to fluctuation, so long will capitalists hesitate to rely upon them, and so long will capital be withheld from agriculture. I can bring capitalists, large capitalists, who will prove to your Lordships that in the clear opinion of the monied men of London, a repeal of the Corn Laws would in a few months produce a steadiness of profits—of farming profits—which would cause capital to be invested in land: would let loose millions, now invested in the funds and yielding a profit of only 3 per cent. And nothing, I take it, would be more beneficial to the landed interest, especially to any portion of it which may happen to be in distress, than the application of large capital to purchases. It would further be a great advantage to the landowners, if the protecting duties on manufactures were taken off, so that manufactures might be sold cheaper; so that they could buy goods of the various descriptions that are manufactured in this country and are consumed by the farmers, either cheaper than at present, of a better kind, and without any increase of price. I need not stop to show that till the Corn Laws are repealed, no man in his senses would venture to propound so extravagant a measure, as depriving the manufacturers of their protecting duties, and at the same time keep up the protecting duties in favour of the landowners.

My last observation on this subject is one of a striking nature. I beseech and earnestly implore the best attention of your Lordships to what I have already stated, and solicit your attention to what I am going to observe. I began by saying, that not a word should cross my lips in depreciation of the agricultural or landed interest, of landlords or farmers, whose great influence and rank in the community I acknowledge,—whose being mixed up with the fate of the country, from the high stake they have in it, I am the last man to deny or hesitate most amply to admit. But so neither will I say one word against the manufacturers, or breathe a whisper which might tend to undervalue those most respectable, useful, and essential members of the community. I have lately seen with the greatest astonishment from a noble friend—I mean one of the present ministers—a statement made on some election occasion I suppose it must have been; but even that would not justify it—a statement which places in the most invidious contrast the merit of the manufacturer and the merit of the landholder, with respect even to morality, with respect to tranquillity, with respect to all the qualities which make good men and good citizens, and which represents, and wantonly represents, the manufacturer in this most odious inferiority. In all things relating to morality, to steadiness of conduct, to tranquillity, and to character as good subjects, he conceives it to be a wild imagination, a dreamy fancy, to compare the manufacturing with the landed interest. My Lords, this is not my sentiment; but it is that of my noble friend (Lord J. Russell) who also then expressed the greatest dismay at the prospect of the Government touching the Corn Laws. He said, "I am afraid this government (he was in opposition then) means to give up the Corn Laws to the manufacturers." The experience he has lately had has altered his views. He has found these Corn Laws not so good now, and he prefers a fixed duty. My Lords, it is not a statesmanlike view of the subject to give such a preference to one class of our fellow citizens over another. I am of that old-fashioned opinion which held all interests to be blended in one; and though it came from a trader rather than a statesman, I think it contained more of political wisdom—it was more sound, more practical, and more statesmanlike than the noble minister's doctrine which I have cited. I refer to those memorable words of Sir Josiah Child, "Land and trade are knit together, and together they must wax and wane; so that it never shall be well with land but trade shall be the better, nor ever trade shall suffer but land shall feel." Comparing this with the Huntingdon address, in political wisdom few would doubt that it is infinitely superior. It may be couched in a plain and homely style, which the ill taste of these days may undervalue, though I hold its diction to be infinitely finer; but that it is the doctrine of a wise statesman I am well assured. It is the sound view of the subject; and the last member of the sentence I especially commend to your Lordships' attention—that "it never shall be ill with trade but land shall feel."

I will now, my Lords, show you what trade has done for you, aye, and I will bring you a test by showing you the prices of wheat before and after the time to which I refer. I allude to the spring our commerce and manufactures took about the year 1770. Before 1774 there was a bounty of five shillings on exportation, and we must deduct that amount from the prices I am now about to recite. In the fifty years commencing in the reign of George I. and ending in 1771, the average price of wheat in the English market, deducting the bounty of five shillings, was 26*s*. The average price was 31*s*. 8*d*., and the deduction of the bounty makes it 26*s*. The average price of fifty-six years, ending in 1825, was 62*s*. Deduct from that period the years from 1800 to 1820, which includes a period of great scarcity, and also the period of the depreciation of the currency, leading until 1819 to a rise in the market price of gold above the current price, until it was restored to its level by Sir Robert Peel's bill—deduct these years from the whole period, you will have for the average price of the remaining years 52*s*., which is exactly double the price of grain before 1770. But most true is the saying of Sir Josiah Child, that it never shall be ill with land, but trade shall suffer; nor ever well with trade, but land shall feel it. The bounty was taken off in 1774, and then began the period the most remarkable, the most brilliant, and I will say the proudest, in the history of the English nation. Then were the mines of this country and of Wales, teeming with wealth, fully explored, serving not only to aggrandize their possessors, but to call into life and action innumerable tools, engines, machines of the most exquisite and powerful description; all the land swarmed with workmen, and the air resounded with the cheerful noise of labour; rocks were blasted, trees felled, the forests cleared, the earth broken up, all rude produce worked into the finest shapes with infinite skill; the bosom of the earth poured forth unbounded crops, while manufacturing industry added to the wealth which she so profusely yielded, till those mighty engines, and that omnipotent labour, assisted by the extraordinary feats of the new power of steam, enlarging the sphere of human dominion, and giving man a new existence and a new sway on the globe, changed the whole face of nature, and made the aspect of the country what it now is, and which God forbid it should ever cease to be, one vast, industrious, expert, and skilful workshop of the most laborious, the most ingenious, I will add from intimate knowledge, the worthiest, I wish I could say the wealthiest of mankind. These were the miracles of manufacturing industry. This was the period of manufacturing prosperity. And yet we were not blessed with tranquillity all the while. But in spite of broken peace, bearing up against an enormous and wrongful war, overcoming by the skill and industry of one class so many evils fatal to both, which the profligacy of another class would have brought upon them—notwithstanding twenty years of one war and ten years of another—notwithstanding the triumphant resistance of Washington—notwithstanding the mighty genius of Napoleon, neither the fleets of America could shake your dominion over the seas, nor the armies and the decrees of France repress the energies of your commerce. Art and manufactures, exposed to the most formidable enemies, flourished and advanced in the hands and under the indomitable exertions of those

> Quos neque Tydides, nec Larissæus Achilles
> Non anni domuere decem, non mille carinæ.

When you thus survey these rich gifts of manufacturing industry—when you observe that during those years of commercial advancement, the price of agricultural produce was doubled, can you have the slightest doubt that Sir Josiah Child was right? Seeing, then, that manufactures were the cause which doubled the rental of every estate in the realm, I ask your Lordships on what principle can you refuse to hear the evidence which I am tendering to prove that the Corn Laws are rapidly driving away from us those very manufactures which while permitted to flourish, doubled, in forty years, the value of every estate in the country?

These, my Lords, are the grounds on which I have founded my request to your Lordships. I offer to prove on oath the destruction of the corn trade—by the Corn Laws. I offer to prove on oath the removal of all security against famine—by the Corn Laws. I offer to prove on oath the fluctuation of all prices at all times—caused by the Corn Laws. I offer to prove on oath the equalization of prices abroad and at home—prevented by the Corn Laws. I offer to prove on oath our manufactures destroyed —by the Corn Laws. I offer to prove on oath the destruction of our export trade, and the closing of the foreign market to our goods—by the Corn Laws. My Lords, I thus close this my tender of evidence by stating the same proposition with which I set out: that if my request is refused—if I am not allowed to prove my statements by evidence at your Lordships' bar, the refusal can only be grounded on one of three positions—either that fully admitting them to be all true, you require no evidence to prove them; or that they are so false that no possible evidence could be brought to prove them; or, that, whether true or false, the point at issue is so immaterial as to make it absurd to examine evidence one way or the other. My Lords, I know that the two latter propositions are altogether impossible and absurd; and I, therefore, conceive that any refusal of yours to hear evidence can only be grounded on the first supposition, that you admit what I advance to be true; and in the event of your refusal, I shall accordingly take my statements to be virtually admitted and on the six propositions which I have stated, my Noble Friend, who is not now present, will, in all probability, ground a motion for some alteration in the system.

But, my Lords, I earnestly implore you not to reject my request; for believe me, if you reject it, the day will come when you shall say, "Better had it been for us if we had thought twice before we shut our ears to the truth." But also the day will come when this reflection may be too late, and when your repentance then will not supply the place of a wise compliance now. When I say this, I am quite conscious that your Lordships are a body of men the last in the world to be influenced by any thing bearing the most remote semblance of menace, and I am the last man to advance anything which could have that construction; at the same time I know that advice is not lost on your Lordships, and that you are ever disposed candidly to take what is proposed into your best and most serious consideration. I shall add but one word more to gain a hearing for the prayer for the petitioners, who earnestly implore to be heard, not by council, but by evidence, at your Lordships' bar. Whatever resolution you ultimately come to, supposing even that it be to do nothing against the present Corn Laws—stick to them, if you will, in the minutest detail—re-enact them as often as you will—resolve not to hear a word said against them—but for God's sake do not form this resolution till after you have heard the evidence I tender you. I protest to you, that if I were the most strenuous advocate of these Laws—if I were the most unalterably fixed in my resolution that nothing should make me judge against them—if I were determined beforehand, though this would hardly be a rational determination, though this would hardly be a proceeding worthy of a judge whose business it is to hear before he decides, but even were I thus predetermined that nothing whatever should induce me to give up the Corn Laws, I should consider this predetermination on my part, not as an argument for refusing to go into the inquiry, but, on the contrary, as the strongest inducement I could have for permitting the investigation before I published my final resolution to the world.

My Lords, let me conjure you most seriously

to reflect what will be the consequences of such a fact going forth to the manufacturers as that when evidence was offered at the bar of your House in proof of six propositions, every one of them vitally affecting the interests of the trade, the manufactures, the commerce, the well being of the country—the deep importance of which no man denies, the possibility of proving which no man can reasonably call in question, the truth of which is so solemnly asserted, the proof of which is so distinctly tendered on oath—what will be said, I ask, if those propositions are arbitarily thrown to the winds—are put down by the mute eloquence of numbers, by the mere force of an overwhelming Parliamentary majority—and the people of England are told, "Parliament has made up its mind about the matter: go your way, return to your empty shops, repair to your ruined manufactories; or hie away to foreign countries; do what you like; we want none of your evidence; we care not for your testimony; we despise your facts; we have made up our minds to this foregone conclusion; and, lest your evidence might shake our determination, we won't run the risk of listening to it at all?" Rely upon it, my Lords, that a refusal on your parts would be accompanied by the most unwelcome suspicions and the most rigorous comments on the part of the country—suspicions which I might regret, without being able to remove—comments, which I might dislike, and yet could not gainsay. It is a much more pleasing task to contemplate the happy effects of an opposite course—of your acceding to my request that you hear this evidence. I can conceive no earthly event which would tend more to reconcile—if there has ever been a falling out—the people of this country to the established state of things, to the order to which your Lordships belong, than your candid consideration of, your paternal listening to, the application of those petitioners—your opening wide your doors to the people's prayers—your not shutting out the proffered evidence as to their distresses, and the remedy which they propose for them.

My Lords, returning to you my best thanks for the patient and indulgent hearing which you have granted me, while addressing you on the part of the whole People of this Country, I will now conclude with moving you that the petitions on the subject of the Corn Laws be referred to a Committee of the whole House, in order that Evidence may be heard at the Bar.

THE END.

Norman and Skeen, Printers, Maiden Lane, Covent Garden.

SUBSTANCE

OF THE

SPEECH OF VISCOUNT HOWICK

ON THE

CORN LAWS.

MARCH 13TH, 1839.

LONDON:
RIDGWAY, PICCADILLY.
1839.

Sir Henry George Grey, Viscount Howick, and, from 1845, 3rd Earl Grey (1802–94)

Like Lord Brougham Viscount Howick, the future third Earl Grey was in a contrary mood. A member of parliament since 1830, he had been appointed secretary at war in 1835 but, like his father, the second Earl Grey, he disapproved of most of the Prime Minister Lord Melbourne's policies, and later in the year he resigned from the Cabinet.[1] Charles Greville recounted in his journal on 24 June 1839 an account by Lord Tavistock, the future seventh Duke of Bedford, of Howick's behaviour in cabinet.

> [Howick's] temper was so intolerable that there was no going on with him; the spirit of contradiction eternally moves him, and especially in the Cabinet, where he makes a point of contesting almost every opinion that is suggested by anybody else. It is impossible to form an idea of the difficulty which he causes to [Lord] John [Russell, home secretary and leader of the Commons] and what he has to endure on his account; and all this is the more provoking because Howick is the only man who assists him in the way of hard work and in mastering the details of measures,[2]

But, unlike Lord Brougham, Viscount Howick remained consistent in his support of the repeal of the corn law and of the League.

[1] See Spencer Walpole, *The Life of Lord John Russell*, vol. 1, London: Longmans, Green, and Co., 1889, p. 336.
[2] Roger Fulford (ed.), *The Greville Memoirs*, London: B. T. Batsford, 1963. pp. 164–5.

SPEECH.

Sir,

I can assure the Honorable Member, who has just sat down (Mr. Wodehouse), that I give the fullest credit to the assertion with which he concluded his speech, that if he were satisfied that the existing Corn Law were really injurious to the community at large, he would offer no opposition to its repeal, however severe might be the sacrifice which such a measure would involve of the interest of the owners of land.—I am convinced that this is the real feeling both of the Honorable Gentleman and of the great body of the Landed Proprietors of this country, and I cannot, therefore, refrain from observing that, though I have perceived with satisfaction, during the course of this debate, a great improvement in the tone of those who have advocated a Repeal of the Corn Laws, and much less of imputation upon the motives of their opponents, than we have heard upon former occasions, still, I do think that the gentlemen connected with the landed interest have great right to complain of the manner in which, out of doors, they have been represented, as resisting any change in the Corn Law, from the most sordid and selfish motives; as obstinately maintaining a system which they are well aware is deeply injurious to the nation at large, for the sake of their own personal advantage; totally regardless of the sufferings they thus impose upon others. I must say, that I consider this to be a most unjust accusation against the landed interest. I think indeed that those connected with this interest are much mistaken in clinging to what is called the protective system, but we ought not to forget that if this is an error, it is one sanctioned and countenanced by the whole course of our policy and legislation up to a very recent period the exclusion from our market of every article which could compete with the productions of our domestic industry was for 200 years the principle universally acted upon, and so little is it true that the principle of protection has been applied by the landed interest for their own exclusive benefit, that, as was truly observed last night by the Honorable Member for the North Riding of Yorkshire (Mr. Cayley), they have passed a great number of laws imposing high protecting duties upon many articles of which they are themselves the principal consumers. It is only within a very few years that even an approach has been made to a system of greater commercial liberality, and we must not forget that till very lately indeed a great majority of those very persons who now charge the landed proprietors with such extreme selfishness for maintaining the principle of protection with regard to corn, themselves insisted upon adhering to the very same principle in respect of those manufactures in which their own interests were concerned. Surely then, it is most unfair to ascribe to nothing but selfish and sordid motives, the refusal of the landed proprietors at once to abandon a system which had so long been approved by all parties, and more particularly by those who are now most clamorous for a change.

But, Sir, though I think the gentlemen connected with the landed interest have been most unfairly and unjustly attacked, I trust they will not suffer these attacks to have the effect of preventing them from giving their calm and deliberate consideration to this momentous question; I hope that the hostile spirit in which a change of the existing law has too frequently been demanded will not lead them hastily to conclude that such a measure must necessarily be injurious to them, or that it must be supported for the purpose of being so. I must beg leave to remind them, that in advocating a change of the existing law, I at least cannot be suspected of any views or feelings hostile to the landed interest. I have the honour of representing the Northern Division of Northumberland, a district exclusively agricultural, and I believe I may confidently assert that no county in the kingdom stands before it for the skill, the energy and the success with which its inhabitants have prosecuted this great branch of national industry. That influence, therefore, which the wishes and interests of our constituents always have, and ought to have, upon the views of their representatives, must dispose me to wish well to agriculture, and certainly my personal interests are not less deeply involved in its prosperity. I must be supposed to be worse than insane by any gentleman who can imagine that I am actuated by any feeling of hostility, or even of indifference, towards the landed interest. I may be wrong in my judgment, but, in forming it, I certainly have not been influenced by any sinister interest; I may be mistaken, but at least the opinion which I entertain has been formed without bias, upon much consideration of this momentous subject, and has been confirmed by my observation of what has actually been the effect of the existing law.

Sir, I consider this as a question which ought to be judged of far more by experience than by mere abstract reasoning. I wish, therefore, to bring it practically to the test of experience; to look back at what has occurred since the law of 1828 was passed, and to compare the results by which it has been followed with the anticipations of those by whom that measure was recommended to the adoption of Parliament.

Now, Sir, what were the grounds upon which it was so recommended to us?—The first consideration which was urged, and that which was most strongly pressed by the advocates of the measure, was, that it would ensure great steadiness in the price of corn. The Hon. Member for the North

Riding of Yorkshire (Mr. Cayley) denied that the law was expected to produce this effect; he asserted that no Corn Law could possibly ensure steadiness of prices, and that we had no right to look for impossibilities. I confess I was surprised to hear this statement, which certainly is by no means in accordance with the arguments advanced by the proposers of the present Law, at the time it was brought forward. My Right Honourable Friend (Mr P. Thomson) last night quoted the language of Mr. Canning, who said that he expected as a consequence of the measure that the price of wheat would range from 55*s.* to 65*s.* a quarter. All the most distinguished advocates of the plan expressed a similar opinion; and, more than this, I find that when the law had been nearly five years in operation, Lord Ashburton then Mr. Baring, on the occasion of a motion brought forward by Mr. W. Whitmore, on the 17th of May, 1833, expressed his conviction that the law was not only intended to ensure great steadiness of price, but that it had actually succeeded in doing so. The following is an extract from his speech upon that occasion:—

"I know it has been stated that prices have fluctuated between 52*s.* and 71*s.* during the last five years; but these must be extreme points, and I am sure that if the price ever reached 71*s.* it was only for a short time. Every body connected with agriculture knows that the price has continued steadily at about 60*s*. sometimes a little higher, sometimes a little lower.

Let me ask how this confident prediction of Lord Ashburton's has been realized? Is it true that the price of corn has not fallen below 52*s*., and that if it has reached 71*s*. this must have been its extreme point, and one at which it would be maintained only for a very short time? On the contrary, the average price of wheat for the whole year, 1834, was only 45*s*. 11*d*.; for the year 1835, it was 39*s*. 5*d*. and at one time, at the close of the same year, it was as low as 36*s*. a quarter; on the other hand, instead of 71*s*. being, as Lord Ashburton stated, the extreme rise which would ever take place, and a price only to be sustained for a very short time, the fact is, that the average of the whole period, from the month of August last, to the present time, has been 72*s*. 8*d*. and in the month of January, the average of one week was as high as 81*s*. 7*d*.

Then, Sir, the next effect the law was to have, was that of making the trade in foreign corn equable and steady, instead of our being exposed to what Mr Canning described as an alternate deluge and drought. But what has been the effect of the law in this respect? Instead of a regular and moderate influx of foreign corn, for six years the entries for home consumption were reduced almost to nothing; and then again, in a single week, nearly a million and a half of quarters were entered at a nominal duty. We were also told that the measure was to cause the capital of the country to be employed in dealing in British rather than in foreign corn and here again the result has been precisely the opposite of that which we were taught to expect Lastly we were told, that by the operation of the law, the consumer on the one hand, and the farmer on the other, were to be effectually protected from the distress to which these classes are exposed, from very high or from very low prices. Instead of this we know that the great body of our population are at this moment suffering most severely from the high price of food while the extent of the distress to which farmers have been exposed from the opposite extreme of low prices in many of the years which have elapsed since the passing of the existing Corn Law is too well known to admit of dispute I hold in my hand a record of this distress in extracts from speeches delivered from the Throne which I will refrain from reading to the House as they were last night quoted by my Right Hon. Friend. But there is one description which has been given of this distress, of greater authority even than those speeches, inasmuch as it was founded upon careful examination of evidence with which I must be permitted to trouble you. The Report of the Committee upon Agricultural Distress, of 1833, contained the following passage :-

"The Committee of 1821 expressed a hope 'that the great body of the occupiers of the soil, either from the savings of more prosperous times, or from the credit which punctuality commands in this country, possess resources which will enable them to surmount the difficulties under which they now labour.' Your Committee, with deep regret, are bound rather to express a fear that the difficulties alone remain unchanged, but that the savings are either gone or greatly diminished, the credit failing, and the resources being generally exhausted;' and this opinion is formed, not on the evidence of rent-payers, but of many most respectable witnesses, as well owners of land, as surveyors and land agents."

Sir, I think the advocates of the existing Corn Law can hardly deny the accuracy of the statement I have now made,—they can neither controvert the facts, nor dispute the wide difference between these results, and those which we were assured in 1828, would follow from our passing the bill which was proposed to us. It is possible they may be able to account for what has happened; they may be able to shew, that without this law, we should have been in a worse situation than we actually have, and that its provisions have, in no degree, tended to produce that alternate distress of the farmer and the consumer, which we have witnessed: they may be able to do this, but, at all events I think they must admit, that in all fairness of reasoning it is incumbent upon them to do so;

that at first sight, at least, there is an apparent failure of the law to produce the effect anticipated, which it is necessary for them to account for. But, though several Gentlemen, advocating the maintenance of the existing Corn Law, have entered most elaborately into the whole question, they have one and all avoided touching upon this point, the Right Hon. Baronet in particular, who spoke last night, (Sir E. Knatchbull), having been challenged by my Right Hon. Friend near me, to account for the difficulties to which the landed interest had been exposed, had only this answer to make, that the Agricultural Committees of 1833 and 1836, had not attributed the distress of the agriculturists to the existing Corn Law. This is perfectly true. But the Right Hon. Baronet must remember, that in the Committee of 1836, the draft of a report was prepared by my Hon. Friend, the Chairman, (Mr. Lefevre), in which an alteration of the existing Corn Law was recommended, and, although this draft was rejected at a meeting of the Committee, where, if I mistake not, 17 out of 23 gentlemen who were present, were connected with the landed interest,—no attempt even was made to assign any other cause by which the then existing distress of the agriculturists could be accounted for.

I think then, that, as the advocates of the law have shrunk from the attempt to reconcile the apparent contradiction between that which has actually taken place since it has been in force, with the predictions of its authors, this circumstance alone, in all fair reasoning, would justify us in pronouncing that it has failed. But, Sir, I am prepared to go further; I think it can be clearly shewn, not only that the Corn Law has failed to avert the inconvenience which has been occasioned by the great fluctuations in the price of corn during the last ten years, but that it has greatly aggravated, if it has not produced, this evil. I think that we can trace, by a reference to facts, the operation of the law, both in further depressing the price of corn at the time when from favourable harvests, it must at all events have been low, and also in still further increasing the dearth which the present deficiency has produced.

In the first place, I will endeavour to show how it is, that, at the present moment, the inconvenience occasioned by high prices is increased by the provisions of the law. We know that the chief argument in favour of the fluctuating duty, was, that in case of a deficiency of our home-supply, it would enable the consumer to obtain foreign corn unburthened by any duty, and thus give him all the benefit of a free trade in corn. Now, this argument is obviously founded upon the assumption, that there is always to be found abroad an unlimited supply of foreign corn, ready to flow into this country whenever it is wanted, if we are willing to receive it. This assumption is utterly unfounded. Corn can no more be grown in foreign countries than it can here, except to meet an anticipated demand; and if it is grown upon the expectation of a demand which does not arise, the consequence must be, an extreme depression of its price, and great distress amongst the agricultural classes. But the effect of our fluctuating duty, is, to render it matter of extreme uncertainty whether the foreign grower can calculate upon a demand from this country or not. In the first five years, which followed the passing of the law, there was so high a range of prices, that the ports were never closed for any long period together, and the whole amount of foreign wheat, entered for home-consumption, was no less than 5,725,000 quarters; but, in the six following years, up to last harvest, the averages were constantly so low, that the duty was always kept above the rate which would admit of any profitable importation. What must have been the necessary consequences of these changes? The supply required in the first five years, must have created abroad an expectation of a demand in this country, and, when afterwards the ports were practically closed for so long as six years, it is impossible that the want of the anticipated market should not have occasioned very great distress to the cultivators and dealers in corn in other countries.

From reasoning, we may conclude, that such must have been the case, nor would it be difficult to produce evidence that it really was so. I hold in my hand a document, which I will not trouble the House by reading, which shows what was the effect abroad of the state of things I have described. It is an extract from a Hamburgh newspaper, of the year 1836, stating in much detail, the inconvenience occasioned to the holders of corn in that port, from the length of time for which they had in vain waited for a demand in this country, and strongly recommending that other channels of trade should be sought for, abandoning all idea of deriving any benefit from the corn trade with England under our present system.

The Landholders in those parts of Poland, whence in previous years, supplies had been drawn for our market, are stated to have experienced very great difficulties, in consequence of the extreme depression of the price of their produce. But it was, of course, impossible that the foreign merchants or growers should long persist in a losing trade, the unnaturally low price of grain, occasioned by the glut arising from the failure of an expected market in this country, could not therefore be of long continuance. But I must observe in passing, that while it lasted, this state of things must have acted as a premium to our foreign competitors in manufactures. The unnaturally low price of food must have had all the effect of a bounty upon the productions of the foreign manufacturer, and though it is true that this is an advantage, he could not long enjoy it,—we know that the first moment of entering upon the field of competition with an established trade, is always that of the greatest difficulty; so that the effect of our fluctuating duty must have been to help our rivals through the critical period of first getting up their infant manufactures. I do not, however, wish to dwell upon this part of the subject, which has already been sufficiently noticed by preceding speakers. I wish rather to point out that the effect of the long closing of our ports must necessarily have been to compel the foreign growers gradually to abandon our markets, and to cause new channels of trade to be opened, so that when we were again in the last autumn in want of a supply from abroad, we could not expect any preparation to have been made for meeting a demand which had been so long interrupted.

Under such circumstances, it was in vain that, with the rise of the averages, we had a reduction of the duty upon foreign corn; this was now too late to be of any real service to the consumer. The sudden opening of our ports, no supply having been raised in foreign countries in anticipation of such an occurrence, produced a great rise in the prices of wheat abroad. The unexpected demand of so rich and populous a country, in a season of defective production at home, coming upon the European market without any preparation. had necessarily a very powerful effect in raising prices generally, and thus both depriving our own consumers of the benefit which it was anticipated they would derive from the opening of the ports at a nominal duty, and producing much inconvenience to the consumers of those countries from which we draw our supplies.

A regular and constant trade in corn with this kingdom would be of inestimable advantage to the great agricultural countries of Europe; a supply would be created to meet the anticipated demand, and the intercourse would be mutually beneficial to both parties; but the case is widely different when, under the existing law, a demand arises from a deficiency of our own harvests, and our ports are, consequently, opened. The supply we require can then only be obtained by drawing upon that which foreign countries raise for their own consumption. Our superior wealth enables us to do this; we can afford to pay a price for wheat which attracts it from all quarters; but, in doing so, it necessarily also raises the price abroad far above its ordinary level. So sudden an increase in the price of food cannot take place without inflicting very great distress upon the foreign consumer, and thus the capricious and the irregular admission of foreign corn into our markets becomes almost as great a nuisance to the countries from which it is drawn, as our at other times refusing to receive the produce which has been raised in expectation of our demand. The Hon. Member for Lincolnshire (Mr. Christopher), adverted to the riots which lately took place in some ports of France, to prevent the shipping of corn to this country, as an illustration of the danger to which we should be exposed, by making ourselves dependent upon other countries for a supply of food. In my opinion, it would have been impossible to have adduced a stronger proof of the very dangerous dependance upon foreign countries to which we are now exposed. I confess that I am in no degree astonished at the conduct of the French populace, or of the French Government, in this matter: what has occurred is the natural consequence of our own legislation. If we refuse to conduct a regular trade in corn with foreign nations, and thus prevent them from growing a supply for our market, is it to be supposed that, when the supply is defective, and when the people of other countries are suffering from the high price of the chief article of subsistence, it will in such a time of general scarcity be endured that England should come forward, and, by her superior wealth, run up their prices, already high, 100 or 200 per cent. above the level of ordinary years? Such a system would be intolerable to other nations, for the prices, so raised by the superior wealth of England, would be famine prices to the people of other countries. I contend, therefore, that the effect of the existing law is to raise up difficulties in the way of our obtaining a supply in the time of our utmost need. The House will do well to recollect that we are, at this moment, shut out from the grain market of a very extensive part of the Continent. If I am not greatly mistaken corn is not now permitted to be shipped for England, from any of the ports of the northern and western coasts of France, from those of Belgium, and of the greater part of Italy including the Austrian dominions in that country, the territory of the Pope, and the kingdom of Naples. From none of these places is the exportation of corn to England now allowed, and the prohibition is, in my opinion, the direct and natural consequence of our own law.

But, independently of the interference of foreign Governments to prohibit the exportation of corn, and of the insufficiency of the supply provided to meet an unexpected demand, the existing law further operates to raise to the consumers the price of foreign corn when it is wanted, by the extreme uncertainty and hazard, which it produces in carrying on the trade in corn. When the duty, after having been for a long period, at a very high rate falls by a rise of the averages to one that is merely nominal, there is always the greatest doubt how long it may remain at this amount, and consequently there is a sort of struggle amongst speculators, to enter for home consumption, the largest possible quantity in the shortest possible time. Owing to this, freight (there being an urgent demand for it,) rises to an unusual price, and all the other charges of importation are increased in a similar manner. The holders of corn, knowing that time is all important to the speculators, and that, therefore, the competition of corn which has to be brought from a greater distance can have little effect, are enabled to insist upon higher prices than they could otherwise obtain. Upon this point, I confess I was surprised to hear one of the advocates of the existing law, gravely quote as a proof of the advantages of the system, a letter from the Continent, in which it is asserted, that some of the Prussian merchants were anxious for the continuance of our Corn Law, because it enabled them, whenever our ports opened, to realise higher prices than they could otherwise obtain. No doubt such is the effect of our system of duties, but, however advantageous it may be in these cases to the Prussian merchants to be relieved from all effective competition, from those of Odessa, or other distant markets, and to be thus enabled to insist upon higher prices than they could otherwise expect; surely this is any thing but an advantage to the consumer in this country, by whom these higher prices have to be paid.

It is true, that, with such a deficiency as we have this year experienced, supplies are obtained from Odessa, and other distant places, but in importing from these quarters, the merchant is exposed to the risk of having the duty again raised, before he can bring his cargoes into the market, and for this danger he must of course be compensated by an additional profit if the adventure should succeed. Thus the uncertainty of the continuance of the low rate of duty raises the price of foreign Corn to the consumer, whether that Corn has to be brought from a distance, or can at once be entered for home consumption, because in the latter case the holder is not exposed to effective competition, and because in the former, the merchant, though he may buy cheap, incurs so much risk that he cannot venture to carry on the taade, except with a view to high profits.

Nor is this the whole extent of the burthen, thrown upon the consumer, by the uncertainty in the trade, occasioned by our varying duties. It is a principle so clear, that, but for some of the very extraordinary arguments and doctrines, put forward by the supporters of the Corn Law, during this debate, I should hardly have thought it necessary to state it, that no trade can be carried on, for a series of years, to a loss; if in any particular branch of commerce, great losses are at times experienced, they must of necessity be compensated by corresponding profits at other times, or the trade must clearly be abandoned. Hence it becomes a point of much importance, to ascertain the extent of the losses sustained by speculators in corn, during the period that a prohibitory rate of duty was maintained, since these losses, must, sooner or later be made good by the consumer. If we can discover the amount of loss, incurred while the ports remained closed, we shall be able to judge in some degree, what must have been the additional charge thrown upon the consumer, when the averages rose so as to allow of the admission of foreign corn at the low duty.

One of the witnesses examined by the Agricultural Committee of 1836, estimated the losses which had even then been incurred in this way, in the few preceding years at not less than £3,000,000. I have every reason to believe that this is no exaggerated calculation, but as Honourable Members, opposite, may not be inclined to attach the same credit that I do myself to a general estimate, of which the particular grounds have not been stated, I have endeavoured to ascertain from data, which can hardly be disputed, what may be considered the lowest amount of expense which must have been incurred in holding foreign corn in bond in this country during the six years preceding the last harvest. It is obvious that this expense can form only a very small part of the losses incurred in the trade in foreign corn for our market; many other very heavy items of loss would still remain to be ascertained, but without reference to these I am anxious to show to the House, how very large an expense must have been incurred by the importers, during the time that the high rates of duty were maintained, under the single head of keeping foreign corn in bond in the ports of this country.

With a view to calculate the amount of this expense, I have obtained a statement, shewing the quantity of foreign wheat imported, the quantity taken out of bond, and the quantity remaining in bond, at the end of each half year, from the 5th January, 1833, to the 5th July, 1837. From this statement, it appears, that there were 507,764 quarters of foreign wheat in bond, on the 5th January, 1833, and that in the 9 following half years, to the 5th July, 1837, there were imported, 611,749 quarters more, making in all, 1,129,513 quarters, which had passed through the bonding warehouses during the period in question. Of this quantity, there were taken, out of bond, during the same time, 545,079 quarters, and as the duty, in these years, was constantly at a prohibiting rate, and only the small quantity of 6,472 quarters, were consequently entered for home consumption, the wheat taken out of bond must have been for re-exportation, except that which was destroyed, a mode of disposing of wheat that had been kept a long time in the warehouses, which the return moved for, by my Honourable Friend the Member for Leeds, (Mr. Baines) shews in some cases, at least, to have been adopted. Whether re-exported or destroyed, it is obvious that no pront whatever could have been obtained by the importers, to make up for even a part of the expense, incurred in warehousing that corn to which I now refer, on the contrary, an additional and very considerable loss must have been incurred in disposing of it, beyond the charge of keeping it in bond. But confining my attention to the amount of this last charge. I find that the length of time for which the wheat thus unprofitably taken out of bond, must have been in warehouse, was upon an average, 47½ months. I arrive at this result, by assuming, that the corn, first imported, was always that first taken out of bond, of course this would not be really the case, but in calculating the average time, that the whole remained in bond, no error can result from the assumption, since if some parcels of corn would be taken, as having been longer in warehouse than they really had, others would be in consequence, taken as having been so for too short a time, and the average obtained, will, therefore, be correct.

The cost of keeping corn in warehouse has, I find, been very variously estimated; the highest calculation I have seen, is 10*s*. a quarter annually, and the lowest 5*s*., and I am led to believe, that in taking it at 6*s*., I am not exceeding the truth. Upon this calculation, the actual charge for keeping in warehouse, 545,079 quarters of wheat; for an average time of 47½ months, will amount to 649,474*l*., and in the 4½ years, in which our markets were entirely closed against the admission of foreign grain, a loss to that extent must have been incurred by the importers, under this single head of expense. But of the 1,129,513 quarters of foreign corn, which, as I have said, had been at different times in warehouse during these years, there still remained in bond, on the 5th of July 1837, 584,434 quarters; of this quantity, about two-thirds were entered for home consumption, some at a high rate of duty in the following half year, and the remainder in the course of the last autumn; upon the same principle of calculation as before, I find that the average period for which it had been in bond, before it was taken out, to have been nearly 30 months, at an expense of 419,762*l*., making a total charge incurred in keep ing in bond, the 1,129,513 quarters, which had been imported during the time our ports were closed, of no less a sum than 1,066,236*l*. or about 19*s*. a quarter.

Sir, I am aware it may be said, that so far as regards that portion of this wheat, which was eventually entered for home consumption, at a low rate of duty, the calculation I have just made is fallacious, in as much as under any mode of conducting the corn trade, wheat imported, must be kept very frequently for considerable periods in warehouse, and the charge so incurred upon this part of what was imported before July 1837, cannot therefore be regarded as a loss occasioned by the existing law. I am not disposed to deny altogether the force of this answer, I am aware that the whole expense of keeping this wheat in warehouse, cannot fairly be attributed to the operation of the law, but far the larger part of it undoubtedly must be so, and against the amount, whatever it may be, by which I may have over-estimated the loss incurred under this head, there has to be set all the very much heavier loss which must have been thrown upon the importers, by being compelled at a great sacrifice to dispose of the very considerable quantity of wheat, which, I have shewn they were compelled to re-export, and some of it actually to destroy. When it is considered that I have allowed nothing for any loss of that kind or for that sustained upon corn warehoused in foreign ports, on account of English capitalists though I have reason to know that there were considerable stocks of wheat held at a very serious expense in some of the foreign ports of exportation, it seems to me impossible to doubt that the loss incurred by the dealers in foreign corn since 1833 must far have exceeded the sum of 1,066,236*l* at which I have calculated it.

I will, however, take it at this amount only, and, I contend, that in seeking to ascertain what is the direct charge which has been imposed upon the British consumer of foreign corn by the existing law, we may fairly assume; (upon the principle, that the loss incurred in the trade at one time, must be compensated by a corresponding profit at another) that this sum together with the actual amount of duty received, must have been repaid by the increased price put upon foreign corn admitted for home consumption. But the amount of duty received, upon foreign corn in the last two years, has been 439,963*l*., which added to the loss I have calculated at 1,066,236*l*, will give a sum of 1,506,199*l*., as the whole direct charge upon the foreign wheat admitted for home consumption since July 1837, and, as the number of quarters entered for consumption from that time, to the 5th January 1839, has been 1,941,990, the impost cannot be considered at less than 15*s*. 6*d*. a quarter, in addition to the further and very heavy tax which we have had to pay in the shape of increased price to the foreign holder of corn, and of increased charges for importation, arising from the uncertainty of our system in the manner I have already shewn.

There is another mode of estimating the charge, which the existing law has thrown upon the country, under the circumstances of the last season notwithstanding its having admitted of the importation of a considerable quantity of foreign corn, at a nominal rate of duty.

It is now about six months, since the deficiency of our home supply of wheat became apparent and produced a considerable rise of price; in September the averages attained the point at which the duty is reduced to its lowest amount yet, in consequence of the restricted supply obtainable from abroad, the importations were only able to lower the price of wheat for a short time; the temporary fall which followed the entry of a considerable quantity of foreign wheat, was soon more than recovered and the average price of the last six months, has been about 72 shillings. Now, Sir, it is, I think, quite impossible to suppose that so high a price could have been maintained for so long a time, under a different system of Corn Laws, and if we assume that, while the 1*s.* duty has been generally chargeable, the want of a more abundant supply of foreign wheat, has raised our market prices only 5*s.* a quarter beyond the rate, which, under a more certain system, might have been expected to prevail, I am convinced, that we shall very greatly indeed under estimate the amount of the burthen thrown upon the consumers of wheat, in one of those periods of scarcity, during which it was the great argument of the advocates of the law, that by the contrivance of the varying scale of duties, we should enjoy all the benefits of a practically free trade. But, as the annual consumption of wheat in this country, is estimated at from 12 to 14 millions of quarters, it will follow, that, at the lowest calculation, an addition of 5*s.* a quarter, to the price of wheat, during six months, must have been equivalent to a tax levied upon the consumers, of no less a sum than 1,500,000*l.*

These considerations seem, to me, clearly to establish the conclusion, that the relief which it was supposed the consumer would derive, from the reduction of the duties upon foreign corn by means of the varying scale, has been proved by experience, to be altogether fallacious and imaginary; we impose, on the contrary, as heavy, or rather, a much heavier burthen upon the country, than if we levied a high fixed duty upon corn, the only difference is, that while we impose the burthen, we carefully contrive to do it in such a manner, as to bring in no revenue to the State. Surely this can hardly be defended as a wise arrangement; it may perhaps be true, as I have heard some gentlemen assert, that we ought not to levy a revenue by a tax upon the food of the people, but the objection to such a tax is surely not the revenue it brings in, but the burthen it imposes, and if we are required to submit to the burthen, we should at least take care that we do not lose the revenue; I cannot, therefore, regard it as otherwise, than a decisive objection to the existing law, that it imposes a charge upon the country, at least as severe as a fixed duty, which, in the last few months, would have brought in 1,000,000*l.*, or 1,200,000*l.* to the Exchequer, while it has been comparatively unproductive of revenue. Can we regard it as otherwise than a most improvident and thriftless waste of the resources of the country, to throw away so large a sum which might have been realized and applied towards the reduction of some of our other burthens, without throwing the slightest additional charge upon the people?

Sir, I will now proceed to that which I consider a yet more important branch of my argument, and

I will endeavour to shew that if in a time of scarcity our fluctuating duty presses heavily upon the consumer, in periods of abundance, it has pressed no less heavily upon the farmer; in the one case it enhances the too high prices, and aggravates the difficulties of such a season as the last; in the other, it increases to a degree absolutely ruinous to the producer, that fall of prices which an unusual plenty must at all times occasion. The very fact, that in unproductive years, our Corn Law, as I have endeavoured to shew, restricts our supply from abroad, and thus enhances the price of wheat in the home market, must, of necessity, produce the opposite effect upon a recurrence of seasons of a contrary description, from the unnatural stimulus which the high prices must give to an increased growth of wheat. The first four or five years after the passing of the Act of 1828, we required from the deficiency of our own crops a considerable supply of wheat from abroad, and, under these circumstances, the effect of the law was undoubtedly both to raise the prices of wheat higher than they otherwise have been, and to inspire the producers with false hopes, that these prices would be maintained. A powerful stimulus was thus given to the increased cultivation of wheat, and favourable harvests having followed, there was a redundant supply, which produced the great depression of prices and agricultural distress, which were so severely felt from 1833 to 1836. I am aware that this statement is not in accordance with that made by the Agricultural Committee of 1833; in the report of that Committee, it is asserted that the produce of wheat in this kingdom had fallen off rather than increased since 1821. Sir, I should not have the presumption to ask the House to prefer my authority to that of the Committee, but the authority of facts is before either, and this is in favour of the statement I have made. In 1821, it was shewn that upon an average of years we did not at that time produce as much wheat as sufficed for our own consumption; but from the harvest of 1832 our consumption was, for six years, almost entirely supplied by our own produce, the amount of foreign corn entered for home consumption, during that time having been too trifling to deserve notice. Yet between 1821 and 1831 our population had increased from 21,193,000 to 24,271,000, and the consumption between 1833 and 1836, was augmented far more than in proportion to the increased population owing to the cheapness of corn, and to the high wages, which, from the commercial prosperity that prevailed during the greater part of the period, were paid in the manufacturing districts. It is notorious also, that wheat, in consequence of its very low price, and the comparatively less abundant supplies of other sorts of grain, was used to a considerable extent for malting, and also for feeding cattle and sheep. This immensely increased consumption, which, for six years, was supplied by our home produce, without any assistance from importation that deserves to be noticed, affords the most conclusive proof of a very greatly increased production of wheat; this increased production sufficiently accounts for the depression of prices during the period in question, and can itself only be attributed to the artificial stimulus caused by the high prices, which immediately followed the passing of the existing law, and by the hope this law encouraged, that similar prices would be maintained.

Sir, I perceive that the Hon. Gentleman (Col. Wood) admits the fact of the greatly increased production of British wheat in the period to which I refer, but implies that this increase must have been a benefit to the nation. Undoubtedly, if the increase in the growth of wheat had been a natural and healthy increase, it would have been a great national advantage, but the forced and artificial increase which took place, not of cultivation generally but of the growth of wheat, too often in place of other crops, and to the permanent injury of the land, was very far indeed from being in any respect beneficial to the country.

But this is a point upon which I do not wish now to dwell; the unnatural stimulus which had been given to the growth of wheat was certainly one powerful cause of the very low prices, which for some years prevailed, but it was not the only, nor, perhaps, the most injurious mode in which the existing law operated in this direction. It appears to me impossible to doubt that the discouragement of trade in British corn, by the varying duties upon foreign corn must have had a very great share in producing the extreme depression of the price of wheat from 1833 to 1836. The tendency of our present scale of duties so to discourage trade in British corn is sufficiently obvious since the very object of the progressive reduction of the duty upon foreign corn with every rise of the averages, is to check that tendency to a rise in the markets, by which alone the speculative purchaser can hope to obtain a profit. It may be contended, indeed, that at the very low prices to which British wheat fell at the close of 1835, the present scale of duties upon foreign corn could not have had any effect in discouraging speculation, since there was ample room for profit between 36*s.* or 40*s.*, at which wheat might at one time have been bought, and 66*s.* or 67*s.* to which at least the average price must have risen, before the rate of duty could possibly allow any considerable quantity of foreign wheat to be entered for home consumption. I should certainly have been inclined before hand to suppose that such would have been the case and that the existing law would have had little effect, at very low prices, in discouraging the trade in British corn, but experience has shewn the fact to be otherwise. This may perhaps be accounted for, partly by supposing that the disadvantage of dealing in British corn at particular prices, from the rapid reduction of the duty on foreign corn as the averages rise, produces a general dislike to the trade, which does not cease to operate even when this reason for it no longer applies; and still more effect is probably produced by the large amount of capital locked up in foreign corn to which it is attracted, by the much higher profits resulting from a successful speculation in this than in British corn. A rise in the markets, it is obvious, only adds to the value of British corn to the extent of that rise, but it adds to the value of foreign corn in bond, not only to this extent, but to the much greater extent of the reduction of duty it occasions. It is true that these high profits are only to be obtained by incurring a proportionate hazard of loss, but I fear that a trade is not rendered less attractive to the generality of men by holding out the prospect of great but uncertain gains, rather than of moderate advantages and diminished risk. Be the explanation of the fact, however, what it may, there is no doubt that during the time the existing Corn Law has been in force, the trade in British corn has languished, and that the want of speculative purchasers has greatly contributed to depress its price. We have the concurrent testimony to this effect of very numerous witnesses, of the most opposite pursuits and opinions, some of them farmers, others corn dealers, some opponents, and others advocates, of the existing law. I will only refer to the names of Mr. Hodgson, Mr. Sturge, Mr. Scott, Mr. Calthorpe (a great advocate of the existing Corn Law),

Mr. Evans David, and of Mr. Blamire, whose practical acquaintance with all that relates to agriculture, and whose sound judgment upon questions of this kind cannot fail to be appreciated by this House, of which he was so lately a member. These witnesses, and many more whom I might mention, all concur in stating that there has been a marked absence of speculation in British corn under the existing law. I will not, however, trouble the House by reading the evidence they have given, but there is a short extract from the evidence of one of the witnesses examined in 1833, which seems to me so clear upon this point, and so important, that I must venture to call your attention to it. The witness to whom I allude is Mr. Low, Professor of Agriculture at Edinburgh, and a Land Surveyor, extensively employed, as it appears, in the celebrated corn district of the Lothians. His evidence is as follows:—

"11453. What are the advantages you contemplate from a fixed duty, which a shifting scale does not afford?—I think that one of the practical inconveniences of the present system, is, that the attention of the trader in corn is directed more to the foreign trade in corn than to the home trade in corn. In the case of the foreign trade, there are two contingencies to calculate on; the decrease of duty, and the increase of price. In the case of home produce, the trader only calculates upon the contingency of the increase of price. Therefore, there appears to be a greater inducement to invest capital in the foreign than in the home produce; and I think that experience has shewn it to be so, since the operation of the law. And I conceive this practical inconvenience may be the result. When a farmer is threshing out to supply a present necessity, there is no capital between him and the consumer; whereas, if the capital of the trader in corn was more directed to the home produce, the farmer, at such a period, would be relieved.

"11454. The result of your experience, leads you to think that the speculators in corn, under the present law, speculate entirely in foreign corn, and not in home-grown corn?—Not entirely, but certainly more, comparatively, in foreign than in home-grown corn.

"11455. Have you observed the effect that has been produced on stocks in hand at harvest, either in the hands of the farmer, in his granary and stack-yard, or the miller and jobber; are the stocks as large as they used heretofore to be?—I think not, on a series of years.

"11456. In average years, the farmers in Lothian have as much wheat on hand in harvest as they used to have?—No, I do not think the farmers have the same stock in general at harvest that they used to have.

"11457. Has it diminished materially?—It has diminished to a considerable extent."

Sir, I think this evidence sufficiently proves

both the discouragement of speculative trade in British corn, by the existing law, and the great injury which results to the farmer from this discouragement. But what most particularly, in my opinion deserves the attention of the House, is the statement as to the diminution of the stocks of corn usually left in the country, when a new crop comes in. Mr. Low's evidence on this point was confirmed by that of a very great number of witnesses; and the Committee were so satisfied of the fact being as it was represented, that, in their Report, they adopt the conclusion, that the usual stock of British corn, left at harvest, which used formerly to be about equal to six months' supply, had not, of late years, been more than a fortnight's consumption. I am convinced that this statement of the Committee is correct; indeed, when we remember, that their Report was drawn up by the Right Hon. Baronet, the Member for Pembroke (Sir J. Graham), one of the ablest advocates in this House of the existing law, it is very little likely that any such statement should have been adopted upon insufficient grounds, or that any conclusion, making against the present system, should have received the sanction of his authority, unless it had been most clearly and satisfactorily established. I assume, then, that under the operation of the Corn Laws, the stock of British wheat, usually in reserve at the time of harvest, has been reduced, as stated by the Committee, from a supply equal to six months' consumption, to one sufficient for a fortnight only; and I would call upon Hon. Members, who wish to maintain the law as it stands, seriously to consider how important are the inferences to be drawn from this fact. It affords the most conclusive proof of the degree to which our existing law has tended to discourage that natural and healthy trade in British corn, which, if left to itself, would form our real security against either the extremes of high, or of low prices.

The diminution of the stock of wheat usually kept in hand can only arise from a decrease of the speculative purchasers by which such a stock is accumulated, and by which, at the same time, a supply of more than usual abundance is prevented from causing a ruinous depression of the markets. This must be highly injurious to the farmer, in times of plenty, but it is a still more serious consideration, how greatly the effects of a deficient harvest must thus be aggravated. It is reckoned a very great and unusual deficiency, when the crop of wheat is one-fourth below that of an ordinary year; the Honourable and Gallant Member opposite (Colonel Wood) says, such a deficiency would be almost a famine. Sir, my fear is, that under the existing law, it might turn out to be, not almost, but quite a famine, and though, happily, so great a deficiency as I have mentioned, is a very rare occurrence, it is one, by no means unexampled;

the failure of the crop in 1816, has, I believe, upon the best authority, been considered as having been not to a less extent. I ask the Honourable Member, then to consider what would be the situation of the country, under the visitation of such a crop as 1816, under a system by which the usual stock of corn at the time of harvest, has been reduced from a six months' to a fortnight's supply ? With a six months' stock in hand, it would require two successive harvests, deficient to this extraordinary degree, to exhaust the resource we should thus possess against a defiency of food, even, though we were to fail in obtaining any supply from abroad ; but with only a fortnight's stock of corn before hand, a single harvest of this description, would render it necessary for us to import at least 2½ millions of quarters to avert all the distress of a positive want of the first necessary of life. The habitual existence of a considerable reserve of corn in the hands of the farmer, and of the merchant, is what alone can effectually mitigate that pressure upon the population, which a defective harvest must always to a greater, or less extent occasion, and yet the existence of any such reserve, it is, upon the shewing of the advocates of the Corn Law themselves, the effect of that measure to prevent. Sir, we are at this moment suffering from this operation of the law ; our present high prices are owing not merely to the restrictions of the supply of foreign corn, to which I before adverted; but to a deficiency of

British wheat occasioned both by the discouragement of trade, of which I have just endeavoured to shew the effects, and also by the diminished cultivation of wheat, which is known to have been caused by the low prices, from 1833 to 1836; for the Honourable Member, who regarded as a national advantage, that increased production of wheat, to which he admitted, that I correctly attributed the very low price which prevailed 4 years ago, would do well to remember that this increased produce, and the glut which it occasioned, were necessarily followed by a subsequent contraction of cultivation. Thus, in every way, the existing Corn Law acts and re-acts in aggravating the inconvenience which results, either from a dearth, or from a glut.

Sir, this is a result at which we have in my opinion, no right to be surprised, when we reflect that the natural course of trade, with which I have shewn, that the cumbrous and complicated regulations of our law, so greatly interfere, is the instrument obviously designed by Providence, for regulating the supply of food to society, and for moderating, as far as they can be moderated, those inequalities in the prices of the produce of the soil, which the varieties of the season are calculated to occasion. To judge of the full importance of this effect of trade, we should look to what occurs in those states of society, where it is able to exercise but little of its salutary influence. In rude and barbarous countries, were the want of capital and security cripple the energies of commerce, the fluctuations which take place in the prices of corn, are found to be very great, because on the one hand, as the producers must sell to meet the charges to which they are liable; while the consumption of food can never undergo a very sudden and considerable extension, where there is little demand, except that for immediate consumption, a comparatively small excess of supply, must produce a more than corresponding depression of price, from the competition of sellers; and on the other hand, as the consumption cannot without extreme inconvenience be much restricted, when there is no reserve in the hands of capitalists to meet a deficiency, even a small deficiency may occasion a great rise of prices, from the general struggle of all to obtain their usual amount of subsistence.

Accordingly, where, by any circumstance, the operations of trade are subjected to great difficulties and discouragement, it has often been observed, that the price of grain varies very much, not only according to the different degrees of productiveness of different seasons, but with the different periods of the year. Very low prices immediately after harvest, and very high prices before a new crop comes in are, in such a state of society, almost habitual, while the extreme cheapness of productive seasons is most fatally compensated by the corresponding intensity of dearth which a single season of scarcity is sufficient to produce.

In those parts of the world in which civilization has made but little progress, examples of this are to the present day to be found. My Right Honourable Friend (Mr. Thomson), last night, stated that he had known wheat in some parts of the interior of Russia, to sell for only 5*s* a quarter, and it was in the very same part of that Empire, that two or three years ago, there prevailed a dearth so severe, that it might almost deserve the name of a famine.

In the earlier periods of our own history, instances of the same kind are not wanting; the prices borne by wheat in this country, in many years of the 13th and 14th centuries, have been recorded, and I will take the liberty of reading to the House, some instances which I have selected of the very violent alterations from high to low prices, which in those days took place.

In the year 1244, the price of wheat, in money of the present day, according to Adam Smith, was 6*s*. a quarter: two years afterwards, in 1246, it was 48*s*. a quarter; in 1270, it is said to have reached 16 guineas. I need not observe, that at this period, it did not constitute the food of more than a very small part of the population.

In one part of 1288, the price was as low as 3*s*, and in another it rose to 28*s*. It was in 1289, 36*s*; it fell in the same year to 6*s*, and rose again to 60*s*. In 1317, the price was 72*s*, fell to 42*s*, rose to twelve pounds, and fell again to 20*s*.

Sir, I might quote many other years in which

similar alterations of price took place, but it is needless to do so, those I have given sufficiently exemplify their violence at this period. I need not say that these are extremes of prices, to which in these days, and even under our existing law we have seen no approach; they go far beyond what occurred even in the calamitous period at the commencement of the present century, when we had an alternation of productive seasons, with others of almost unexampled severity, of which the effect was aggravated by the desolation of so large a part of the civilized world, by war and commotions. Nor need I observe, how grievous to all classes of the community must have been the distress to which such irregularities as these in the supply of food, must necessarily have given rise. And to what is it that we owe our exemption from the same evils? Simply to the dealings of the trader; it is by these, and by these only, that we have secured to us the inestimable blessing of the comparative steadiness in the price and supply of food, which in these days we enjoy. The manner in which commerce operates in producing this effect, is one of the most important discoveries of modern times. We now understand that the merchant in buying corn, when it is plentiful and cheap, though he may be looking only to his own advantage and future profit, is in fact performing the most essential service to the community? By the additional demand, he thus brings into the market, he checks that fall of prices, which to the great loss of the farmer, and therefore to the ultimate injury of the consumer, must inevitably take place, if with an extraordinary supply, the only purchasers were those for immediate consumption. And while he thus checks the ruinous fall of prices in plenty, he is at the same time making the best provision against future scarcity, and by bringing out upon such occasions, the reserve he has before accumulated, he mitigates the severity of the distress which the diminished supply of food must otherwise occasion. Nor is this all, by causing a timely rise of price as soon as a deficiency is known, he enforces a wise economy of consumption during the whole year, and thus arrests the horrors of a famine at its close.

Sir, I greatly regret that I have been compelled to trouble the House with these general remarks, on the nature and effects of trade, but I have thought it necessary to advert to these, now well-known, principles, because they are of vital importance in considering the subject now before us, and my whole argument on the effect of the law in discouraging trade, entirely hinges upon them, while they seem to have been completely lost sight of by the speakers on the other side.

And, in speaking of the manner in which the supply of food to a large and civilized community is regulated by trade, I am reminded of the argument of the Noble Lord, the Member for Shropshire (Lord Darlington), that the present high price of corn caused no distress to the labourer, because his wages had risen in the same proportion. Surely the Noble Lord would have perceived that this is utterly impossible, had he reflected that the rise of prices, which always takes place in consequence of a deficient supply, is nothing more than the effect of that natural mechanism of society, which seems to have been contrived by Providence for the purpose of guarding us against the evils of famine; it is by high prices that such an economy in the consumption of food is enforced, as may enable a short crop to last until another can be obtained. Now, if wages rose in proportion to the rise in the price of corn, this object would be defeated; it is, therefore, quite impossible that a rise in the price of corn should produce an equivalent rise of wages, and the very statement of the Noble Lord shows that, in the case to which he refers, it had not done so. The usual wages, he tells us, of a labouring man, in that part of Lincolnshire in which he resides, were, in 1835, 12*s*. a-week, and they have now risen to 15*s*. Sir, I fear this increase is by no means general; that the country with which the Noble Lord happens to be acquainted has been, in this respect, unusually fortunate; but even in this favoured district, the increase of wages which has taken place is but 25 per cent., while the price of wheat has risen 100 per cent. in the same time. An Hon. Member opposite asks whether a labouring man spends all his wages in bread. Certainly not; nor did I mean to argue that, in order to enable him to have the same supply of food as before, his wages ought to have risen 100 per cent., because the price of wheat had risen to this extent; but I do mean to say that, considering the proportion of his earnings which an agricultural labourer is usually compelled to spend in purchasing bread for himself and his family, his wages ought to have risen, not 25, but more probably 75 per cent., to prevent him from being exposed to privations by the present price of wheat, as compared to that of the winter of 1835.

But, Sir, this is a topic to which I did not intend to allude, and on which I will not further remark; my aim, in the observations I have addressed to the House, was, as I stated in the outset, to show that the evil of too high, and of too low prices, which we have experienced, at different periods, within the last ten years, has, in both cases, been aggravated by the operation of the existing law, and I think I have now proved this to have been the case. It appears to me clearly to follow from the facts and arguments I have stated, that this law, of which the object and avowed intention was to secure, by its complicated regulations, a forced and unnatural equality of prices, has, on the contrary, in its practical effect, tended to increase and aggravate those fluctuations in the price of the produce of the soil, which the variations of the season must always, to a greater or less extent, occasion. It has done this by impeding and interrupting the course of trade, which is the natural regulator of prices, and thus carrying us one step backwards in civilization—one degree nearer to the irregularities in the supply of food, which, in barbarous countries, where trade is not permitted to flourish, I have shown to occasion so much inconvenience.

Sir, I am persuaded that such will ever be the result of our interfering, by means of complicated and artificial regulations, with the natural order of things, and with that beautiful mechanism of society, which seems to me to bear so clearly the impress of unerring wisdom and divine benevolence. That more mischief has not ensued from our legislation may well, I think, be matter of congratulation; and it is a new proof how admirably contrived and adapted to its intended objects is the constitution of human society, that greater disturbance has not been produced, even by such ill-judged and perverse interference with its natural arrangements, as that of which we have presumed to be guilty. Yet, let me not be misunderstood, as saying that much harm has not been done by our legislation upon this subject. Far from it; great evil, though less, I think, than we have well deserved, has resulted from the existing Corn Law; and the greater part of that evil, as I believe will always happen, in such cases, has fallen upon the heads of those for whose special benefit the law was intended.

Sir, I say the greatest share of the evil consequences of the law has fallen upon those for whose benefit it was intended; and in support of that assertion allow me to read the account which was given of the manner in which the agricultural interest has suffered under its operation by one of the witnesses examined in 1833. Mr. Cooper, a land agent, and also himself a proprietor of land, gave the following evidence:—

"9667. Amongst the farmers that are made insolvent, are there many of industrious and prudent habits?—Yes.

"9668. Men that had at the outset a capital adequate to the cultivation of their farms?—Quite equal to it.

"9669. Is that class very numerous?—Yes, that class is numerous who had a property quite equal to the capital required upon their farms, but now their capital is diminished, and, in many cases, gone.

"9670. Do you think those men, in taking their farms, acted with the average prudence, or were there instances of improvidence in taking farms?—The value of a farm has been very difficult to ascertain, both as regards the land and the produce; because the prices of produce have been so fluctuating, that no man could value land accurately.

"9671. It is hardly possible for a man to judge at what price he would be safe at taking land?—No.

"9673. Has the farming of land been a kind of lottery lately?—Yes.

"9674. Was it the custom at former periods for farming to be a dangerous trade?—No.

"9675. Was it considered as being a safe pursuit?—Yes.

"9692. Do the farmers generally keep as great a stock of grain as they did formerly?—No.

"9693. Is that visible in their yards and in their barns?—Yes.

"9694. To a considerable extent?—Yes, to a very considerable extent it is visible."

Such is the description, given by a witness entitled to the highest credit, of the practical consequences of the system we have pursued; and I cannot too earnestly call upon all who are interested in the welfare of agriculture seriously to reflect upon this statement, of the issue of the fatal experiment in which we have now for four-and-twenty years persisted. For that long period we have now given the fullest trial to the principle of what is termed protection; in 1815 this principle was carried to its furthest possible point, and a Corn Law was passed in strict conformity with the wishes of the agriculturists; it turned out that in granting them what they had asked, the most fatal boon had been conferred upon them; and it was after a few years all but universally admitted by all parties that the law of 1815 had proved an utter and complete failure. Accordingly in 1828, another and the most improved method of applying the same principle of protection was adopted, a new act was passed, and in framing it the agriculturists, the advocates of prohibition, and the friends of artificial regulations, were again the parties who were listened to, and whose views were adopted. And what has again been the result? I have shewn that during the period of ten years, which has since elapsed, the time of Parliament has been occupied at least half of those years in listening to the loudest, the bitterest, and I must say the justest complaints of agricultural distress. The first years after the passing of the act, deficient crops produced high prices, and these prices, with the false hope that they would be maintained, with which our legislation inspired the farmers, gave an unnatural stimulus to production; more wheat was sown, higher rent was offered for land, and a delusive appearance of agricultural prosperity was for a time created. But favourable harvests succeeded, and notwithstanding the complete monopoly of the home market the prices of wheat continued to fall; the farmers could no longer pay, or could pay only out of their capital the high rents which had been promised upon the expectation of those prices which it was the professed object of the Corn Law to secure; and one common and wide-sweeping distress involved both the landlord who had calculated upon receiving the rent for which he had let his land, and the farmer who struggled to the last to fulfil his engagement.

I appeal to those gentlemen who served upon the Agricultural Committees of 1833 and 1836, whether this is not an account far from exaggerated, of the distress of the agriculturists from the great depression of the price of wheat in those years; and how, I ask, is this distress to be accounted for in a period of profound peace, of constantly diminishing taxation, and generally of great commercial prosperity, except by the operation of our ill-judged legislation. But now the landed interest is in a more prosperous situation. The Hon. Member for Lincolnshire, (Mr. Heathcote), said, the other evening, that the landed interest was just beginning to revive, owing, I suppose, to the blessing of a deficient harvest. If this is so, what must be the state of things in which the landed interest can only prosper from a deficient harvest, which used justly to be reckoned one of the severest visitations with which Providence could afflict a nation?

Such has been the issue of an experiment of four and twenty years of the protective system; let us contrast with this result that which has followed from a different system. My Right Hon. Friend, the President of the Board of Trade, last night adverted to the case of the Wool Trade; but that case is so strong that I must make one or two observations upon it. The House must be aware, that in 1819 a heavy duty was imposed on foreign wool; it was a fixed duty, indeed, and, therefore, unlike our mischievous and fluctuating duty on corn, it did not interfere with the trade in wool of our own growth. Still it was a heavy protecting duty. In 1825 it was repealed, and soon afterwards, from causes, as I believe, quite independent of this repeal, there occurred a very great fall in the price of wool. The utmost alarm was excited amongst the gentlemen of the landed interest. In the year 1828 innumerable petitions were presented to this House, all complaining of the competition of foreign wool. The Members for the great wool growing counties, in presenting these petitions, most earnestly supported their prayer; amongst others, I remember well, that my Hon. Friend, the Member for Wiltshire, (Mr. Bennet), whom I now see listening to me, predicted the absolute ruin of the South Down farmers, unless the high protecting duty upon foreign wool were again imposed. In the other House of Parliament, a Committee was appointed to inquire into the subject, and witness after witness was brought forward, from amongst the farmers and owners of land, all declaring that the low price was entirely occasioned by the glut produced by the large importation of foreign wool, and that unless this importation were restrained, there must be an end of the growth of wool by the British farmer. It was asserted that there were large districts on the Continent in which the land would immediately be devoted to the production of wool, and one of the principal witnesses examined, Mr. Elman, declared, that no lower duty than one of 33 per cent. would be sufficient for the protection of English wool.

No less fortunately for the agriculturists than for the country at large these gloomy predictions were not listened to, and the legislature refused to re-impose the former heavy duty upon foreign wool. And what has been the result? Has the ruin they anticipated fallen upon the growers of wool? I hold in my hand a statement of the prices given for different descriptions of wool, in each year since the peace, by one of the most eminent dealers in the North of England, who purchases a large proportion of the produce of wool in the county which I have the honour to represent, and in which, sheep farming, as it is well known, is carried to a very great extent.

From this statement it appears, that the average price of Leicester wool during the six years from 1819 to 1824, when the high duty was in force, was 13*d.* to 13½*d.* per. pound. At Midsummer, 1828, the price had fallen, and was from 10½*d.* to 11*d.*, while the average of the last six years is from 17½*d* to 18*d.*. This, as compared to 1828, when we were told that without the re-imposition of the protecting duty, a further and ruinous fall must take place, shews an increase in the price of this description of wool, under the system of free competition; with foreign wool of no less than 63 per cent, and of 30 per cent, as compared to the period when the heavy duty was in force. Cheviot wool, from 1819 to 1824, was sold on an average at from $8\frac{1}{2}d.$ to $9d.$ per. pound. At Midsummer, 1828, the price was from $4\frac{1}{4}d.$ to $4\frac{3}{4}d.$, while for the last six years, the average price has been $10d.$ to $10\frac{1}{2}d.$, being, as compared to the former period of the same number of years, an increase of 17 per cent. South Down fleeces have only for the last six years, maintained the same average price as during the six years of the protecting duty; the average of both periods having been $17\frac{1}{2}d.$, but, as compared to the year 1828, the rise of this kind of wool is also very great; the price at Midsummer in that year having been only $8\frac{1}{2}d.$; the average of the last years shewing, therefore, an increase of 100 per. cent. Such, Sir, notwithstanding the free competition of foreign wool, which was so greatly dreaded by our agriculturists, has been the extraordinary improvement in the value of their own produce, and this improvement has taken place while, at the same time, the importations from which so much mischief was apprehended, have increased from 30 to 60 millions of pounds; and thus it has turned out, that Parliament, by refusing to listen to the unfounded fears and urgent demands of the landed interest with regard to wool, has both benefited that interest, and preserved an important branch of our national manufactures from the ruin which must inevitably have fallen upon it, from the re-imposition of the heavy duty upon the raw material with which it is carried on. I think the case I have just stated is very strong, as proving the utter extravagance of the apprehensions which are so often expressed of the effect which foreign competition would produce upon our agricultural interest but I have one which seems to me still stronger, to which I would call the attention of the House. In the Agricultural Committee of 1836, Mr. Fison made the following statement.

"12701. There is an immense quantity of land on the Continent that might be appropriated to the growth of rape-seed. Rape-seed is now bearing a good price in England; I suppose from 60*s* to 64*s* a quarter; which is fully as high as the average price, when there was 20*s* a quarter protecting duty upon it."

I see, Sir, that Hon. Gentlemen opposite consider rape-seed a very trifling article; but, in the year 1836, when the statement I have quoted was made, we imported considerably upwards of half a million of bushels, while English rape-seed, as it appears, still bore a very fair remunerating price. How, let me ask, could this have been; if, as we are told, the foreign grower can so completely undersell? Surely the same land and the same labour, which might be employed in the growth of wheat for one market, might equally be employed in the production of rape-seed; and if the apprehensions of Hon. Gentlemen, as to the effects of foreign competition, were well founded, it would be impossible for the English farmer to attempt the cultivation of this article, unprotected as it is.

Looking to these considerations, if the question this night before us, were, whether we would maintain the existing Corn Laws, or would consent to the total repeal of all duties on foreign corn, I should unhesitatingly say, that, even regarding this in the narrow light of merely a landowner's question, and not considering the other great national interests which it involves, I should give my vote in favour of a total repeal. But this is not the question before the House; and I will fairly tell the Hon. Member who brought forward the motion, that I shall not vote for going into a Committee with any view to the total repeal of these duties, falsely, in my opinion, called protecting. It is true, the whole system of what is called Protection, I consider to be grossly delusive, and most injurious to all classes of the community. I should much wish to see the time, when no duties whatever should be levied in this country for any purpose but that of revenue; but though this is the opinion as to what would be best for the country, which I most sincerely entertain, and which I therefore will never shrink from avowing, still, Sir, I cannot help feeling that it is necessary to consider the artificial condition to which, by our long perseverance in a bad system, this country has been brought, and, more especially, the amount of our taxation, and the necessity of raising a considerable revenue by duties upon imports. Looking to all these things, I think that the proper course for the

Legislature to pursue, would be that of establishing a moderate fixed duty upon corn; and this is the object which I have in view, in supporting the present motion. The Right Hon. Baronet, the Member for Kent (Sir Ed. Knatchbull), last night, taunted the supporters of the motion, with the absurdity of asking for a Committee of the whole House, instead of at once stating the measure we should propose to adopt, and, I believe, he alluded to some arguments which I ventured to address to the House, on a former evening, against a proposal for taking evidence at the bar.

But truly the Right Hon. Baronet must be well aware, that what we propose, is not a mere Committee of Enquiry. He must know, that by the forms of our proceedings, our going into a Committee of the whole House, is a necessary preliminary to any alteration whatever, of the existing law, and the vote which we are now to give, will be, in fact, simply on this question, whether we are prepared to adhere to the Corn Law, as it now stands, without any alteration whatever; whether we are determined to maintain our present system of fluctuating duties, or whether we will endeavour to effect any kind of improvement. The Hon. Member for Lincolnshire, (Mr. Christopher) fairly admitted that this was the point at issue, that it really is a question of whether or not we shall declare our unreserved and entire approbation of the existing law. This being the question, let me remind Hon. Members who agree with me in wishing for a fixed duty, but who are alarmed by the manner in which the present motion has been brought forward that if we should go into Committee, there is but little danger of our being out-voted by the advocates of a total repeal of all duties upon foreign corn. Surely, no one can suppose that the temper of this House is so adverse to the landed interest, that there is the slightest danger of the fair claims of that interest, not receiving under all circumstances, the fullest and most favourable consideration. I trust, therefore, that Hon. Members connected with the landed interest, will not be deterred from supporting the present motion, by their dread of any extreme measure. I attribute the greatest importance to their votes upon this occasion, because, I believe, that such votes would have a powerful effect upon those who look up to them, and are disposed to follow their opinions. By supporting this motion, they will be telling the farmers of England, that there is no ground for their extravagant apprehensions of foreign competition, which they have been taught to entertain, and that they ought not to trust for their future prosperity to a delusive system, which has produced, and can only produce disappointment, but that, on the contrary, they ought to rely upon their own industry, their own energy, intelligence, and enterprise. I am convinced that they are not the true friends of the

British farmer, however fond they may be of arrogating that exclusive title, who would inculcate upon him, a reliance upon the artificial regulations of Acts of Parliament, instead of upon his own exertions. Nor, can I help observing, that it is not a little remarkable, how much louder have been the complaints of agricultural distress, in former years, and how much greater the clamour for the maintenance of the system of protection, from those districts of the country which are most behind hand in their system of cultivation. From the agricultural counties of Scotland, from the county I have the honour to represent, and from the North generally, Parliament heard comparatively little of that cry of distress, which was raised so loudly in other parts of the country, from 1833 to 1836. Undoubtedly, the distress which then prevailed, did make itself felt, and felt, I am sorry to say, severely, even in the districts I have mentioned, but the clamour for further protection, and the expectation of obtaining relief from legislative measures, instead of from their own exertions, were chiefly confined to some of the Southern and Midland Counties. Now, let the House for a moment compare the state of agriculture in these, and in the Northern Counties. Look at the inartificial system of cultivation pursued in the Southern Counties, their antiquated rotation of crops, their heavy and clumsy plough, hardly improved from the ancient instrument, of which, as schoolboys, we have read a description in the Georgics, and, I ask, how can those who adhere to such a system as this, who are so backward in improvement, expect to compete with the northern farmers, with their improved modes of husbandry, their amended rotation of crops, their light and well constructed plough, doing more work, in a single day, with one man and two horses, than the other can accomplish in two days, with a man and a boy, and with three or four horses following each other in a string.

It is by carrying into agriculture generally, the intelligence, and the enterprise, for which some districts are already distinguished—It is by thus increasing the productiveness of the soil, and diminishing the expenses of cultivation, and not by being bolstered up by protecting duties, that the prosperity of the landed interest must be secured.

Is this, Sir, only my opinion? No—it is one which rests upon far higher authority upon agricultural matters, than I can pretend to. I allude to Lord Tweeddale, one of the most distinguished agriculturists, as the House is aware, of the present day. Some months ago, I saw with great pleasure an account of the proceedings at an agricultural dinner, in the South of England, at which that Noble Lord was present. Some of those speeches so usual with certain gentlemen, upon such occasions had been made, calling upon the farmers to defend their rights; to resist the slightest change or modification of the Corn Laws, and so maintain their claim to protection; when Lord Tweeddale administered a reproof to those who held this language, of which the satire was not the less from its having been, I believe, too fine to be perceived by those against whom it was directed. He told his audience, that what really deserved their attention, was the improvement of their system of agriculture; that in many important points, they were greatly behind hand, and that, if the farmers of England exerted themselves, they would soon make two ears of corn grow, where one grew now, and that by doing so, they would practically repeal the Corn Laws. Lord Tweeddale's advice was right, and it is remarkable that in the committees of 1833 and 1836, of which I was a Member, I observed almost universally, that those witnesses who seemed to have carried on their farming operations with most spirit, and most success, were those who the least relied upon the artificial protection of the law. Three gentlemen, Mr. Bell, Mr. Hope, and Mr. Howton, who gave a most interesting account of the highly improved system of cultivation, which they had carried on in the Lothians, concurred in objecting to the present Corn Law. Some of the English farmers who have entered upon the same career of improvement, expressed a similar opinion; I will mention only Mr. Crowther, who farmed, if I am not mistaken, 2000 acres of land in Liecestershire, and Mr. Ellis, who had an extensive farm in Leicestershire. All these gentlemen, whose success in their agricultural pursuits, was the best proof of their skill, expressed a most decided opinion as to the unfavourable operation of the existing Corn Law upon the interests of the farmer I do not mean that they all agreed precisely as to the change which should be adopted, some proposed one alteration of the law, and some another, but they all were agreed as to the fact that the present Corn Law, is not really beneficial to the enterprising farmer.

In conclusion, I have only to entreat Honourable Gentlemen to consider how deeply important is the question they are about to decide It is now in our power in altering the Corn Law, to substitute one resting upon a sounder principle, and at the same time to avert any sudden or violent change. But, if we neglect this opportunity, who can tell what may be the result?

If, after the high prices of the present year, and the stimulus which I am informed this price has already given to the increased growth of wheat, we should have two favourable harvests in succession, the table of this House will again groan beneath the burthen of petitions complaining of agricultural distress. But if, on the contrary, we should be visited with the misfortune of another bad crop, the consequences will be far more serious. We have been more fortunate than we deserved in this year obtaining, even at the high price we have been compelled to pay for it, the supply we so greatly needed. But we may rest assured, that while we maintain our fluctuating duty, the foreign grower, after the losses already sustained, will not venture to make any preparation to meet a demand for our market. If, therefore, now that the stocks of foreign corn before accumulated are exhausted, another deficient harvest should compel us again to seek for a supply from abroad, is it improbable that this demand may cause so much difficulty in the chief grain growing countries, that they may all follow the course which has this year been adopted by France? In such an event, we might be exposed to an absolute deficiency of food, and can any man contemplate, without the most serious apprehension, the possible effect of such a state of things in our densely peopled manufacturing districts? Even that degree of scarcity under which we are now suffering, with the high prices it occasions, if it had fallen upon us only a year ago, when we should have had at the same time to struggle with the difficulties arising from the stagnation of trade, would have produced an extent of distress in those districts which would have been a source of the utmost danger.

The question then is, whether we are needlessly to incur so great a hazard; whether we are to leave such interests as these to the chances of the seasons, or whether we are to avail ourselves of the opportunity we now have of securing ourselves, as far as it is possible to do so, against the ruinous fluctuation in the price of corn to which we have been exposed, and against the alternate distress thus occasioned to the commercial and agricultural classes of the community, by once more putting the trade in corn upon a sound and natural footing, free from all the risk and uncertainty to which it is subjected by our scale of variable duties.

THE END.

NORMAN AND SKEEN, PRINTERS, MAIDEN LANE, COVENT GARDEN.

ON THE CORN-LAWS.

THE SPEECH

OF

HON. C. P. VILLIERS, M.P.,

IN THE HOUSE OF COMMONS,

ON

WEDNESDAY, 1ST OF APRIL, 1840.

EXTRACTED FROM HANSARD'S PARLIAMENTARY DEBATES.

1840.

Charles Pelham Villiers (1802–98)[1]

Villiers, the third son of the Honourable George Villiers, was born in 1802 and was educated in Haileybury and St John's College, Cambridge. He was called to the Bar at Lincoln's Inn in 1827 and in 1833 was appointed examiner in the Court of Chancery. In 1832 Villiers, who had come under the influence of Bentham and the Philosophic Radicals, became one of the assistant commissioners of the Poor Law Royal Commission. He stood unsuccessfully for Hull in 1826 and was elected in January 1835 as one of the two representatives for Wolverhampton, a seat he held until 1885 when the constituency was divided into two, after which he represented South Wolverhampton until his death in 1898.

Villiers came of a well established Whig family. His older brother George William Frederick, fourth Earl of Clarendon and fourth Baron Hyde (1800–70) was Lord Privy Seal, 1839–41, President of the Board of Trade, 1846, Lord-Lieutenant of Ireland, 1847–52, and Foreign Minister, 1853–8 (during the Crimean war), 1865–70. Villiers however adopted free trade in the 1820s and his independent positions appear to have been responsible to his attaining cabinet office at the relatively advanced age of fifty seven.

Villiers first presented what was to become his annual motion for free trade in March 1838. It was in the form of a motion for the House to go into a committee of the whole House to consider the Act of 9 George IV., c.60 relating to the importation of corn, thereby insuring the support of all critics of the corn law whether they were complete repealers or in favour of a low fixed tax. In 1838 95 voted in favour, 300 against. By 1840 the protectionist majority dropped to 116, in 1841 it increased to 303, and by 1845 it declined to 132. His annual motion became one of the main foci of the anti corn law campaign although after Cobden's election to parliament in 1841 Villiers could no longer be regarded as the leader of the free traders in the Commons.[2]

[1] See W. O. Henderson, Charles Pelham Villiers', in *History* New Series, vol. 37 (1952), pp. 25–39.
[2] McCord, *The Anti Corn Law League*, pp. 95–6.

SPEECH, &c.

SIR,

In rising to propose the question of which I have given notice, I beg to apologize to the House for its postponement till this evening. I assure the House that it proceeded from a cause which I could not control, arising as it did from indisposition—an excuse, indeed, which I could offer with great force this evening, but learning that many persons expected that the subject would be discussed this week, I determined that, if possible, no other delay should occur on my account. The circumstance, however, only adds to the many considerations that now present themselves to my mind to make me regret that it is still in my hands to make this proposition to the House. The subject is now assuming a very serious aspect in this country, it is engaging the attention, as it is affecting the interest of the great mass of the community, and whatever the House may think, questions of this character, affecting as they do the commerce, the employment, and the condition of the people, excite among them an interest far exceeding any other. I wish, therefore, that the question was with those who could do more justice to it than myself, and still more that it was with those who had the power to do the people justice. I had, indeed, well hoped that 'ere now, that the landed proprietary of this country, would, in consideration of that deep distress which is now pervading and bearing down the productive classes of our community, have given some sign of intending to relax the rigours of their law, and that what has hitherto been denied to the claims of justice, might yet have been granted on the grounds of mercy. Three months have, however, passed away since the Parliament assembled, and not a whisper of such an intention has been heard; on the contrary, the same querulous note has been sounded in another place about agitation, and the same haughty and ill-placed observations respecting its object; while, in this House, we have seen that the usual efforts have been made to procure some proof of opinion in favour of the law, but, in truth, proving nothing but the influence so commonly used by the landholders over their dependents; and showing nothing, as it appears, but the determination of the class to maintain the law unchanged. Having, however, mooted this matter before in this House, some confidence is placed in me that I will not suffer it to slumber; and I cannot, therefore, allow more time to escape without asking the majority of this House to reconsider the decision they gave on it last Session, and seriously to review the grounds on which they rested their opinion, and which I apprehend to have been, that the law works well, that it has satisfied the purpose for which it was enacted, and that it ought to be maintained. A bold conclusion, I think, to have pronounced last Session, but one I think, that will require more courage to repeat; I, therefore, shall restate some of those facts and arguments which have led me to the honest conviction that the law is bad, that it has worked ill, that it has caused, and is causing great loss and suffering to the productive classes, and that it now casts upon the community a fearful addition to those burthens which it is at all times compelled to endure: and were I to state further what prompts me to press this matter again on the House, it is that I believe that a day has not passed since the last discussion, that either from personal suffering or greater intelligence, fresh converts have not been made to the repeal of this law, while I do not believe that one human being would be produced, who having been either indifferent to the law before or opposed to the law, has since become a convert to its continuance; and I regret the importance which I know I must attach to this circumstance, for I fear it will greatly outweigh any argument that I could adduce on the subject. For I cannot persuade myself, that unless there was a general impression in both Houses of Parliament, either that great ignorance or general indifference prevailed among the people on the question, that those who take a prominent part in these discussions, would utter the things which we hear on the subject. For not only do we hear that the Corn-law is a necessary evil, but that it is a positive advantage; and the advocates of repeal have it thus cast upon them to prove that an abundance of the essential of life, which in its abundance gives further means of satisfying the wants of life, is better than that dearness and scarcity that deteriorates the condition of all. However, if this task has to be performed again, the moment is, perhaps, favourable for the purpose. For it is almost difficult to believe, that if those who argued in favour of the law last year, could have known that their statements would have followed so close upon the heels of events which afforded to them such complete denial, that they would have uttered them, or indeed perhaps if it could have been expected that we on this side should have had the sad advantage which the distress of the country this year affords us, the decision on the question might have been different. I am not going to deny, however, that there has been great misapprehension on the subject of the Corn-laws, that mystery has been artfully thrown round the question, and that thousands are only, at this day, viewing the question in the true simplicity of its character. I shall, therefore, consider it with all the calmness and deliberation which should attach to a question that admitted of dispute; and I shall, as I have done on former occasions, proceed to consider the object of the law. The object of the Corn-law, then, may be simply stated to be, to limit the quantity of food imported from abroad, for the purpose of raising and maintaining the price of that which is grown at home, this is the object as it is to be collected from the avowed purpose as well as the provision of the law. The policy of such legislation seems to belong to the present century, and we are now living under the third legislative experiment that has been made for the purpose. In 1804, Mr. Western's bill passed into law, this was followed by the law of 1815, and we are now living under the enactment of 1828. Each of these laws have professed the same purpose, namely, to keep lands in cultivation, to keep the people in employment, and to secure to the cultivator a certain price for his produce; to each, also, have the same objections been offered, namely, that such policy may be at variance with the public good, that the interests of the community may be sacrificed by maintaining particular soils in cultivation; and that, as the price of produce depended upon circumstances beyond the reach of legislation, that the law was only calculated to mislead those who relied upon it. The justice of such objections with respect to two of those laws is now matter of history. Mr. Western procured his bill by stating that thousands of acres would otherwise be thrown out of cultivation, and that a proportionate number of labourers would be thus rendered destitute. Now, Sir, I believe I state the fact, when I say that after the passing of that bill, that the ports never were closed; and that so far from land going out of cultivation from this circumstance, that within six or seven years after it had passed, produce had risen nearly 300 per cent above the price that he had fixed as remunerative. Next came the law of 1815, which proposed to make the community pay for its food at the price which it had reached during the war, and in a depreciated currency, and that for ever. I have a right to say, that that was the deliberate intention of the Legislature, because there was an hon. Member, at that time in this House, whose eager and able exertions on that occasion to expose what he called the iniquity and injustice of the law, excited general attention, and he made a distinct proposition that if such a law were to pass, that it should not exist beyond the time when we should place our currency on a more sure basis—in short, when we should resume cash payments. I need not say I allude to Mr. Baring, who has since become Lord Ashburton. He made that proposition to the House, but it was rejected. Sir, it is no longer matter of question, that that law was a failure in every respect. It failed to give profit to the producer—it failed to give plenty to the people—it failed to maintain steadiness of prices, and it failed even in that which might have been expected from it, namely, in giving wisdom to those who projected it. It was introduced amidst the curses of the people—it seems to have expired without more favour from its friends. But in 1828, its failure did not seem to be ascribed to the purposes which it sought to obtain, but only to the means which were adopted for its attainment. It was thought, still, that it was possible to fix the price by law at which the produce could be sold, and to secure the cultivator the price which he expected. It was only considered the means had not yet been discovered by which that object should be attained, and it was in 1828 that this discovery was thought to have been made, and the scheme of a sliding scale was suggested for meeting the wishes of the agriculturists; and I take it we are now to consider whether this scheme, which was devised in 1828, has succeeded or not. There are some who think that it has worked well—that it has accomplished every object intended, and I hope they will prove their case. I certainly am of opinion that it has only verified every prediction of evil that was likely to attend it, and I think I can show it has done so. I do not think the public require much information on the subject; but they are watching this discussion, and I trust that they will consider well on which side the truth prevails. Now, Sir, I contend that the present law is a complete failure; and when I say so, I refer, perhaps, rather to its avowed object than to that which may have been intended, though not avowed, I contend that it has failed to benefit agriculture, though perhaps it has succeeded in greatly raising the value of land. And it is very important here to distinguish clearly between what is called agriculture and the ownership of land. These interests are, in many respects, distinct; because, however, in some degree, they are the same, the landowners claim for themselves all the arguments usually advanced in support of the law that have only reference to agriculture. Now, the fact is, the connexion is not nearer between the cultivation of the land and its ownership, than between a house and the business carried on in it; or between the merchant and his banker, who may lend him the capital to conduct his business; or between the manufacturer and the person of whom he purchases the raw material. These interests are in some material points distinct, and nobody confounds them; and there is no more reason for confusion between the cultivator and the owner of the soil, than between those interests. The landowner may hardly know where his property is, he may be unable to distinguish one kind of produce from another; he may live abroad, and know no one connected with his property but the receiver of his rents; and again, the cultivator may be equally ignorant of any circumstance connected with the ownership of the land, beyond the price he pays for its use. The distinction, however, is so obvious that I would not have troubled the House by stating it, but for a singular confusion which is made in this respect in arguing for the law, and that under the general term agriculturists, we hear the most exaggerated pretensions put forward, based on the assumed interest of landlord, farmer, and labourer. These interests, however, being in so many respects distinct, it is important that they should be so viewed. Now, with respect to the necessity or policy of legislating at all for the particular interest of the agriculturist or the farmer; what does it consist in? What would he desire the law to do for him if it could? Why, probably, to enable him to get the return for his capital that he expected, and that is, what I suppose, every capitalist would wish; in fact, to be made sure in his calculations, and obtain the profit he expects; and this is, in truth, what the Corn-law promises it will do for him, and does hold out the expectation of something like certainty and steadiness in this respect. We have now to examine how far it has realized his expectations: the first fact then that is to be observed is, that since the passing of this law, there has been every variation in the price of produce, and that the farmer has experienced great distress, and disappointment, which at least seems to lead to the conclusion that this law has not averted the evil apprehended by the agriculturists. But the next question is, whether this has not been actually caused by the law? This I believe can be almost demonstrated, and I collect the proof of it from the agriculturists themselves—not to have referred to their opinions as it has been collected by this House, seems to have been an omission in the previous discussions upon this question; the fact is, that those who complain of this law, are usually so much occupied with showing the gross injustice of the law, that they have as yet paid little attention to the evidence against it by those for whose interest it is professed to be maintained; but there has, however, been a great body of evidence collected by the House, and given under circumstances which compel us to give it credit; and to which the public ought to have its attention directed; for I do say, that if there is one conclusion before another to which a candid inquirer would arrive after reading that evidence, it is, that the law is extremely prejudicial to the farmer—and that it has occasioned distress and disappointment to all of that class who have trusted to it. This is an important consideration, because there are many now who distinctly see the injustice of the law, but yet from fear of the consequences of its repeal to the persons who have invested their capital upon the faith of its continuance, are yet slow in calling for its repeal; and now, at the risk of wearying the House hoping to be excused by the importance of the question, I shall proceed to read some extracts of the evidence collected in 1836, by the agricultural committee appointed in that year. The first person whose evidence I will advert to is that of Ellis, a Leicestershire farmer, who is asked whether the distress of the time had any connexion with the Corn-law—and he says in reply that he thought the present duty too high, because it gave a fictitious value to land, and that it gave the farmers an expectation of something that could never occur; and on that account, it holds up the value of land fictitiously. This question is then put to him; then you think it induced the tenants to make larger offers than in the result they have been able to pay? I think so, farmers are prone to expect high prices, and they have been expecting something that was not likely to occur.—

Mr. Parker, an Essex farmer, is asked:—

"Do you consider, that the distressed state of those farmers can be at all attributed to the rents not having been lowered sufficiently in time?—I should say very materially, the landlords not prudently lowering their rents earlier than they have done.

"The farms would have been in better condition?—Yes; it has been by persisting in the high rents that the farms would have been worked out of condition, and then no person would take them except at a very low rent.

"Do you think, that they (the Corn-laws) hold out hopes of a continuance of a higher rate of price than can ever be realised?—The Corn-laws have been in operation but a few years, they commenced with large foreign supplies; we have been only put on our own growth the last four years; I do not think if the present laws continue, that we should be often interfered with by foreign supply.

"Take the whole of the farmers in the county of Essex, do you think, that they are possessed of as much capital now, as they were in 1821?—Certainly not.

"Then they have been labouring now for fifteen years, and have expended a great deal of industry, and skill, and capital, with no return at all, as a body?—They have been parting with their capital, a great many of them, to their landlords, and to other persons, whose charges upon them were excessively high."

Mr. Cox, of Buckinghamshire, gives this evidence:—

"For the last three years you have been farming that land to a profit?—Decidedly not to a profit.

"Should you say that the cultivation of Buckinghamshire has fallen off within the last eight or ten years?—I should say so, in the neighbourhood in which I live.

"In what respect?—The land is getting very foul and overcropped; in some places, driven further than it should be."

Mr. John Houghton, a gentleman of great experience, states:—

"Have you not arable farms in the county of Buckingham, over which you are steward? —Yes, I have.

"What is their state now compared with the state of the grazing farms to which you allude?—On the heavy clay lands the distress is very great, more than it is on the turnip and barley lands, or grass land.

"How do you account for that distress upon the clay lands?—From the low price of wheat.

"Do you find, that the capital of the farmesr has been dimishing?—Certainly; I think the great distress has been on the heavy land farms.

"Have their farmers been paying their rents out of their produce, or out of their capital?—If you take the heavy clay land, certainly out of their capital.

Mr. John Rolfe, farmer of Buckinghamshire, gives this evidence:—

"Do you use wheat for any other purpose, but that of human food now?—I have not done it; some have ground wheat for the pigs; some have given it to their horses, but that was principally the grown wheat of the last harvest but one.

"What is the cost of the cultivation of your farm per acre now, as compared with what it was some years ago?—The cost of cultivation is very much the same; there is a little difference in the price of labour.

"Can you state how rents are paid in your district?—Rents have heretofore, till the last two years, been very well paid.

"How have they been paid since 1833?—They have been paid very badly.

"Even on the light soils you speak of?—Yes.

"There is more wheat grown upon land now?—Yes.

"Supposing there should not be a corresponding demand for wheat in proportion as that class of land increases, it must make the heavy clay land less profitable?—Yes.

You do not complain of the price of mutton now?—No.

"Of wool?—No.

"Of barley? you cannot expect much increase in that?—No, not much.

"Oats?—Oats we should wish for a little increase.

"Beans?—If we had 4s. a quarter more, we should not have much fault to find.

"The chief complaint is on account of the depression in the price of wheat?—Yes, that is where the farmer is suffering most; that is where he looks for his rent in the spring of the year, when he should have the price of his wheat to raise the money for his rent; when he is looking for a large sum of money to meet his payments; when he comes to thresh out and carry to market, his expenses almost take the whole price.

"What will become of the landlord?—We shall be all beggars together."

Mr. John Curtis, another Buckinghamshire farmer says—

"Has the capital of the farmers in your opinion diminished?—I should say considerably.

"Will you state in what way farmers are worse off?—In the first place, they have cropped their land hard, and it is now getting into bad condition; it is getting foul, and the stock diminishes.

"Now looking at the different descriptions of soils; first of all the grass, has the produce of your grass enabled you to pay the rent upon the grass land?—What little grass I have is very good; that is the best part of my farm.

"You have stated that the condition of the labourers is good; you mean those that are employed?—Those that are employed; and there are very few out of employment.

"Chairman: Has the poor-rate been reduced lately?—Yes; the Poor-law bill works well with us."

Mr. John Kemp, an Essex farmer gives this evidence:—

"Do you consider, then, that the quantity of wheat in the market has been the cause of the depression of the price?—I should say so.

"Has the capital of the farmers in your neighbourhood, and under your knowledge, diminished or not?—Very much diminished.

"What was the rate in your parish previous to the passing of the Poor-law Bill, and what is it now?—Our expenditure in the parish used to be 1,600*l.*, and last year it was not more than 1,200*l.*

"What is the state of the small farmer about you; the man who rents an hundred acres?—As bad off as the poor man.

"Are farmers paying rents from their profits or their capital?—From their capital.

"Taking the labourers as a body, are they as well employed as they used to be?—They have been very well employed for the last three years.

"Do you think, that upon the average, the higher price, from a scarce season, compensates the farmer for the deficiency of his crop?—No; for at the time when corn was so high, about six years ago, during the wet seasons, we were certainly worse off than we are now, and wheat was much higher."

This is from the evidence of Mr. Thurlwall, of Cambridgeshire:—

"What, in your opinion, is the condition of the tenantry generally in your neighbourhood?—I think verging on insolvency, generally in the most desperate state that men can possibly be."

Mr. Charles Page, in Essex, farmer, is asked:—

"Have you lost or gained this last year upon your farm?—In fact, I have lost every year since I have been in business.

"Have you lost principally upon the wheat or the barley crop?—The loss upon the wheat crop I think is the most material."

Mr. George Babbs is asked:—

"Do you believe whether the farmers are paying their rent out of capital, or out of the profits of their farms?—I believe the farmers have been paying their rents out of the capital they employ.

"Is that your case?—It has been my case.

"Has the land been cropped harder in your neighbourhood than it used to be?—I think it has."

Mr. Charles Howard is asked:—

"Taking the period since the last committee sat in 1833, what do you consider to be the comparative state of the farming interests now and at that time?—Decidedly and progressively worse.

"Do you take into your consideration every species of land, or one species of land more than another?—I think upon the sheep farms, the upland farms, from the increased demand which there has been for sheep, the distress has rather decreased; sheep have been very high.

"Then with respect to the low-land farms?—Their situation has been progressively much worse.

"You stated that in consequence of the depressed state of the farming interest of that country, the landlords have permitted a considerable portion of the old grass lands to be ploughed up; has that tended to precipitate the affairs of the tenant, or otherwise?—It has kept the tenant longer upon his legs.

"But it has more materially deteriorated the condition of those farms upon which the permission was given?—Decidedly so.

"Either you think that the land will go out of cultivation and produce a diminished supply, or you think that the Legislature will interfere in some way so as to produce a rise in price?—Exactly.

"And you think that is the view of those persons that buy those farms at present?—I do believe it."

Mr. Robert Hope, a Scotch farmer, gives the following evidence:—

"Have you ever thought anything about the present Corn-laws, whether they are beneficial to the farmer or not?—Yes, they have been often discussed, but it is a very general feeling among those that pay corn-rents, that they have not been hitherto beneficial, but the very reverse of being beneficial.

"What is your reason for that opinion?—It induced men to offer more than has been well realized by the price of corn, because it was generally expected from the Corn-laws, that prices would be kept up to something like what they promised; that the import of foreign corn would be restricted, and by that means, keep up the price of the home growth to 70s. or so.

"How has the Corn-law disappointed your expectation?—Because it led those that took farms at money rents, to give a much higher rent than they would have done.

"Then is it the opinion of you and those other gentlemen that have considered the subject in the way you mention, that the present Corn-law ought to continue, or do you think, that any change would be beneficial to the farmer?—From what we experienced in the year 1831, I am disposed to think, that a change might be more beneficial to the farmer, by reducing the scale at which foreign corn is imported.

"You have stated, that the existing Corn-law you consider is prejudicial to the farmer; is your opinion founded upon the circumstance of there having been a miscalculation as to the effects to be produced by the Corn-laws, or upon the working of the Corn-laws themselves?—I think by the present working of the Corn-laws, that it may run prices too high for the interest of the farmers in years of scarcity, before any foreign corn can be admitted into the country, prices may be run up so high as to be prejudicial to the interest of the farmer, because, in such a year as we had in 1831, we could not grow so much wheat as we had to pay in rent.

"If the result of this Corn-law should be to produce great fluctuations in price, you would think that effect would apply to all farmers?—I think it has been prejudicial to those that even pay a money rent, because I am sure, that if it had not been for the Corn-laws, they would not have given so high a money-rent."

Mr. James Tisen, an English farmer, gives this evidence:—

"What causes have there been to depress the state of the farmers of stiff land?—High rents; it is my opinion, founded on the testimony of farmers themselves, that many of them are farming under war-rents, while they are selling their corn at peace prices.

"Mr. Loch: The consequence of the rents being kept up too high has been that the land has been overcropped?—Yes; when I have conversed with farmers, this appears to be the conclusion they have come to, that they have paid their landlords what they ought to have paid to the labourers. If they had paid it to labourers they would have had value for the money; whereas they paid it to the landlord, and, of course, received nothing back, and they had so much less to lay out upon their farms.

"On the light soils, have the tenants been met by the landlords with a reduction of rent?—They have not needed so much reduction as they have upon the heavier soils.

"It appears from your evidence, therefore, that it is a question very much between landlord and tenant, as to the present condition of the farming interest; that is to say, that the landlord has more in his power than can be done by the Legislature?—Decidedly; I do not see what the Legislature can do, except with respect to the Poor-law, to benefit the agriculturist effectually.

"Mr. Wodehouse: Looking at Mr. Coke's estate, in Norfolk, could any number of his tenantry afford to give him any rent whatever, with wheat at 5s. a bushel?—Yes, I think with a good crop they could.

"Then you think that the want of intelligence and the want of skill has gone a great way towards producing the depressed state of the farmers?—According to my view of it, such is the state of society in this country, that for a person to do well in any branch, whether in agriculture, manufacture, or in commerce, there must be a combination of intelligence, practical skill, capital, and industry; and if any of those be wanting, whether it is in agriculture, or in mercantile affairs, a person is almost sure now to go wrong; and when I have traced a great number of cases of individual distress among farmers to that cause, one of those has been wanting.

"What do you conceive to be the effect of the present Corn-laws upon the consumer?—I think they have a very unfavourable effect; they operate as a very great hinderance to the extension of trade, to the manufacturing and commercial interests, because, under the present system of Corn-laws, we can receive nothing in return from those countries which would take our manufactured goods, if they could send us their corn in return; for instance Prussia; our trade would be immense with Prussia if we could take their corn in return.

"What do you think is the average price which may be fairly calculated upon by the farmer under the existing Corn-law?—Under 50s. a quarter for wheat."

Mr. Thomas Bennett is asked:—

"Do you think, with reduction of rent, and the reduction of prices, the farmer can cultivate his land at a profit?—Looking to the seven years back, and having taken those farms under very low prices, I have not a question that some may do it profitably, and I have no doubt some will.

"Sir James Graham: At what price do you

estimate wheat for the next seven years?—If I was going to take a farm myself, I should not expect, nor would I calculate for the next seven years, to have wheat above 5s. to 6s. a bushel.

"Will the Duke of Bedford's tenants, who have retaken those farms, be able to pay the rent for which they have just agreed, with wheat at 5s. a bushel?—I think they will. I think the majority do not expect to see it at much more."

Mr. Andrew Howden, a Scotch farmer, gives this evidence:—

"If you had been sold off in 1820, do you think you would have been better off than you are now?—I do not know that mine is a fair case to be taken as a general case, because I started very poor in life, and I have had a hard struggle, and other circumstances that contributed to assist me. I am the only remaining farmer in the parish where I was brought up; except myself, there is not a farmer, nor the son of a farmer remaining within the parish but myself.

"What is the reason of their having all gone away?—The money rents that where exacted of them. They all conceived that they were to have 80s. a quarter, and their calculations were made upon that. It soon appeared that that could not be realized, and they were not converted, and ruin has been the consequence.

"Then there has been a great change of tenancy in your neighbourhood?—There has been.

"And that has been caused by the fall of prices?—Yes, and the want of accommodation on the part of the proprietors.

"In your opinion did the Corn-law that was made in 1815, deceive both the landlord and the tenant?—It did. I believe that the calculation upon which they took at that time was almost universally 4*l.* a quarter.

"The Corn-law having promised a price of 80s., failed to perform it?—Yes."

Mr. William Bell, a Scotch farmer, is asked :—

"What is your reason for supposing a fixed duty would be preferable?—By the present Corn-law, when the price approaches near the rate at which the foreign corn can be brought into the market with a profit, the prices may possibly be run up to that rate by artificial means. Thus a great quantity of corn would be improperly liberated and thrown upon the market, and this might probably depress the market for the whole season. Now, at a fixed duty, that could not take place."

Mr. George Robertson, another English farmer, gives this evidence :—

"Supposing that mutton had borne the same proportionate price when wheat fell to 40s., do you think the Scotch farmer would then have been enabled to make a good living?—The Scotch farmer would have tried something else than wheat; he would have extended his grass cultivation, and that would have tended to reduce the price of meat still more, no doubt.

"And if the price of barley had been also reduced?—Those are all regulated by the demand of the manufacturing and commercial classes.

"Do you know anything of the sale of the manufacturing and commercial classes?—My belief is, that they were never more prosperous.

"How long has that been the case?—It has been gradually coming on for years.

"In the face of that increasing prosperity, has there not been a decline in the price of wheat?—That may be accounted for by the great additional average crops for a series of years.

"Are you able to perceive a great increase in the demand of the operative classes?—Very great in flour and meat, and I have no doubt, the increased price of barley is caused by a demand for malting in England.

"Supposing the supply and demand for

labour to remain the same, will not eventually the price of labour fall in proportion to the fall in the price of food?—At present the demand for labour for the manufacturing interest is so great, that we can scarcely get hands for necessary operations of agriculture.

"You have been asked, with reference to the price of wheat governing the price of meat, can you anticipate a very great falling off in the price of meat, when you consider that the population of this country is increasing so rapidly, and that the manufacturing employment of that population is so great as it is at present?—No. I think the price of agricultural produce must keep up; that is to say if the manufacturing classes prosper and live as they are doing."

I shall not, however, trouble the House with any further extracts. It is impossible to read that evidence without being convinced that the farmers are induced by this law to promise rents for their land, which it does not enable them to pay, and that they are tempted by the price of which the law professes to assure them, to devote much of their capital to the growth of wheat, which, as it is the most expensive plant they can grow, if they are disappointed in the price they expect, the loss they experience is proportionally severe. And I think, Sir, I may venture to state this with confidence to this House, since I find in the admirable address you published to your constituents, that this was the conclusion to which you arrived, after devoting more attention and time to that committee, and to the subsequent consideration of the evidence than perhaps any other Member. And I find, that your conviction is, that the law is actually prejudicial to the farmer, and in the manner in which I have stated it to be so, and you, Sir, seem to agree in the conclusion to be drawn from much of the evidence given by agriculturists themselves, namely, that they must not depend for fortune upon the adventitious aid of such legislation as the Corn-law, but upon what all other capitalist must rely upon, namely, the skill, experience, and intelligence, which they bring to their pursuit. But now I wish the House to mark the consequence of the farmer being tempted to direct his attention chiefly, or to apply his capital so largely to the cultivation of wheat, and by neglecting the culture of other products and by the overproduction of wheat, lowering its price below the sum that could be remunerating: namely, that he becomes suddenly alarmed and disappointed at his loss, and withdraws much of his capital from such employment, and thus narrows the breadth which he sows with wheat, and then we see how another purpose which the law is supposed to have, is fulfilled--namely, to supply the community with food at a reasonable rate. Why, the first consequence of growing less wheat has been of course to raise the price, which occurring at the time of a bad harvest, the public have been suffering for the last eighteen months, and are now suffering, from an unusual deficiency, and have been paying a great additional price for their food; neither have they any prospect of improvement. There is every probability that prices will keep up, and that great sacrifices will yet have to be made by the public for food. But, supposing that all the assertions about the present season and all the usual predictions respecting the coming harvest were true, and that the price was greatly to fall in consequence of the rotation of the crops being disturbed by a greater breadth of wheat sown this year than was ever known before. Why, how will that benefit the farmer? We shall have the same story of distress over again, and we shall see that class as badly off as they were in 1836. And this is, indeed, the regular operation of the Corn-law, namely, either to ruin the farmer or greatly prejudice the public. Yet this is the law which is sought to be identified with all the cherished institutions of the State, and if any one assails it, he is charged with designs against the constitution itself. But who is benefitted by this law, if the farmer is thus injured and deceived? it is usual to say in these discussions, that by making prices high, particular soils are kept in cultivation, and the labourers are thus secured employment, that wages rise with the price of food, and that, in fact, the labourer is thus made better off by high prices because his wages are higher. This was deliberately said last year; will that be repeated? I trust not—I dont think it creditable to have urged it at all—it certainly is not true. It is almost cruel to the labourer to say it, seeing that he can have no doubt of the privations he is obliged to endure from a high price of food. There is not a pretence for asserting, that when provisions are high the agricultural labourer is well off. The contrary has always been the case whenever such periods have occurred. In 1797, a year of great scarcity and high price, so far from its leading to higher wages, it was the time when the system of pauperising independent labourers commenced, and wages were made up from the rates for the very purpose of escaping from what is said to be the result of high prices, namely, raising wages in proportion to the price of food. Again, in 1810, 1818, 1830, and at the present time, there have been great complaints of their sufferings, and during each of those years the prices have been high. But it is a fact not less striking, in contradiction of what is assumed, that whenever provisions have been low, the labourers have been well off, that there has been a great demand for their labour, and that their wages have given them a greater command over the necessaries of life. Not certainly astonishing to any person who reflects for a moment on the subject, because it is clear that, as every body is more or less an employer of labour, and that he is so according to his means, that in proportion as his means are greater or less, so will be his demand for labour, and so consequently will be the wages of the labourer, as it is the proportion which their number bears to the demand for them, which must determine their condition—but if there can be any doubt as to the influence of high prices or the condition of the people, it will be well to view what really is the case at this moment, and I own, as far as my own enquiries have gone, I can learn nothing but that either the wages though raised, have not risen in proportion to the price of food, or that, not having risen at all, the labourers have in many cases endured the greatest privations. And here I will just read to the House a report of some cases occurring a short time since, which have appeared in a provincial paper, into the truth of which I have enquired and to which I merely refer to show how incautiously it is asserted here that the agricultural labourers are not affected by the price of food:—

"In the southern part of this county 6*s.* a-week is commonly given to agricultural labourers. Within the last fortnight at the petty sessions held at Salisbury, a farmer, living at Durnford, was summoned by a labourer named

Blake, for refusing to pay him 6*s*. 6*d*. for a day's work. The complaint stated that he worked on "*the Stem*," sometimes for one master, sometimes for another, at 6*s*. 6*d*. *a-week, the rate agreed to by the farmers at a vestry meeting*. His employer had refused to pay him more than 6*s*., which Blake would not accept, as it was not sufficient to maintain himself and wife. The master, in his defence, told the magistrates that the farmers of Durnford had "*stemmed*" the surplus labourers of that parish *at* 6*s*. *per week, which was as much as they could afford to pay*. The Bench expressed their surprise—as well they might—at the practice pursued by the farmers at Durnford towards the labourers, and ordered the defendant to pay Blake the full amount of wages agreed on 6*s*. 6*d*., and to remunerate him for his loss of time in seeking redress. This week we will take a different district, and name Rushall, a parish standing comparatively in favourable circumstances, where the poor have advantages which in many other places they do not enjoy. This parish is divided into three large farms, the land is chiefly arable, and of excellent quality, producing on an average, certainly not less than eight sacks of wheat, and ten sacks of barley per acre. On this fertile spot the highest wages of able-bodied married labourers with families are only 9*s*. per week (we except harvest work, for which, of course, more is paid); those without children, and single men, although equally able, aye, and willing too, to do a good day's work, are put off with 5*s*., 6*s*., and 7*s*. a-week. We do not understand why this is; it appears to be an act of injustice, and we should be glad to know upon what principle the distinction is made:—If an able man's service be worth 9*s*. a-week, then is the single man deprived of his due by being paid only 5*s*.; but if an able man's services be worth only 5*s*. or 6*s*. a-week, then must the difference between that and 9*s*. be considered as parish allowance for the children; it is high time this were properly understood, for if the latter be the case, the *real* rate of wages is much lower than it is represented to be. Of course, with such wages, destitution and distress abound. Many families are unable to obtain more than *one* meal a day, and in many instances that one meal consists of *potatoes and salt*, without meat, and with only a small quantity of the coarsest bread. Very few even of those who are the best off get wheaten bread, but are obliged to have recourse to a mixture of barley and wheat, the latter being of a very inferior description—tail wheat. Meat is hardly ever eaten by any of the labourers, they never buy any."

I think I have a right to refer to such cases when I read addresses to the peasantry, such as have been made by a noble Duke (Buckingham), who takes a lead in maintaining the Corn-laws and asks them to believe that while they maintain those laws they will ever be prosperous. Why, Sir, if it was for no other reason but the one that the Corn-laws tend to make land dear, it is prejudicial to the labouring class, who are always better off when land is accessible to them, and nothing tends more to their contentment and comfort than the possession of land. Another circumstance I might mention which tends, in my judgment, to shew that the people are badly off and discontented now in the agricultural districts, namely, that there have been a greater number of the agricultural labourers who have sought to avail themselves of the provision for emigration this year than ever they did before. Why should this be the case, if the people were well paid and well employed? but the fact is, that there is less means for employing labour this year because the price of food is so high, and the poor are driven from the farmhouse to the poor-house, and from thence to the State, to implore of it to send them out of the country. And, really, if we will not allow the food to come to them, it is only merciful to send them were the food is produced; but in God's name, why are they to be driven from their homes, when, if provisions were low as they were in 1836, they would get plenty of employment, as the admission of all the farmers themselves they did then. Who is it, then, after all, whose interests are benefitted by these laws? I say, in the first place, none can be permanently so at the expense of the rest of the community, but immediately and for the while, there is no doubt whatever that the owner of the land has an advantage in them—and it is an advantage in this way, that it enables a certain class of inferior soils to be cultivated with wheat, and which doubtless could not bear the expense if the produce of better foreign soils was brought into competition with it; and these soils being thus articifically enhanced in value, tend to raise the value and consequently the rent of all other land; and the owners of land, therefore, without reference to the effect of the law upon other classes of the community, have this interest in the law; and it is well that the truth should be avowed and known, and that it be allowed that they have a temporary advantage in the Corn-law, and though the farmers and the labourers cannot benefit by rent being thus artificially raised, it is clear the landowners do, and it is to them alone to whom we must deliberately turn for redress, and appeal to them on the score of injury and injustice done to the community at large, and ultimately of injury to themselves, by impairing the fortunes of those on whom they must depend, by means of their custom for the permament value of their estates. It is reasonable, therefore, to direct our whole attention to that class, for certain am I, that, notwithstanding the delusion of some of the farmers on this subject, that if some of the more distinguished of the landowners in both Houses of Parliament, were to rise in their places and express an opinion that the law ought to be changed, that all alarm among their tenants would at once be dissipated and allayed. I am not, however, inclined to join in any wholesale denunciation of the landowners of this country; it would be unjust to do so; because I know that there are among that class men of great intelligence, high minded men, men of generous feeling, some who are ready and anxious to change this law, knowing it is prejudicial to the country at large, and some who seeing their own advantage in it, yet will not adhere to it at the expense of their country; it is right, therefore, to discriminate among them, but certainly it is fair to fix upon those among the landlords, who obstruct and oppose all change of the law, all the consequence, and all responsibility that results from such a course; and I say this the more confidently, because it is not in their power to shew, that the law rests upon any ground of justice or of public good. The landlords in any other country but this might allege that they were exclusively taxed, that they bore more of the burdens of the state than any other class, and were entitled to have a law that should give an artificial value to their produce. I say in this country they cannot allege this. Will they go into an inquiry? Is there any particular burden they bear from which other classes are exempt? Will they say that they are not exempt from burdens that others bear? They are not entitled to this protection on the ground of advantage to the community. It cannot be shown there is one burden that they bear that other classes do not equally endure. What, therefore, is the ground for their exclusive protection? What is the ground that they themselves take? They say, if you allow the produce of foreign countries to come into competition with our own, you will throw out of employ many of the labourers on our own land. What is the principle of that, supposing it to be true? Are the interests of the country to be sacrificed that certain lands shall not forego a particular cultivation? We wish, for the benefit of the community, to resort to soils more productive, whence we shall get food cheaper—and the landowner forbids us on the ground of protection. What might the mechanic not say? What says the hand-loom weaver? They might say, do not introduce a machine that shall make labour cheaper. They do say tax machinery. The principle is the same. There seems to be no difference in the policy. What is the truth then? The proprietors not being exclusively taxed, but, on the contrary, being rather exempted from taxation, have no ground in justice for claiming protection, whatever may be their power for enforcing it. Before I quit what may be called the agricultural part of the question, perhaps I may be allowed to refer to what may in the course of this discussion be adduced in support of this law, namely, that Ireland is an agricultural country, and that it is an advantage to Ireland that the present law should be continued. I should be sorry to let anything fall from me that could possibly give offence to that country. We have done enough to offend that country already: but I must say, that of all the groundless and unreasonable pretences for supporting this law, the case of Ireland seems to me to stand beyond all others. Ireland, that has of late years been sending us less and less wheat; Ireland, where the mass of the people are too poor to consume wheat, where the husbandry is the worst in the kingdom, where the landlords have a larger share of the produce for rent, and spend it more out of their own country than any other landlords in Europe; Ireland, moreover, where agriculture would thrive more by not cultivating wheat, and where no country would benefit more from the prosperity of manufacture here, or its introduction there—for Ireland has always felt and instantly so, the benefit of the prosperity of manufactures in England; and what condition would she now be in, if English manufactures were to decline with her new liability to maintain her poor. That is a question for Irish landlords to consider. But before the committee on agriculture to which I have referred, there is positive evidence that where Irish agriculturists have prospered, it has been referable to their abandoning the culture of wheat and applying the soil to other purposes. How, then, are the real interests of Ireland consulted by a law which by the price it promises offers peculiar temptation to the cultivation of wheat? If I thought the present Corn-law of great advantage to Ireland it would have great weight with me, but what is to be gathered on this head from the avowed opinions of men who have studied and sought to promote the interests of that country, and I allude more particularly to the opinions of Mr. Sharman Crawford and the Member for Dublin, Gentlemen differing on many matters, but agreeing in condemning the Corn-law, as tending to make land dear and as repressing manufacturing enterprise in their country. I cannot think, under all these circumstances, that Ireland offers us any ground for upholding the Corn-law. And now, Sir, I think I have said enough with regard to the wisdom of this law, as it respects agriculture, and how far that interest can be said to have thriven under the influence of monopoly. I must now turn to the great and general question involving the principle which should be the test of every law, namely, its effects upon the community at large; for I have hitherto examined its effect on the partial interest alone for which it was professed to be passed, and it is one thing which the public will expect to learn from this discussion, namely, how far they are effected by paying more or less for food in this country, and this, I think, can be shewn. It is indeed among the advantages of the agitation of a great question of this kind, that it brings a great many intelligent minds to its consideration, which tends to illicit truth where doubt prevails. And here I am glad to be able to point to a very intelligent work recently published, entitled "Influences on the Corn-laws," by Mr. James Wilson, for this author appears to me to have made some very faithful and accurate calculations, as to these effects of the Corn-laws. He takes as the basis of his calculation, the amount in quantity, and the rate at which the people have been annually paying for food for the last seven years. He adopts the general estimate as to the quantity annually consumed, which is sixteen millions of quarters, and the average price of the last seven years, which has been about 52*s.* a-quarter. From this it will be found that the annual cost of wheat to the community, is 41,600,000*l.* It follows, therefore, that whatever is paid more or less than this sum, is gained or lost to the community, and it can, therefore, be shewn what this has been of late years, and what is the amount now lost to the community. Mr. Wilson in his work, presents in one table what has been the sum paid at home and abroad for wheat during the years 1834, 1835, 1836, 1837, 1838, 1839. For instance: in 1834, the total cost of wheat was 36,933,333*l.*, while the total cost of foreign wheat was 101,750*l.*, in 1835, the total cost of wheat was 31,400,000*l.*, and of the latter 34,654*l.*; in 1836, of the former 38,800,000*l.*, while of the latter 51,177*l.*; in 1837, 44,666,000*l.*, and of the latter 499,430*l.*; in 1838, 51,666,000*l.*, and of the latter 4,594,014*l.*; in 1839, 56,533,000*l.*, and the latter 7,515,800*l.* It thus appears, that during the last three years, we have as a nation spent more in wheat grown at home, by 45,793,000*l.* than in the preceding years, and paid more by 12,420,000*l.* during the latter years for foreign wheat, than during the three preceding years. The illustration, however, will be still more simple, if we compare the two last years, namely, 1838 and 1839. In the beginning of the year 1838, we find the price of wheat is at an average of 52*s.* a quarter. In the autumn of the same year it suddenly rose to 75*s.* being more than 20*s.* a quarter higher—therefore, taking the consumption at 16,000,000*l.* the country was suddenly called upon in September 1838, to pay 300,000*l.* a-week more for food than was paid in the six preceding months, and 450,000*l.* a-week more than it paid in 1835, and this increased sum was paid during the whole year following. This then is a sum suddenly abstracted from the capital and income which, under existing arrangements, was finding useful and convenient employment elsewhere, and must be considered as thus lost to those departments of industry to which it was giving employment. It seems, moreover, that what invariably attends a high price of food in this country is, importation from abroad, the amount of which, in late years, has been stated; but with our present relations with the corn growing counties, to pay for grain we are compelled to export bullion: we have, therefore, on these occasions, a certain amount of the currency of the country invariably abstracted to make this payment. We have thus an additional abstraction from the means usually devoted to the employment at home—a very important consideration in a commercial point of view, since the absence of so much bullion is of necessity followed by a contraction of the paper currency. The public, therefore, have to view the law connected with this twofold evil, high price and contracted currency—thus doubly checking the operations of capital and labour. The same author, to prove the connection between the price of food and the currency in this country, has collected in a tabular form the annual amount paid for wheat, the amount of bullion, and the amount of deposits in the Bank of England, and the amount paid for foreign wheat—and this for a period of above twenty years; and there appears from this table a close correspondence between the different amounts of bullion and deposits in the Bank, and the different amounts paid for wheat at home and abroad—the former declining as the latter encreased, and with that regularity as to render it impossible not to conclude that a necessary connection exists between them. From 1817 until the present time, as grain has been imported from abroad, and prices have been high, the deposits and the bullion have declined. The diminution of the deposits would result from the increased payments required for food, which lessens the amount of surplus capital in the country; and the amount of it in the Bank of England would indicate pretty much what surplus was in the country generally. In support of which I quote the opinion of a mercantile man who says,

"When money is everywhere abundant and prosperity general, the resource of the Bank of England must be very great; at such times the surplus of every man throughout the country finds its way to his banker; a portion of the surplus of the bankers throughout the country finds its way to their agents in London for employment; and the surplus of these agents, as well as all the London bankers, finds its way to the coffers of the Bank of England, as the most accredited place of safety; and thus constitutes an index, not of the wealth and capital of the Bank of England, but of the extent of surplus capital possessed at any given moment by the whole country."

It seems to be reasonable to expect, that if great and sudden demands for the national means were made, that it would manifest itself in this way, and the facts to which I have referred, seem to establish that it does so. Now we observe, that from the end of 1838 till October 1839, there appears to be a diminution, from month to month, of bullion and deposits, during the whole of which time we were importing food from abroad; and we know farther how bitterly the commercial classes have complained during that time of the contraction of the currency. The great importance to the public of this circumstance is, that they may know the truth respecting the sources of those fluctuations in the value and amount of the currency, which occasions such serious and alarming embarrassment in this country, and though I do not stand here as the apologist of the Bank of England, against whom, if only judged according to the rules it has laid down for itself, there is abundant ground of complaint, yet it is well to know, that what is imputed entirely to the mismanagement of the Bank of England, must in great measure be referred to the operation of the Corn laws. And now, Sir, it becomes us to consider, after having proved that there has been a contraction of the currency, an increase in the price of food, and a large sacrifice of the national means to meet it—what has been the effect of these circumstances upon the commercial interest of the country. I will first allude to the cotton trade. The facts I am now about to state, I believe, will prove that, whereas there had been a greater export of manufactured goods, the consumption of manufactures at home had been less. I quote these facts to show that the whole trade of the country was worse in the years in which the price of provisions was high. I take the years 1838 and 1839. The quantity of cotton exported in 1838, was 269,000,000lbs.; in 1839, it was 262,000,000lbs.; being a deficiency of 7,000,000lbs. In 1838, the home consumption of cotton was 155,000,000lbs.; in 1839, it was 122,000,000lbs.; being a deficiency of 33,000,000lbs. Of wool, the home consumption, in 1838, was 56,000,000lbs.; in 1839, it was 53,000,000 lbs., being a deficiency of 3,000,000lbs. But the export of woollen goods had increased. In 1838, the quantity exported was 6,000,000lbs.; in 1839, it was 6,600,000lbs. Of flax, the home consumption, in 1838, was 1,600,000lbs.; in

1839, it was 1,200,000lbs., and so on with respect to many other articles which he would not then stay to enumerate. It appeared also that the articles which contributed to these staple manufactures of the country, had also greatly fallen off in consumption. From the returns I have quoted, the House will perceive, that whilst the goods entered for home consumption had materially diminished in amount, the quantity of manufactured goods exported had increased. Doubtless some persons in this House will think, that this proved that the country was prosperous. I advise such persons, however, first to consult their manufacturing friends, or indeed any competent authority connected with our foreign trade, whether the increase of exports was a sure sign of prosperity, and whether it was not compatible with the manner in which business was conducted in this country, that the exports should increase when the consumption at home declined, the manufacturers being driven by necessity to procure somewhere a sale for goods cast back, as it were, on their own hands, and whether it was not usual for them then to consign these goods, on their own account, to houses abroad to be disposed of, and whether this has not, from distress, been done during the last year, to a very great extent. Indeed there was evidence of it in the complaints which had come from different countries of the sales of our manufactures which we were forcing on their markets. I find in a letter addressed to one of our most influential journals, from its correspondent abroad, speaking of the extraordinary quantity of British goods brought into foreign markets, says, I would wish to give a hint to those British manufacturers who continue to send over goods to be sold at forced sales, at any price; if that practice be continued the loss will be enormous. Mr. Biddle, who was well known in America, in a letter he addressed to this country last year, spoke of the injurious extent to which British merchandise was forced into the American markets. I might indeed quote much more evidence to shew that goods are frequently exported for want of a market at home for which they have been produced, and which, for some reason has failed, and which, in this case, I chiefly ascribe to the heavy payments that have been required for food. Another proof I might give of the depression at home would be the diminished consumption of certain articles on which revenue is collected, as that, at least, is shown by the amount collected on the different quarters, ending in January 1839 and 1840. I will take four articles of ordinary consumption.

		£.		£.
Hops	in 1839	298,343	in the year ending 1840	280,079
Malt	—	5,211,798	—	4,845,948
Soap	—	1,047,545	—	7,400,000
Spirits	—	5,451,792	—	5,412,477

But, Sir, I will fortify my opinion, that there has been a diminished power of consumption at home owing to the influences that I have traced to the Corn laws, by the authority of a gentleman, whose name I am sure will be received by the House with great respect, I mean Mr. Jones Lloyd, and who in a pamphlet recently published, in which he inquires into the cause of the commercial distress for the last year in this country; he places first in order.

"The succession of two bad harvests in a country afflicted with laws which render such an occurrence peculiarly oppressive to the community, and by a peculiar felicity in mischief, contrive to make monetary derangement, and consequently commercial pressure, the inevitable accompaniment of the misfortune of the seasons. The poison of impolicy is thus thrown into the fiendish cauldron of injustice,

" 'For a charm of powerful trouble
Like a hell-broth to boil and bubble.'"

Now, in referring to this Gentleman, I am not naming a person likely to express himself rashly or incautiously, or one who had no stake in the country, as it is called, but I am referring to one who was probably the possessor of more property than any of those who would take part in the discussion this evening—property of every description, not only in money but in land, and whose judgment was held in high esteem wherever he was known. And now, Sir, we will just consider what are the consequences of this monetary derangement and commercial pressure of which Mr. Lloyd speaks; for there ought to be something to correspond in the actual condition of some of our manufacturing towns, if these things were true, and I think I have here a report from one of those districts which will enlighten the House upon that subject. I will read the result of an inquiry made at Bolton a few weeks since:—

"In the cotton mills alone, about 95,000*l.* less have been paid during the last twelve months. Many of the mills have been entirely stopped for all or part of the time, and with only two exceptions, all have worked short time for a considerable portion of the past year. I have made a very careful calculation from extensive personal inquiry, and assert most confidently, that, altogether, there must have been at least 130,000*l.* less paid in wages in the Bolton Union. Now, add this 130,000*l.* less in wages to the 195,000*l.* more for food, and there is a total loss to Bolton of 325,000*l.*! What are the consequences? There are now in Bolton 1,125 houses untenanted, of which about fifty are shops, some of them in the principal streets. Here is a loss to the owners of 10,000*l.* to 12,000*l.* a-year. The shopkeepers are almost ruined by diminished returns and bad debts. There were, a short time ago, three sales of the effects of shopkeepers in one day. Distraints for cottage rents occur daily. The arrears of cottage rents, and the debts to shopkeepers, are incalculable, but they must amount to many thousand pounds. The pawnbrokers' shops are stowed full of the clothing, furniture, and even bedding of the destitute poor. Fever is also prevalent. Mr. R. S. Kay, one of the medical officers of the union, and a young practitioner of great promise, lately took the infection of malignant typhus fever, and last week fell a victim to his harassing duties. He had latterly worked almost day and night. A short time ago 590 persons were relieved by the poor-law guardians in one day, in amounts varying from six to eighteen pence per head per week. In many cases two or three families are crowded into one house. In one case, seventeen persons were found in a dwelling about five yards square. In another, eight persons, two pair of looms, and two beds, in a cellar six feet under ground, and measuring four yards by five. There are scores of families with little or no bedding, having literally eaten it, *i. e.* pawned or sold it for food! The out-door relief to the poor is three times greater in amount than on the average of the three years ending 1838. South of Bolton, four miles, a large spinning establishment, giving employment to 800, and subsistence to 1,300 persons, has been entirely stopped for nine months. The proprietor has upwards of 100 cottages empty, or paying no rent, and, although possessed of immense capital, finds himself unable to continue working his mills to advantage. Entering Bolton from Manchester, another mill, requiring 180 hands, has been entirely standing for eighteen months. In the centre of the town, another, 250 hands, stopped several weeks. North of Bolton, one mile, a spinning, manufacturing, and bleaching establishment, on which 1,200 persons were dependent for subsistence, has been entirely standing for four months. Several machine makers and engineers are now employing one or two hundred hands less than usual, at wages varying from 15*s.* to 40*s.* a-week. A public subscription, amounting to nearly two thousand pounds, has just been raised to mitigate, in some degree, the sufferings of the destitute poor; in fact, to deal out a scanty pittance, just sufficient to keep them from actual starvation, to a body of workmen who possess, perhaps, greater skill and industry than any population of similar numbers on the face of the globe, but who are forbid, by the inhuman policy of our landowners, to exchange the produce of their labour for food in the open market of the world!"

And that really was the cause of their distress; and this melancholy state of things is unfortunately by no means confined to the cotton districts, as I know well myself from information which I have procured from the place which I represent. And is it not strictly in point, I would ask, to bring these matters before the House? I am not one who would advise the Legislature to interfere simply because there was distress; but when great evil and great distress can be traced to the law, then I think it is the duty, as it is in the power of the Legislature to interfere. I believe, in this case, that it is in the power of this House to give instant relief—I believe it is possible to give permanent relief. The people are now suffering from the high price of provisions, and they are suffering for want of commerce with those countries where the food is grown cheap. The warehouses here are full of foreign grain, and the countries where it is grown are ready to negociate with us for a regular interchange of products. But the people are starving, and we forbid them to touch the cheap and abundant food within their reach; the people want employment, and we refuse to allow them to work for corn-growing customers and employers; our manufactures are stopped, because payments from abroad are not made for goods already supplied from the scarcity of money; they offer us flour in payment for our manufactures, and our manufacturers are willing to take it, and would at once be willing to execute fresh orders upon receiving it, but the law forbids the people to touch it without payment of the duty, and stops the payment that would thus be readily made by the merchants in America to the manufacturers of this country. This is no opinion, it is the fact—America owes a large debt to our merchants in this country; owing to their own monetary embarrassments they have no means of paying their debts, but large quantities of flour have been sent to this country on American account; could this be admitted, not only would those debts be paid, and thus relief be given to our manufactures but they would be ready to execute fresh orders, and thus give employment to our people who are starving for want of it. We are moreover now left without a pretence for saying, that the states from which we might export our corn, have not always been, and are now, ready to admit our manufactures on terms of reciprocity. I do not understand the denial of it, if that proceeds from any authority. Is it intended to imply that the late President of the Board of Trade stated what was false, when he said he had, besides the official communications which he read to the House, perused many other letters from foreign ministers all to the effect of shewing the willingness on the part of those foreign countries to reduce there tariffs on our applying the same principle to their product; and what does the able report of Dr. Bowring but distinctly confirm the impression which these official documents, read by Mr. Thomson, had made, and proves, even at this hour, the readiness of those countries to trade with us? I believe what is contained in Dr. Bowring's report, for it corresponds exactly with the information I procured myself when in those countries, and I have heard no reason since to question its correctness. The effects already of our system in compelling those States to employ their population in manufacture, may be shewn by the following official statement, taken from the first and last year of the tables of the Board of Trade relating to our trade with the corn-growing countries:—

MANUFACTURED GOODS EXPORTED TO RUSSIA, GERMANY, AND PRUSSIA, IN 1832 and 1838.

	1832.	1838.
Cotton Manufactures	£1,273,355	£946,433
Hosiery	359,157	197,615
Linen Manufactures	6,429	25,111
Silk	20,888	17,629
Woollen	952,450	815,785
	£2,612,279	£2,002,573
Deficiency, notwithstanding a great increase of population		609,706

To enable these countries to employ their population in manufacturing clothing, to make up the deficiency of their imports, the following statement, from the same source, shows the yarns to them in the same years:—

	1832.	1838.
Cotton Twist and Yarn ..	£2,935,775	£3,502,186
Linen Yarns	65	29,871
Woollen	137,082	229,572
	£3,072,922	£3,761,629
Increase of Material to work into Cloth	688,707	

But as it is needful, in order that these countries shall successfully rival England at home and in neutral markets, that they shall have our coals, iron, and steel, and more especially our machinery and millwork; the following statement, from the same source, shows the progress of our exports of these materials, in the same years to these countries:—

	1832.	1838.			
Coals	£27,790	£56,350	increase	100	per cent.
Iron and Steel	75,295	190,222	,,	250	,,
Machinery and Millwork ..	7,863	97,479	,,	1,250	,,
Total ..	£110,948	£344,051	average	300	,,

The result is a reduction in the export of manufactured goods, which would employ our labour; an increase of yarn to employ their own labour; and an increase of machinery of 1,250 per cent., to render them perfectly independent of us in their own countries, and to rival us in neutral countries.

But it is not only with the German state, that it would be important for us to negociate at this moment, but it is the moment which is yet left to us, to engage in fresh treaties with the United States and Brazil—and here I must hope that the President of the Board of Trade will tell us exactly the truth on this matter, and whether the general impression is correct that the present tariff of the United States will cease in 1842; and that, about the same time, our present treaty with Brazil will expire; and that our future relations with those countries, will very much depend upon the terms, that we may be enabled to offer them. I hope, at least, that the people will be under no delusion on the subject, and that if we are to continue these fetters on our commerce, at least it shall be done deliberately and with our eyes open. The future well being of this country must now depend upon the extension of our commerce, there is no other mode of providing for our population, or averting the decline of our country. The foolish and impolitic fetters with which we now restrict the commerce of this country are now pressing upon the vitals of the people, and their cry for relief is to be heard in this motion before the House. There are some who think our foreign trade has been carried too far, and that we should have been better without it, that may be true or not, but the complaint is too late, and our foreign trade is now essential to our existence, and we cannot lessen it or destroy it without jeopardising our whole financial and commercial system. We must look to it for the maintenance of our credit, and the collection of our revenue. Most certainly this is not the moment to weaken the sources of our revenue when our expenditure has increased and is increasing by the price we pay for our sustenance, and by the steps we are taking to subdue our colonies, I cannot, indeed, see how the deficiency in the revenue is to be supplied. The great sources of our revenue are found in the capacity of the people to consume the articles that are taxed. I cannot see how it is possible to expect that any fresh tax upon the daily consumption of the people can be collected—for while the price of provisions was thus enhanced by the Corn-law, and the prospects of trade remained as they were, how could it be supposed that if a fresh tax was imposed, that some other branch of the revenue would not fall off. The only resource which in wisdom or justice I can think it possible to resort to would be a property tax. In the year 1830 the country was then tending to the condition in which we now find it. The price of food was then high, and the taxation was grievously felt by the productive classes; Mr. Huskisson then in a most able speech and the last that he made in this House on the state of the nation, drew the attention of the House to the sources of our revenue, and the difficulties which there would exist in collecting the same amount of revenue if trade declined, and the productive classes remained depressed, he did then point to our only alternative, in the imposition of a tax upon property. These were his words :—

"The more general considerations to which I now claim the attention of the House are these. First, that no other country in Europe has so large a proportion of its taxation bearing directly upon the incomes of labour and productive capital. Secondly, that in no other country of the same extent—I think I might say in none of five times the extent of this kingdom—is there so large a mass of income belonging to those classes who do not directly employ it in bringing forth the produce of labour. Thirdly, that no other country has so large a proportion of its taxation mortgaged (in proportion to the amount of that mortgage are we interested in any measure which, without injustice to the mortgagee, would tend to lessen the absolute burden of the mortgage). Fourthly, that from no other country in the world does so large a proportion of the class not engaged in production (including many of the wealthy), spend their incomes in foreign parts. I know I may be told, that by taxing that income you run the risk of driving them to withdraw their capital altogether. My answer is, First, that ninety-nine out of every hundred of these absentees, have no such command over the source of their income. Secondly, that the danger is now of another and more alarming description—that of the productive capitals of this country being transferred to other countries, where they would be secure of a more profitable return. The relief of industry, is the remedy against that danger."

I believe that the people will now turn their attention to this mode of obtaining relief, and certainly I doubt if any new tax but that on property will be submitted to. I am afraid, that I have now exhausted the patience of the House by detailing the mischievous results of these laws, and I will proceed no farther; but I cannot conclude without exhorting those who had hitherto opposed any change, to pause well before they pronounce their decision again upon this question. I ask them whether they perceive anything in the appearance of circumstances around them that encourage belief that the people would adopt their views? Do they think, that any change of opinion since the last Session has occurred in the public mind? Do they not, on the contrarv, know that great numbers have come forth and declared their opposition to the existing law who were silent before? Were there not many classes, who had never spoken before, now eager upon the subject? I ask the attention of the House to the fact, that some of the most cautious and conservative persons in the community—men who were supposed to preside over the monetary system of the country, and who were most averse to change, have come forth, and declared their opinion that this law is most injurious to all the great interests with which they are connected. Have not a greater number of persons of the working classes, pronounced their opin on upon this question than have ever done so before. I want, therefore, to know what it is that is expected to result from the rejection of this motion. The hon. Member for Rutland has declared his determination to oppose this motion, and I certainly admire more the bold injustice of the hon. Gentleman than the insidious proceeding of the hon. Member for Cambridge, who has proposed an amendment but who left the real mischief of the law untouched. I wish to ask what these Gentlemen expect to gain by such a course? Do they expect that all those who have come forward and devoted their attention to this subject, who have sacrificed their property in the cause, and have pledged themselves for the future to agitate this question until it was brought to a satisfactory conclusion."—[*Opposition cheers.*] Yes; he thought it was the best test of the earnestness of men when they devoted their money to promote an object. [*Hear, hear!*] Did hon. Gentlemen who opposed his motion expect that by its rejection all those persons of whom he had spoken would go home and admit themselves to be in error? Did they expect those persons would say, "We certainly did think we were right, but we have found, after discussion, that we are wrong; that all those who have agitated the question are in error; and that this law is a gain and a blessing to us. Let us forget our folly, and never revert to the matter?" Was it reasonable to suppose that the great mass of the people would quite reverse their language upon this subject, and adopt that quiescent and convenient course, if this motion were rejected? If hon. Gentlemen did not expect this, what was it that they conceived would be the consequence of that rejection? Why, the people would return to their homes in the conviction that they were right and at the same time satisfied that the House of Commons would not do them justice. And what prospect did that present? Would it settle the question? If there was difficulty now in making arrangements in the settlement of property, would the mere rejection of this motion facilitate their views. Would it allay the anxiety of the public mind on the subject? What was there to induce the people to admit that they were wrong? They did not doubt themselves, that they were cruelly injured by the law. What eminent authority was there, what person of that kind had lately appeared to shake them in this conviction. And yet, what year passed that some fresh person whose interest or intelligence entitled him to credit, did not appear to denounce it? On all other great questions there had been drawn forth men of ability, advocating opinions in favour of, as well as in opposition to, the proposition advanced; but with respect to this particular question, there was hardly a single man of eminence and intelligence who had undertaken to write in support of the present law. [*Ironical cheers from the Opposition*] If any able publication had appeared in favour of the views of the hon. Gentlemen opposite, he was unaware of the fact, and should certainly feel great pleasure at having the opportunity of perusing it [*Hear, hear!*]. But while there was comparative silence observed by the advocates of the existing system, men of the greatest talent and most extensive information, were coming forth daily with publications of their opinions against it. What, then, could hon. Gentlemen expect to result from their resistance to any change. I pray the House therefore, to pause before they come to a decision, that they will resist all enquiry. I have abstained from stating my own views of what consists with justice and policy; in what should be substituted for the present law. I have satisfied myself with pointing out the evils that resulted from the present law. There was no pretext, therefore, for resisting the motion on the score of the known opinions of the mover. Supposing that the House should now resist all enquiry, how long will those who vote in that way abide by their decision—let them reflect how soon it may be, that they will be called upon to vote in the directly opposite way — and whether that will reflect great credit either upon the House or themselves — for this reason then, I ask the House to pause before they oppose all changes. It is no use to say, that because I propose this question, that they would not assent to it, or because I wished to see the law totally repealed, that they who had the power to resist all change, who have the power to determine the precise amount of change, would not consider the subject. The people would not be deluded by such distinctions and pretences as those. The motion is now made by one who has a perfect right to make it; and those who vote against it, will be very justly considered the friends and advocates of the law. And when they decided thus to maintain the law, did they consider who were the parties who were arrayed against them? It was no question simply between landowners and manufacturers. That was the weak invention of the enemy to assert, and said for the purpose of throwing discredit on the question. No! The question was above any other that could be named, one in which the great majority of the community were interested one way, and a comparatively small section of it, deemed themselves interested the other way; and the advantage which the minority possessed, was in their position in the legislation where their interest greatly prevailed. But was it wise simply to rely on this power? As far as I have been able to collect the opinions of that great and intelligent portion of the population termed the working class, they had rested their claims to the Suffrage chiefly and with great distinctness on these grounds; that they considered that their interests and those of the community at large, were not duly represented in the House of Commons, that they were bound by laws enacted and maintained by those who had no fellow feeling with them—and that the general conduct of the Legislature was their strong argument for widening and altering the character of the constituency. And as far as he could collect the views of the many thousands of this class who had petitioned to repeal the Corn-laws, it was as a sort of test of the character and constitution of the House, which they might point to hereafter as a ground for the assertion of their claims. But do the working classes stand alone? Had not other classes attached themselves to them? Were not the classes immediately above them acting cordially with them upon this occasion? The working classes certainly spoke with confidence of the House not doing them justice in this matter. They consented, however, to act with the middle class, whose language to those below them generally was, "act cordially with us, petition the House respectfully, pray for the redress of your grievances, we will join you, do not yet believe that the Parliament will reject your prayer, and refuse you justice." The people then have petitioned, but it is well known that every working man who had signed those petitions this year, had declared, that if they proved abortive, that it was the last they would sign for the repeal of the Corn-laws. The next petition they would sign would be for the reform of the House of Commons itself. There was now upon this question of the Corn-laws an union between the middle and the working classes, and did hon. Members believe, that, under common disappointment, there would not be an union as firm and cordial between those classes, and upon the other the ultimate question which would then be raised. If this motion is rejected, he believed that three years would not elapse before that junction would be formed for the purpose of a further reform in the constitution of that House. The middle classes experienced the mischief of these laws, and they called for their repeal. The working classes suffer from them equally, I believe in a much greater degree, but they have said, that it is useless to call upon this House to accomplish the object, and they tell the middle class, that it is for this purpose that they want the franchise, that they do not call for change for the sake of change, but that no advance will be made in that House, on these questions of national interest, until they can throw their weight into the political scale. And did this House for one moment suppose, that it would be able to change this opinion, thus deliberately formed, and strongly maintained, by the rude rejection of this measure. A few months ago he attended a meeting of the working classes at Manchester, when he witnessed the most gratifying spectacle of upwards of 5,000 working men who had just quitted their daily avocations, and who had assembled together at dinner to express their opinions upon this vital question. A more orderly, respectful, or attentive meeting, and one where those decent observances requisite in public assemblies were more regarded, he never witnessed. Nothing could have been more strikingly contrasted with the conduct of many other meetings which frequently occurred, composed of persons who were accustomed to discredit and disparage the people, than the decorous deportment of that vast assemblage. He did not doubt that, throughout this kingdom, a similar feeling and conduct would be displayed wherever the working people might assemble. What, then, does the House think, would be the effect of the rejection of this motion upon these very men to whom I refer, or on any others in their circumstances, and equally endowed with qualities so justly entitling them to respect? Was it supposed that they would tamely submit to the injury and the affront that you would offer them by refusing an inquiry into the working of this law? Would they believe that they were in error, because those who were interested in the law asserted that they were so? Would they proclaim to the world that they had, on this occasion, met and made fools of themselves, by remaining silent in future? Let, then, the majority of this House make it matter of calculation with themselves, and ask, what they will gain by persisting to maintain the law as it is, and incurring all the odium that attaches to such a course? Whatever the opinion of the House really may be, it should look at this question practically. Supposing that the repeal of the law was an evil, was it not an inevitable one? The people believed the law was an intolerable evil; do you prove to them that it is not, in anything you say, and do they not hear, and have they not heard, from some of the most distinguished men in the land, that they are right? That the law is unjust and unwise, and that they rightly refer their sufferings to it—still I fear that these considerations are not weighing with the majority of this assembly, and that this motion is to be rejected. I shall then only say, that the responsibility of all the consequences that follow from this course must be fixed upon them. Whatever might happen—whatever disturbance might follow — whatever evils that may occur, whether they be social or political, or of a physical kind, as resulting from this law, the whole blame and responsibility must attach to those very persons individually and collectively who give their vote this evening against this motion. The people were now enduring great physical suffering, which, on great professional authority, I may justly ascribe to the miserable food to which this law condemns them: there is discontent pervading the working classes throughout the kingdom, springing from a sense of injustice inflicted on them by this House, and their attention is now being drawn, though at first reluctantly, yet now grown into habit, to the consideration of political subjects, and their feelings, from these circumstances, are becoming hourly heightened by the agitation of this question. The House, then, has at this moment an opportunity of allaying this excitement, and extending to them relief from the pressure which is now bearing them down. Will they throw away this moment? Let them! if they do, they will surely be indebted to fortune alone if they should be enabled to regain it. I will not longer obtrude upon the attention of the House. If I have expressed myself with warmth, I regret it. If I have done so, it proceeds only from the very sincere conviction on my part that I am right on this subject; and from an apprehension that the House may be guilty of the egregious error of resisting the motion, I now move that the House resolve itself, into a Committee of the whole House to take into consideration the act 9 Geo. 4th, regulating the importation of foreign grain.

THE END.

THOMAS CURSON HANSARD, PATERNOSTER ROW.

THE END

OBSERVATIONS ON CORN LAWS,

ON

POLITICAL PRAVITY AND INGRATITUDE,

AND ON

Clerical and Personal Slander,

IN THE SHAPE OF

A MEEK AND MODEST REPLY

TO THE

SECOND LETTER

OF THE

EARL OF SHREWSBURY, WATERFORD, AND WEXFORD,

TO AMBROSE LISLE PHILLIPPS, ESQ.

BY DANIEL O'CONNELL,

LORD MAYOR OF DUBLIN.

"Oh well may we call her, like thee, 'The Forsaken;'
"Her proudest are vanquished, her boldest are slaves,
"And the harps of her bards when gayest they waken,
"Have breathings as sad as the wind over graves."

DUBLIN:

SAMUEL J. MACHEN, 8, D'OLIER-STREET.

1842.

Daniel O'Connell (1775–1847)

During the early 1840s O'Connell cultivated an alliance with the Anti Corn Law League. In addition to sharing the League's objective of free trade, Irish nationalism and the League shared common enemies – the Chartists and the landed interest. In Manchester O'Connell's Irish supporters helped neutralize the physical force Chartists in a series of confrontations in the summer of 1841.[1] It seems that the Irish repealers (of the Union) regarded the English repealers (of the corn law) as a political shield against repression by the government.[2] So that while Cobden, who distrusted and disliked O'Connell, did little to repay the latter's generous advocacy of the League's cause, the Irish nationalists appear to have thought that the League's campaign might help their cause.[3]

O'Connell's *Observations on Corn Laws* was written in response to the Earl of Shrewsbury, *A Second Letter to Ambrose Lisle Phillipps, Esq. On the Present Posture of Affairs*, London: Charles Dolman, September 1841, in which O'Connell's radicalism was criticised. The Earl was prepared to admit the need for a fixed duty '*after* a fair remunerating price were insured to the home grower, by means of a sliding scale.' (p. 51) But total repeal was, in his view, a course of action 'fraught with ruin both to the agriculturist, and manufacturer.' (p. 39)

[1] McCord, *The Anti Corn Law League*, pp. 99–103.

[2] See Oliver MacDonagh, 'Politics, 1830–45', in W. E. Vaughan (ed.), *A New History of Ireland, vol. 5, Ireland under the Union, I 1801–70*, Oxford: Clarendon Press, 1989, p. 183.

[3] On Cobden's attitude see G. M. Trevelyan, *The Life of John Bright*, Boston and New York: Houghton Mifflin Company, 1913, p. 160.

TO THE EARL OF SHREWSBURY,

&c. &c.

MY LORD,

I love the Jesuits—I admire the Jesuits—the greatest benefactors to religion and to literature that the world ever saw. There is a shrewd compactness in the way they embody common sense, greatly to be prized. One of their maxims is, "*that there is no theologian so dangerous to religion as a* VERY PIOUS FOOL." The Jesuit who uses this phrase, does not intend personal offence to any individual; nor, certainly, do I! I use the expression, not as a description or designation: but, admitting to the fullest extent your lordship's piety, I give it as a caution. Do, my lord, I implore you, beware how you mix up foolishness with your sentiments of devotion!

But whatever course *you* shall please to take, you have addressed me so often in your pamphlet, and with such scant courtesy, that you compel me to reply. My complaints are many, but this is my first grievance. I might bear other evils, but I cannot endure that you should have loudly entered your protest, even "*upon religious grounds*," against the abolition of the Corn Laws. You have, for the first time, arrayed Catholicity against a concession to the poor and the starving; you have summoned the English Catholics; and you have more than insinuated, even by the multiplication of your titles of honour, a call on the Catholics of Ireland, to join with you in the sustainment of those laws, which have been characterized (and I think justly) as "*the plunder of the poor for the benefit of the rich.*"

I bitterly deplore that you should take such a part. I pay the most unfeigned respect to your motives; to your charitable disposition; to your animated religious feelings; but I am thoroughly convinced that you act most unwisely—that you stain and tarnish, and, I fear, deeply injure the sacred cause of Catholicity.

The reasons of my conviction are these. For the first time in the modern history of Catholicity, are the English Catholics called upon, as such, to take part in the political pravity of supporting taxation, and of transferring their attachment from statesmen who have ever been their friends, to public men who—we are gratuitously told—are to be no longer their enemies. For the first time, you introduce politics into the very sanctuary. And *what* politics! politics whose frightful consequence is to enhance the price of bread to those who have but little to eat! and to sustain in office the narrow-minded haters of Catholicity—the men who have trafficked on that hatred, until they jobbed on it into power!

You would array the Catholics in this most unseemly warfare; an inglorious warfare even if successful. Not like the Talbots in their battles of old, you, my lord, with pure-intentions, but alas! with perverted ingenuity, would strew your battle field with the carcasses of starved manufacturers.

You have indeed placed yourself in a deplorable position. Because, although it must be admitted by every body who knows any thing of you, that you are reasonably free from sordid or selfish motives; yet your position is that of a man who contends against feeding the poor, in order that he may increase his own means, and augment his own rents, and for the accumulation of his own wealth. But by what modes of action, gracious heaven! By taking from the poor more money for his bread, than that poor person would be otherwise obliged to pay for it! By coming to the table of the wretched widow with a small fixed income, and telling her and her hungry children that before they taste their bread, there must be a toll paid to your lordship, and your co-proprietors of the land! And that the crumbs that are greedily devoured upon her table shall be fewer in number, lest *your* class should not have so much money as at present, to put into your landlord-pocket.

This, my lord, is the unhappy position in which you are placed. I unfeignedly assure you, I deplore—I bitterly deplore that so charitable and benevolent a man as you are, should have placed yourself in so unamiable a position. But I ought to weep more bitterly at the position in which you place Catholicity; in which *you*, a moral and religious man, place the faith you profess—the glorious faith of your fathers. Catholicity was ever the promoter of every species of charity. It allures, by the brightest reward, it commands under the most awful sanction, to feed the hungry, to clothe the naked, to visit the prisoner, to assuage the sufferings of the sick. Such are the "good works," which, (duly performed) are, according to Catholic doctrine, meritorious in the concerns of eternity.

Yet—in what an attitude do you call upon the Catholics of England to place themselves? The poor man is sick from the faintness arising from his scanty food; and the English Catholics are to proclaim, under your lordship's auspices, that his bread shall be still more scarce to him! The operative is naked; and you call upon the English Catholics to tell him that his bread shall be so dear, that all his earnings shall scarce suffice for food, and that there shall be no residue to purchase clothing. As to imprisonment, your poor-houses *are* prisons; and, alas! my lord, you taunt with insult those who, like me, do not relish the imprisonment of a poor-house. As to the hungry; why, the gospel precepts are to be worked out in favour of the hungry, by making their food as scarce and as dear as the suffering multitude *will* endure.

Had you written and published your pamphlet as a private individual of ancient family and high rank; had you published it as a landlord, or as a peer of parliament; had you confined it to *arguments* (such as *they* are!) to statistics, such as they may be; or to political economy, such as it ought to be; you might, my lord—at least I hope and believe you might, as far as I am concerned—have indulged yourself in as many insults and insinuations respecting me as you pleased, unscathed and unanswered. But your trumpet-sounds call Catholicity to battle along with you.

My complaint ought to be, (and my chief complaint *is*) that you have sought to array Catholicity on the worst side of the worst cause that public penman ever supported; that you have thrown into the scale of the rich and the lordly, against the lowly and the poor, that influence which your ancient rank and high station, your generous and benevolent private character, entitled you to possess among the Catholics of England, in order,—you have done so in order to induce them to adopt the worst part, and to be solicitous about bad things.

This, however, my lord, is too sacred a cause to be abandoned, There is an awful duty to be performed. You *shall not*, my lord—you SHALL NOT bring Catholicity into the ranks of the ungenerous and the sordid. You may go over yourself. You may be found, (alas the day!) among those ungenial ranks! But Catholicity still shall elevate her heavenly banner in her proper station. Even I—ungifted as I am—will wipe off the stain you have flung upon her scutcheon; and proclaim that Catholicity still is, as she ever was—at the side of the people; the mitigator of poverty and the comforter of the distressed; the opponent of aristocratic selfishness; the true guardian of the poor of the Lord.

See, Great Earl! what a glorious example the Catholic farmers of Ireland have set to men in higher station. It has often been said that the Irish head is not unfrequently wrong, but that the Irish heart is always in the right. I doubt the former—I know the truth of the latter assertion. The Irish Catholic farmers did not enter into any minute details. They knew full well by the experience of every one of them, that the oft repeated allegation that the Corn Laws increase the rate of wages, was totally false; the wages in Ireland being of the lowest. They know that cheap bread does not make wages diminish. They—the Irish farmers—knew full well, that "*nothing can be politically right that is morally wrong.*" And they, with cordial unanimity, supported the abolishers of the Corn Laws. My lord, I mean not to offend you; but I glory in the contrast between you and the Irish Catholic farmers.

Permit me, my lord, to cite my own situation as a public man, as one of the proofs that vindicate Catholicity from the selfishness of Corn Law advocacy. I have ever been, upon principle, and for reasons of humanity, the decided advocate of the total abolition of the tax upon bread. A fixed duty would, in my mind, be nothing more than a fixed injustice; and if, having no other choice, I am found voting for the Eight shilling duty, it is only as a substitute for the greater and the gambling iniquity of the sliding scale; and as an instalment of that justice which cannot be complete, without a total abolition of all toll or duty upon human food; whether that tax be imposed to relieve the wants of the state, or for the more glaringly iniquitous purpose of augmenting the wealth of the landlords.

Notwithstanding these my opinions, I am at the present moment the representative of two of the largest agricultural communities in Ireland; a significant proof of their coincidence in my views, and approbation of my opinions.

If I have been bitterly ashamed of your lordship's attempt to rank the Catholics on the wrong side in this question, my dissatisfaction does not rest there. I blush deeply at the paucity, and—I am sorry to say it—the shallow sophistry of what you appear to consider arguments in support of the Corn Laws. The grain of wheat in the shape of reason, it is scarcely possible to sift out of the anomalous heaps of chaff, of the same colour and almost in the same quantity, stuffed now in the text and now in the notes, with which you have overlaid the subject.

Your principal argument* consists in asking, "Why manufacturers of various articles should enjoy their pro-

* Pamphlet, p. 38.

tecting duties of from 20 to 30 per cent. against foreign competition, and yet the manufacture of corn be left without protection ?"

I cannot conceal my surprize that any thing so unfair—so replete with *mistake* of facts, should emanate from your lordship. Are you not aware ?—surely you must know—that our manufacturers export from England and sell to foreign nations, probably to the value of sixty millions of pounds sterling per annum, of their manufactured goods. That is, they undersell the people of foreign countries in their own markets to that extent. To talk, therefore, of protection for manufactures under such circumstances, is really, my lord, to talk not wisely. The protection may be in the statute book; but it is as insignificant as if witchcraft were there! Your argument thus is destroyed at the first blush. There is, however, something worse behind: because it is impossible but you must know that the petitions of the manufacturers—the resolutions of great meetings in particular localities, and of delegates from many places, as well as the unanimous voice of the Anti-Corn Law League, with that exceedingly able man, Mr. Cobden, at their head, have, with one consent, disclaimed every species of fiscal protection. This disclaimer of protection has been made so loudly and so often, that you cannot possibly have been ignorant of it. And yet, my lord, you have thought it fair and right and honest, and above all, *religious!* to found your reasoning, involving the interests of millions, and, in particular, involving the feeding of the hungry poor, upon the basis of an immaterial fact; and which, even if it were material, is totally disclaimed by the manufacturing interests, who have called on the legislature to abolish equally all manufacturing as well as agricultural protection.

The next thing that resembles argument is your allegation, in substance thus—"*that a monstrous proposition is set up on the plea of religion—namely, that a large portion of our corn-growing land should be thrown out of cultivation, and the labourers thereon thrown upon the towns.*"—(p. 39.)

I have stripped this assertion of some of the poetic imagining with which you have surrounded it. I wish—I heartily wish I could admit it to be common sense. It is not so—but it has a still greater defect—it is not true! Nobody asserts—not even the "sectarian ministers" whom you charge with combination and agitation—that corn-growing land should be thrown out of cultivation. It is not sought for that any land capable of producing corn, with all the advantages of the home market, should be other than corn-growing land. That which is insisted upon is widely different, and you ought to know it. It is insisted that such land as now grows corn solely by means of an expenditure, which is prompted and compensated for by the unnaturally high price of corn in England created by the Bread Tax, should not have *that* stimulant for the misapplication of its purposes, but should be made to produce other articles of consumption, for which that land is naturally adapted. In the healthy state of the agricultural *trade*, every species of land will be made to produce that which it is best suited by nature to produce. There is no danger of a want of consumers for every species of agricultural produce. In England the population rapidly increases. You never will want consumers of the produce of any land cultivated as its nature requires.

In another passage you bring to the aid of exceedingly defective logic, your Catholic and Christian faith. The passage is this;* "That the prosperity of both classes "(the agricultural and manufacturing) is a reciprocal "benefit, cannot be denied; and each ought to look for "support from the other."—Quite true. It should not only be fair and just, but reciprocal. Your lordship's reciprocity, however, savours of what is called a Hibernian quality, and is "*a reciprocity all on one side.*" You continue: "But the idea of sacrificing the whole landed "property of the country, to satisfy the mania for com-"mercial speculation, is indeed *Anti-Catholic and Anti-"Christian.*"

No less! Anti-Catholic and Anti-Christian!

For shame, my lord! Oh, for shame! How could you combine the idea of Catholic Christianity with the selfish, and I regret to say, essentially sordid notions that were passing through your mind, when you wrote that phrase! Sacrifice of landed property, forsooth! Answer me—what landed property, or what luxury

---

* Pp. 38—39.

arising from your landed property do we ask you to sacrifice? Not any term or estate in your lands: not your splendid mansions, or your luxuriant gardens; not your fisheries or your graperies; not your pineries or your pheasant preserves; not your pampered horses or your stall-fed oxen or sheep. Feed and fatten on these, until appetite provoked by every variety of delicacy is satiated, or at least wearied. We require not your green crops or turnip heaps; not your hay or your grass. No —not your wheat, nor your oats, nor your barley. Send these, as our manufacturers do their produce, to every corner of the globe where you can find buyers. Send them to the home market or the foreign market, as best suits your interest or your fancy or your caprice. Or if your wantonness makes you careless, destroy them if you please; or consume them, either yourselves or by your servants, or even by your pigs and poultry. In short, you are free to use or to abuse your lands and their produce, at discretion or caprice.

What property of yours, then, is to be sacrificed? I will tell you—and you ought to blush that it should be necessary for me to tell you! The property of which we demand from you the sacrifice, is nothing in the world but "the privilege to pillage the poorer classes of the community." What we desire to take away from you, is the power which the Corn Laws iniquitously give you, to compel the operative to pay for your corn a larger price than that which he could get the same article for elsewhere; and yet you assume the air of an awful theologian, and tell us that to take away that power is Anti-Christian and Anti-Catholic.

The wealthy nobleman, "clothed in purple and fine linen" may credit you. *He* may imagine the Catholic religion was so good a thing for the aristocratic classes, that he ought to promote it. But the poor, starving mechanic, who, by reason of your law, has a slice of bread the less to give to each of his children, will despise your reasoning, and may, perhaps, hate that form of faith which *you* obtrude between his hungry family and a full meal. Should he hear your *real* character; should he hear that you really are, as an individual, humane and generous, bountiful and good, may he not on that very account form a loathing against that religion—in itself pure and undefiled—which thus seems to sear your conscience, and which makes you—even *you!* an apostle of starvation, and a preacher of monopoly?

I believe I have now touched upon all that savours of reasoning in your support of the Corn-Laws. You have, it is true, mixed up many details of the statistics of Corn and Currency. But even in that mist of figures, with which you so uselessly surround yourself, the natural benevolence of your disposition breaks out. There is not that iron tenacity about you, which marks the Dukes of Buckingham and Richmond. You are ready to relax the pressure upon the working classes; and that poor and paltry concession, which some others also are ready to make, for the purpose by mitigating harshness to continue delusion, you, from better and purer motives, are willing to concede. Oh! how I should desire to make you perceive, that even the concession so wrung from others, bespeaks the foregone conclusion, that the bread-tax is in its nature too oppressive, to be much longer endured in its present form and pressure.

I do not reply to your statistics on Corn and Currency. I would not take the trouble of confuting some conclusions or elucidating some mistakes. I leave you the full benefit of having them uncommented on and unreplied to. Yet I fearlessly assert that even you yourself cannot be without some consciousness that the Corn Laws are unchristian and uncatholic, because they are unjust and oppressive. The matter lies in a narrow compass.

First—The Corn Laws operate to prevent the workmen in manufactories from earning wages, inasmuch as they prevent the agricultural countries in Europe and America, which want our manufactures, from having a medium of exchange whereby they would obtain these manufactures. If they were allowed to send corn here, they would exchange that corn (or exchange the *price* of it, which is the same thing) for English goods. Thus there would be achieved for England a good with a double aspect. First, it would be good for the English to get an increased quantity of food. Secondly, it would be good for the English to sell an increased quantity of manufactures. But you, my lord, stand in the midst. You will not let the increased food come in; and you thereby prevent the increased quantity of manufactures from going out. And all this mischief you proclaim and sustain, with "*religion*" dropping from your lips in almost every sentence!

Secondly—The crowning injustice of the Corn Laws consists in this: the operative is indebted to Providence for the strength which enables him to labour; and to his own industry for the skill with which he applies that strength. His property is his labour; composed of two elements, strength and skill. There is not in the world a more rightful property. His title is infinitely beyond that derived from the casualties of modern descent, or the chances of ancient plunder. With his skill and labour he has earned money. A limited sum of money it must necessarily be. He wants food for his sustentation and support. He comes into the market for food. It would be the greatest tyranny and iniquity to prevent his buying that food in the market. It is a tyranny and an iniquity, *less only in degree*, but the same in principle, to interpose a tax or other impediment, which compels him to purchase a lesser quantity than he wants, and than he otherwise would be able to purchase. The principle is identically the same; but it would amount in morals to murder, by actual starvation totally to prohibit him. Nor does it appear to me that the guilt is much mitigated by the fact, that the *lesser* process is more slow in its operation, and does not so immediately create death; and only anticipates the period of his demise by the more tedious mode of insufficient sustenance.

The provision-tax, therefore, is in its nature most criminal. It is murderous. It is the most direct violation of the first principles of justice. It is not mitigated even by the fact, that such tax is applied to the necessities of the state and the maintenance of the laws, and thus confers *some* benefit, however remote, upon each individual in that state. The thing is in itself so radically oppressive and unjust, that it is incapable of moral mitigation. However, this tax, though not to be mitigated in its severity by any circumstance, is yet capable of an enormous aggravation of its criminality. This aggravation arises when the tax is not for the benefit of the state or for any public purpose, but is a favour and a benefit given to a particular class of society; when it is levied—*not* for the expenditure of the government, but for the sole profit of a privileged and insomuch a plundering class; when, in short, it is a protection to a particular interest. The protected person, thus, by the voice of the Corn-Law, addresses the workman; "You shall not buy your breakfast, though you have your own hard earned money to buy it with, until you have first paid *me* a heavy tax for liberty to purchase!"

Bread, my lord, is at this moment, in round numbers, at Paris, five pence,—in reality, five pence and a fraction, for the loaf. A loaf of the same size, weight, and quality, costs in England ten pence. The charges of bringing over from Paris to England the materials to make that loaf, would not increase its price one penny. Thus the English artizan, and every English poor person, is defrauded of four pence out of ten pence in the price of his loaf. And that four pence is the plain and manifest plunder committed by the grower of English wheat, under the sanction and by the authority of the Corn Law.

I do not mean the least discourtesy to Lord Shrewsbury, but I cannot qualify my terms. This is a robbery—the worst species of robbery. It is the robbery of the poorer classes to enrich the wealthier. You may talk and write about it what you please—it cannot and will not be long endured.

The English people must not be led by my Lord Shrewsbury, or any body else, to believe that the Catholic religion sanctions this robbery; or that the great bulk of the Catholics, even of England, are favourable to this injustice. Self-interest may delude a great man, here and there; associating with other Corn Law plunderers, he may familiarize his mind to the injustice; but the Catholic religion is by no means responsible for his errors. On the contrary, those errors are in direct contradiction to the principles of that holy religion—a religion promotive of all good works, and the instigator of every charity.

Having thus disposed of your very futile attempt, to sustain the hard-hearted iniquity of the Corn Laws, I turn with alacrity to other topics of your pamphlet. I will first take up your solicitation to the Catholics, to forsake the Whigs now that they are defeated, and to give in their adhesion to the Tories now that they are in power. You, with much *naïveté*, ask, "Why should we follow the fallen fortunes of the Whigs?" Strange chivalry, gentle reader, for an Earl of ancient fame!

You really overrate your powers of seduction, and your capacity to create wholesale desertion. Even the question of creating political renegades, smacks in your language—pardon me!—of something like religious pretension. It would seem that you endeavour to make it a point of conscience, that the Catholics should abandon all political gratitude, forsake the fallen fortunes of the Whigs, and adopt, with a servile alacrity, the politics of the Tories.

Here again the Corn Laws seem to obtrude; for it is impossible to discover any other assignable motive for the desertion—in its own nature unprincipled—of the friends of your earlier political life; or for your embracing the malignant foes of your caste and your creed, with a rapidity more remarkable for its abruptness than for its delicacy or decency.

This, indeed, is strange. This whirling rapidity of transition, from the avowed love of gradual amelioration, to the determined resistance to every salutary change, (for *that* is Toryism) would appear almost miraculous; but for the political creed, which, in your second page, you announce, in all the emphasis of *italics* hashed up with CAPITALS.

That creed may well indeed be called the slippery scale of politics. There is no political conscience that it may not exactly suit. It is everything, and it is nothing! Here is your magnanimous profession of political faith; I give it *verbatim*. As a matter of curiosity it deserves to be preserved; embalmed amidst the no-meaning absurdities of plausible nothingness! You say, "I always "was, and I hope I always shall be, a Whig; by which I "mean, *an advocate for the greatest possible degree of civil* "*and religious liberty*, *and the greatest possible amount of* "*religious toleration*, CONSISTENT WITH THE INSTITUTIONS, "AND THE CONDITION OF THE COUNTRY."*

There it is — a precious document! — a document which the monster, Emperor Nicholas—who, in one of his sanguinary freaks, swept the streets of Warsaw of, and bore for ever away, the children of Polish mothers; and in another fantastic barbarity, compelled nearly one million of his subjects to apostatize from the Catholic religion,—he, even he, might sign this creed together with the Earl of Shrewsbury. For *he*, too, will give all the civil liberty, and all the religious toleration which he deems *consistent with the institutions and the condition of his country*. There is no tyrant, no bigot, who may not cry, amen! to your lordship's creed. They are all ready to go every length for civil and religious liberty; provided they be allowed to qualify and to limit it to that which *they* deem consistent with the institutions, and, above all, with the condition of the country. Shakspeare says that your "if" is a great pacificator. Your

* Pamphlet, p. 4.

"condition" is a great neutralizer of all that is valuable in your first assertion. If any measure to promote civil liberty or religious toleration be asked for, the negative reply at once may be,—"It is not consistent with the *institutions* of the country;—the country is not in a *condition* for such a change."

Really, my lord, it is surprising how a man of your understanding should give us, with all the pride, pomp, and circumstance of typographical dignity, such a bundle of unmeaning words. The efficacy with which they can contradict each other, renders the words devoid of any real meaning.

Surely, you cannot have forgotten that these were the very same cant phrases, with which we were met and opposed while struggling for Emancipation. We were met by the bigots and oppressors, then, with the declaration of a great wish to satisfy all his Majesty's subjects in their demands; but how could Emancipation consist with the *institutions* of the country? And then—only think of the *condition* of the country! England was not in a condition to suffer such a change! Such was then the cry of all our enemies. And the very topics with which you qualify your opinions, would have kept the Catholics of both kingdoms in thraldom for perhaps a century to come, if it had not been for one of us, my lord—you or I—I give you the choice to say which!

I cannot however pass without censure one expression in your creed. Nor can I talk of it with sufficient abhorrence, without violating that personal courtesy which I owe, and am most willing to maintain, towards your lordship. I allude to the word " toleration." Toleration means "permission"—"sufferance." He who claims to be "tolerated" gives up his right of self-assertion. He who talks of "tolerating," assumes that he has the right to refuse permission. Now, my lord, I require the permission of no man, I despise the toleration of any man, for my worship of the adorable Creator and Redeemer, in that pure form in which my conscientious conviction tells me that the truth of God abides. It is *my* right; it is *your* right; it is the right of every christian man! In fact, the word "toleration" admits the principle of persecution. No man can talk of tolerating another, unless in the assertion of the right to persecute. He who admits he has no right to persecute, gives up, necessarily, all title to tolerate. And I, as a Catholic, abhor and repudiate persecution; and on behalf of the Catholic body, I reject *toleration*. Insisting on my own right, at my own awful responsibility to my Creator and Lord, and to him alone, to worship him in the full sincerity of conscientious belief, I assert for every other Christian man precisely the same right at the same awful responsibility.

As I have already, I do hope, cleansed the sacred banner of Catholicity from the stain which you had by your bread-tax advocacy flung upon it—so again do I brighten that banner from the obscuration of your odious word "toleration."

I must not, however, be misunderstood. There is not

in this, my assertion of freedom of conscience, the slightest tinge of indifferentism in matter of religion. On the contrary, no man can be more thoroughly convinced than I am, that it is impossible for any thing to be of so much importance as the truth of the Christian Faith; or that nothing can be comparable in magnitude to the spiritual obligation upon every body to believe and profess the TRUE Faith. But this is a question between man and his God. The obligation of belief is not to our fellow-man, but to the Creator of all. And the awful responsibility of which I speak, relates to an eternity of weal or of woe; and to nothing that human government can give or take away.

From this all-important subject, I now descend to the ludicrous nature of your profession of political faith. It is like a nose of wax; it would fit any face. Or perhaps it resembles more the pledge of an anti-teetotaler, who made boast that he never would again get drunk in any man's company, unless he should be a friend, a relation, an acquaintance, or a stranger.

It is, after all, not so much your political *no*-opinions that I arraign. It is the ungenerous counsel that you give to the English Catholics. It is, permit me to add, the ungenerous example—in speaking to any other man, I would call it the *paltry* example—which you hold forth to the British Catholics. You took your place among the partisans of the late administration, so long as they were in office; so long as they basked in royal favour, and that the Sovereign had it in her power to continue them around her. You were their *prosperity* friend. But, now that they have fallen into adversity; now that the Queen has been compelled to send them back again into the ranks of private life; now that they have no longer ministerial rank, station, or dignity; now that the winter's gale is upon them; you—their "friend" in their season of prosperity—clap up your helm, sail in the squadron, and elevate the flag of their fortunate enemies, exclaiming, "*Why should we bind ourselves to the fallen fortunes of the Whigs?*"

This assuredly is not dignified, or generous, or noble. *You* are disinterested. But yet, what encouragement does not your example give to the selfish, to the servile, and even to the treacherous?

Believe me, it little becomes the name of Talbot to exhibit an un-Catonian specimen of preference given to the victorious but *worse* cause; and the abandonment of the better, though defeated party!

Judging by your conduct to my humble and insignificant self, I should be forced to the conclusion that gratitude was not, in your opinion, one of the cardinal virtues; at least, that it was not an English Catholic virtue; but was rather a quality deserving little estimation. I should, indeed, have feared that this was a judgment formed by me in my natural prejudice in my own cause, if I were not irresistibly compelled to perceive that ingratitude—dark ingratitude—pervades all that portion of your pamphlet which calls on British Catholics to desert the unlucky Whigs, and to join the lucky Tories.

It is impossible to conceal or to deny this ingratitude. Yes, my Lord, it is, I am sorry to say, too obvious. It is, in its nature, too discreditable to be endured in silence.

No man *did* describe—few men have the ability to describe in terms of such glowing eloquence, of bitter grief, and even of agony, as did *you*, my lord, describe the oppressive degradation and contumely which were inflicted on *you*, the premier Earl of England, and upon the English Catholics in their native land, by the iniquitous "penal laws."

Your plaintive cry was this: it bewailed the following grievances: take them in numerical order, as they have been all since redressed. In 1828 you exclaimed:—

1. "A Catholic cannot sit or vote in the House of Peers, and is thus deprived of his most valuable birthright.

2. "A Catholic Commoner cannot sit or vote in the House of Commons.

3. "A Catholic freeholder may be prevented from voting at elections for members.

4. "A Catholic cannot sit in the Privy Council.

5. "He cannot be a Minister of the Crown.

6. "He cannot be a Judge.

7. "He cannot hold any office in any spiritual, equity, or common law court.

8. "He cannot become a King's Counsel.

9. "He cannot hold any office in any of the corporations.

10. "He cannot marry either a Protestant or a Catholic, unless the *ceremony* be performed by a Protestant clergyman.

11. "He cannot settle real or personal property for the use of his church.

12. "Nor for the use of Catholic schools, nor for any other purposes of the Catholic religion."

You added this complaint :—

"From early youth to the last stage of existence, we "Catholics are doomed to bear about us a painful feeling "of inferiority and undeserved reproach."*

In a different passage you justly complained, thus :—

"*We are worse than aliens in our native land;* inas-"much as that an alien is under the protection of an "equal law, which we are not. If an alien be a delin-"quent, or a presumed delinquent, he is entitled to a "trial by his peers; and half those peers are his own "countrymen, and of his own religion; whereas *our* de-"linquency, imaginary as it is, is tried by men who have "no fellow-feeling with us, and who convict us upon "evidence collected, produced, and attested by *themselves.* "We are compelled to endure the stings of insult and "of calumny, frequently without either the opportunity "of reply, or the hope of redress by law. *We are denied* "*the privilege of the meanest malefactor;* that of being "confronted with our accusers. We are excluded from "the places in which the most galling and most influ-

---

* "Reasons for not taking the Test." Second edit.; Appendix, 755.

"ential of the calumnies pronounced against us are "uttered; and if we dare to answer them elsewhere, our "calumniators may sit in judgment upon us, and punish "our audacity with imprisonment."—*Reasons for not taking the Test.* Second edit. p. xiii.

Protesting against that infliction, labouring against that iniquity at the period of your unjust degradation and adverse fortune, was to be found Lord Melbourne, the late Prime Minister.

Advocating the cause of justice and liberality to you, in your then inferior and suffering state, was ranged the manly eloquence of the Marquis of Lansdowne, another member of the late Cabinet.

At that dark period of your political history, Lord John Russell, the late ministerial leader of the House of Commons, sustained, with a power of oratory and argument almost unequalled, your interests, and vindicated your rights.

Need I remind you, my lord, of the sincere zeal and accumulated services in the Catholic cause, of the Ponsonby family? and in particular of that excellent nobleman, Lord Duncannon, another member of the late Cabinet?

Is it necessary to recal to your memory the sincere zeal and power of eloquence of Sir John Hobhouse, another member of the late Cabinet? Why should I unnecessarily multiply individual instances? Was not every man of the late Cabinet, who had a seat in Parliament before Emancipation, the decided friend, advocate, and supporter of our cause! the decided enemy of the Tory iniquity under which we suffered!

They *were* your friends, my lord; your true, your trusty, your tried friends. Your friends in the day of your need—in the day of your distress. Your friends when you could not help yourself. They were the enemies of *your* enemies: the assertors of your rights! Aye, my lord—they were more! They were the vindicators of your unjustly tarnished honour, and of the PRINCIPLE of your calumniated religion.

One thought more. So far from the members of the late Administration having supported the Catholic cause from motives of party interest, or from the ambition of attaining the honours and emoluments of office, the fact is that they actually and voluntarily placed themselves under the ban of the Crown. They, with full consciousness, exposed themselves to the personal hatred, and even malignity, of the two monarchs, George III. and George IV. They, with full knowledge of the consequences, raised, by their advocacy of Catholic rights, an almost impassable barrier against the enjoyment of the favour of the Crown, and the rewards, honours, and dignities of ministerial power. They knew full well that if circumstances forced them on the king, he would soon find means, as he *did* on one remarkable occasion, of dismissing them from office.

They were, in short, my lord, the martyrs of *your* cause. They were *your* political martyrs.

Turn we now to the other side. Let us pass in array

the chiefs of those on whose behalf you have now rushed into print; and whose power you have used all your persuasive influences to support and consolidate.

Let us select one of the leaders of the new Cabinet—the lauded of Lord Shrewsbury—the Right Hon. Henry Goulburn. Was *he*, my Lord, sensible of the cruelty and injustice under which you and the Catholics laboured? Had he the feeling of the wrong—the sense of the iniquity perpetrated against you? No, my lord! no. He rejoiced in that wrong; he gloried in that iniquity. He would have continued it to the present day. His only regret was that the injustice ceased—that the wrong was alleviated. It is his great regret to the present moment. He actually resigned office—and no man ever loved office, perhaps, *so much* as Goulburn; certainly *not more.* Yes. He resigned his office when the Cabinet to which he belonged had determined to grant Emancipation. Nor has he ever relaxed his undying hatred of Pope and Popery. Nor has ever one word betrayed him into the disgraceful inconsistency of favouring the progress of liberality.

I will tell you an anecdote of Goulburn, whilst he was Orange-patronising Secretary in Ireland. There is an Italian—you may have heard of him—named Bianconi; a man of the greatest worth and integrity. He came here a friendless and almost penniless stranger. He has acquired a large independent fortune by opening up all parts of Ireland to very cheap and very expeditious travelling; by maintaining upon the roads what are termed jaunting-cars. He had purchased stations, and built stables for his horses in many localities. In a short time he discovered, from some of the persons in the employment unjustly retaining possession of the buildings, that being an alien and a Catholic, he had no legal power to evict the fraudulent occupier, or to assert dominion over his own property.

He was a Catholic. Had he been a foreign Protestant, no matter from what country, by landing in Ireland he would have been naturalised, and have possessed all the privileges of a British subject. But he was a Catholic; and therefore he continued an alien.

Under these circumstances, he was advised to apply to Goulburn for letters of denization. It was thought he would have got them quite as a matter of course. No man could have a higher character for industry, activity, public utility, and personal integrity. He was, however, a Catholic, and his most reasonable request was refused, by your new ally, Goulburn. A second and a third application met the same fate. Nor was the inconvenience and impediment to his business removed, until those Whigs, whom you so wisely and so gratefully advise us to renounce, came into office—when at once he was made a denizen.

You, my lord, with all your titles, birth, and fame, would continue to be denied the privilege of the meanest malefactor, if Goulburn's vote could have kept you in that unenviable situation—or if it could at the present moment restore you to it, he would be the most unprincipled of human beings if he did not cheerfully pronounce that vote. Yet you call on us to go over to him!

The next of these new allies to whom you vow fealty is Sir Edward Knatchbull: a man whom you must admit to be one of the most unmitigated enemies to the rights of the Catholics in or out of these realms. He never relaxed his hostility. He never avowed, because he never felt, the slightest mitigation in his enmity to the Catholics. He spoke in every debate; he voted in every division *in* the house—he exerted all his influence *out* of the house, to keep us all still slaves. There was a virulence in his hostility, unchanged and unaltered to the present hour. He assailed Peel for yielding to the necessity of granting Emancipation. He it was, who, in the excess of his indignation and animosity against the Catholics, taunted Peel with a "*nusquam tuta fides.*"

What he was on the day when he uttered these words, the same he is at the present day.

I place him second upon the list of your favourites among the present Cabinet Ministers.

The third shall be the Duke of Buckingham. Pretty much on a par with Knatchbull in point of talents, he if possible exceeded him in virulence. And like Knatchbull, he has never relaxed or qualified his hostility. You would still, my lord, "*be denied the privilege of the meanest malefactor*" (oh! how I thank you for the words!)—if the Duke of Buckingham's vote in Parliament could have detained you in thraldom, or could now consign you back to slavery.

But let me not rest with the minor fry of the present Cabinet. Let me proceed to the highest name amongst them all—the Duke of Wellington. Let me confine myself to *your own words*, when I speak of *him*, the most fortunate of the fortunate!

You, my lord, published two editions of your "REASONS FOR NOT TAKING THE TEST:" the first in March, the second in October, 1828. You alluded to the hope which the then preceding Administration of Mr. Canning had inspired. In both editions of your book there is this passage:—

"After many anxious vicissitudes of hope and fear; "after passing through a trying variety of temperature; "the political horizon appeared to have settled in almost "unclouded sunshine upon the Catholics of the empire; "when, to our dismay and horror, it is now again "suddenly darkening around us. We cannot but fear "that the appointment of the Duke of Wellington as "Premier is a fatal omen to our cause: *for hitherto he "has but too often ranked amongst the most signal of our "opposers.*" *

You were right, my lord. You were right. He was, indeed, my lord, ranked amongst the most signal of our opponents; and, I would add, amongst the most ungrateful. You yourself proclaimed his ingratitude.

* "Reasons," &c. 2d edit. cxxii.

Yes. More dishonouring ingratitude was never (*at least until very lately*) exhibited; because he was most deeply indebted to the sacrifice of Irish Catholic blood for his elevation to the dukedom. You, yourself, say, "Were it not for his Catholic troops, the Duke of Wel-"lington had never gathered one solitary laurel; for all "the laurels he wears have sprung from their valour, "and been watered by their blood. But for the confi-"dence reposed in him by Catholic governments, he had "never been carried forward in his career. But for the "honours heaped upon him by Catholic monarchs, his "breast had never blazed with half that brilliancy that "beams upon it now; and many of those high-sounding "titles, which so loudly proclaim his glory to the world, "would have been mute."*

Yet the first vote he gave as a duke, the very first and most deliberate vote for which he left his proxy, was a vote to continue the degrading slavery of the Catholics.

It was, to him, a degrading vote. *You* may speak of him, my lord, as you please. *I* will always speak of him as he really is; as the most lucky of all the ungifted and ungenerous beings that ever were wafted by fortunate chances and accidents to great elevation.

To the passage which I have first quoted, you add, "If the Duke of Wellington be the bigot which many "imagine, our fate is sealed so long as his counsels pre-"vail. But we are willing to *hope against hope*."†

---

* Reasons, cxxii.—† Ib. cxxiv.

Whilst you thus avowed your fears from the bigotry of the Duke of Wellington, you declared your determination not to despair; "to hope even against hope." And yet I may say, by way of parenthesis, that you now come out against me, and bid *me* to despair of carrying the Repeal of the Union, although *I* hope for that event. *not* "against hope," but with events that cluster hopes around me, whether in Spain, in France, in Africa, or in the East—or in America. For, my lord, the moment the Irish are sufficiently combined amongst themselves to obtain that respectful attention which they will then assuredly merit; or—mark me, my lord! the moment that England wants the assistance of the people of Ireland,—that moment England *will* obtain that assistance —but the Union *shall* be repealed.

But to return.

In 1828, you were quite conscious of the Duke of Wellington's bigoted opposition. You denounced him as the enemy of the Catholics. But you may allege that he subsequently altered his opinions, mitigated his hostility, and emancipated the Catholics.

I admit the last fact. He *did* emancipate the Catholics—but he emancipated them because (as he himself avowed) emancipation was no longer to be resisted. We had our moral Waterloo, my lord, and our victory was more useful, if not more glorious. We chained the valiant duke to the car of our triumph, and compelled him to set us free.

But I utterly deny that he altered his opinions or mitigated his hostility. He avowed that his enmity to Catholic rights—that his preference for Catholic degradation, were still the same; whilst he added the plaintive conclusion, that further resistance was impossible. He declared that his hostility was still unmitigated. Nay, he said that the Emancipation would be more useful to the expansion and establishment of Protestantism, by the union of action which would continue amongst Protestants; whilst the Catholics, no longer kept together by political interests, would tarnish themselves by their feuds, and disgrace themselves with their dissentions; and weaken themselves by both.

Was his soul prophetic, good my lord?

The Duke changed his politics and emancipated us; but he never changed his bigoted opinions. He opposed, during the late administration, every concession to the Irish people; every attempt to assimilate the franchises of the Irish with those of the English. It was he who thrust into the Irish parliamentary Reform Bill, the clause which preserved the rights of the exclusively Protestant freemen. And the express grounds on which he perpetrated these enormities, was to preserve, as far as he could, the *ascendancy* of the Protestant church in Ireland.

He more than once, during Lord Melbourne's government, laid it down as a maxim in the administration of Ireland, "that Protestants should be *encouraged.*" By "encouraged" he of course intended, and avowed he intended, that they should be "*preferred*" to the Catholics on all practicable occasions.

With that maxim of his, I leave him for the present, under the protection and special favour of the Catholic Earl of Shrewsbury.

The next that I offer to your lordship's consideration is Lord Lyndhurst. Of *him*, too, you entertain hopes which I shall leave undisturbed; because such hopes are, and must be, intact by any process of reasoning, or any approach of common sense! They can spring only from that species of sensibility, which, when translated into words, is familiarly called "twaddle;" and when confined to mere thought, falls within the category of dotage. You are too young and too wise for either twaddle or dotage; and yet I must, in despair, abandon you to your "hopes" (!) of Lord Lyndhurst. He has been guilty of most mischievous indiscretion: let me call it dangerous, too. It is true that it was only the *Irish* Catholics on whom he affixed the appellation of "*aliens in language, aliens in blood, and aliens in religion.*" It will be well, however, to recollect, that as an "*alien in religion,*" you, even *you*, are stigmatized. Though you are emancipated, he still brands *alienage* upon you! after having in parliament exerted all his faculties, and even availed himself of the excellence of his memory, to detain you in a state worse than that of an alien. Nay, he incurred, to keep you in degradation, all the odium of being a renegade, and of abandoning all his former liberal opinions for the vile love of place and promotion. He poured out against you that speech which was "*once Toby Philpott's;*" and ranked himself at the side of bigotry, in a manner which entitled him to be classed among the most unprincipled and the most narrow-minded of modern statesmen.

Perhaps indeed there may be something in the private life of this nobleman, which inspires you with hopes and encourages your confidence. If so, I am totally ignorant of it. But if it be so, I leave you to the full benefit of its influence.

Let me next point your attention to some of the minor fry of triumphant Toryism. There is Mr. Milnes Gaskell, and there is Mr. Sidney Herbert. The one, it is said, *has been* liberal; I do not vouch for it; but this I know, that at present his disposition is to call *you*, my lord, a "Romanist." But if he were disposed to an excess of civility, perhaps he might condescend to call you a "Papist."

As to Mr. Sidney Herbert, the only way, so far as I can judge, in which he earned office, was by a speech in which he most grossly calumniated the Catholic priesthood of Ireland; distorted the evidence before the intimidation committee; so as to show that he had some ability, and more inclination, to range himself for life as a No-Popery champion.

This, however, as addressed to *you*, is a topic of some delicacy. For you have in your pamphlet, as I shall shortly show, sanctioned some of his charges against the Catholic clergy, and adopted some of his calumnies. But whether coming from him alone, or sanctioned by you, high as you are, it is a subject which forbids mincing delicacy, and compels me to proclaim the charges false as they are foul; unfounded as they are injurious. Yes! the calumniated Catholic clergy of Ireland can set not only him, but even *you*, at utter defiance!

Last but not least, comes Sir Robert Peel. And what is *his* history? He began his career in Ireland by organizing Orangism; by joining with Saurin in that corruption of the Irish Bar, which now promises us a plentiful crop of bigoted, intolerant, and partial judges. He re-organized and armed the Orange yeomanry of the north of Ireland, whose orgies were annually celebrated in the blood of the Catholics; whilst he proclaimed in the House of Commons, that the only fault of those Orangemen was their "excess of loyalty;" those very Orangemen who have been scattered by the unanimous condemnation of parliament. He filled every office with their then sworn partizans. He raised himself from obscurity into notice and high station, as the child and champion of intolerance. There was no dirty dexterity of which he was not capable, even upon the most awful of all possible subjects; but let me give your own charge in your own words:—

"It was asserted," [by Peel] "with much parade "of solemn and momentous accusation, against the most "unimpeachable prelacy in the world, that they were "guilty of the most audacious impiety in cancelling "a precept from the Decalogue; and it was at least "insinuated that they did so in order to flatter their "favourite propensities to idolatry."*

The charge, of course, was false. You have proclaimed it so; and shown the miserable chicanery upon which it was founded. But that chicanery was Peel's—that falsehood was Peel's! On the subject of the Decalogue itself, he was guilty of bearing that false witness against you, and against every one of us, from our highest prelate down to the humblest attendant upon our worship. What was your own description of him? You began by paying him a compliment which he little deserved. You said;

"It is astonishing that a man of Mr. Peel's character "and reputation for fair dealing, should condescend to "use misrepresentation when he finds argument fail him. "But it only shows the extent of his delusion, *and how "fitted his mind is to receive impressions contrary to truth, "reason, and common sense*, when his favourite prejudices "are to be cherished. If that delusion only affected the "individual, we should lament it, without presuming to "correct him; but when the delusion of an individual "stands between the happiness of millions, and that "individual is the champion of A PARTY OPPOSED TO THE "BEST INTERESTS OF THE EMPIRE, then indeed it is a "delusion which ought to be exposed to the whole "world."†

* "Reasons," 2nd. edit. p. xxviii. † Ibid, pp. xxviii. xxix.

There they are, my lord. I have paraded them before you.

I have, indeed, omitted Stanley, because he is an inveterate and malignant enemy of the Irish; and the unhappy Irish are the subject rather of your lordship's sneers than of your sympathy and support. They (the Catholic Irish) may be called villainous perjurers; and but for me, you probably never would have heard of it! *Having* heard of it, you seem disposed not to pardon me for disturbing the aristocratic repose of your indifference to Ireland.

I have paraded them before you. There are Hobhouse and Palmerston; Lord John Russell and Lansdowne; Lord Duncannon and Melbourne—the late ministry—your firm, your disinterested friends; friends at need—friends who sacrificed party interests to sustain *you;* when in your native land you were "*worse off than an alien, and had not the privilege of the meanest malefactor.*"

Recollect, too, that all the rest of the men in office, under the late administration, were, each in his sphere, the decided supporters of the principle of Catholic Emancipation. On the other hand, you have Goulburn and Knatchbull, and Buckingham and Lyndhurst!—and Wellington, who gave his first vote as a Duke against you; and Peel, who falsified the commandments of God, in order to calumniate the Catholics, and to continue their slavery;—Peel, whom you yourself have proclaimed to be "a person, whose mind is fitted to receive impressions contrary to truth, reason, and common sense," when his prejudices are to be cherished.

These are the men who would have kept you "*worse than an alien in your native land, and without the privileges of the meanest malefactor.*"

There now, are both parties before you. Your ancient foes are politically triumphant; your ancient friends politically defeated and prostrate. Representative of all the chivalry of all the Talbots, make your choice between the two!

But pause. Pause one moment. Recollect—(oh! that it should be necessary to remind you of it!)—that one of the principal means by which the constituency of England was, to say the least, predisposed to the present administration, was the incessant abuse and vilification of Catholics, and above all of the Catholic religion. Remember that the great organ of that party denominated the Catholic priests of Ireland "superstitious tyrants," "brutal monsters," "surpliced ruffians." But they spoke of *Irish* priests; and you, it seems, my gentle lord, vouchsafe to be "*scandalized*" (that is your word) with some of them. You may very well afford to forgive the Tories their abuse of the *Irish* priesthood; but can you forget the language they used respecting the Catholic religion? Is the high tide of your ingratitude to your former political friends so strong, as to blot out the recollection that the common epithet applied by the Tories to Catholicity was "a vile superstition;" but that the more favourite name was "an abject idolatry!"

Has your lordship been seduced by being called "vilely superstitious?" Or have you been won by the flattery of being termed "an abject idolator?"

But you may reproach *me* with the fact that the Whigs enacted "a base, brutal, and bloody" coercion bill. Recollect, however, that the *English* Catholics were unaffected by that measure. There is therefore no *English* excuse for a treacherous desertion of your old friends. Push not then your sympathy for Ireland too far. We are in the habit of suffering, and therefore we can bear it more patiently. We are like the eels, accustomed to be skinned alive. Recollect, good my lord, pray recollect—that of two of the most influential members of the present Cabinet, the one, Sir James Graham, was the ardent supporter, and the other, Lord Stanley, was the contriver, fabricator, and triumphant advocate of "the base, brutal, and bloody" coercion bill for Ireland.

Now, my lord, make your choice. Show your highmindedness, your generosity, your noble gratitude for past services; your just indignation against unprincipled hostility. Make your choice———, but, alas! Your choice is already made! The highmindedness is gone; the generous feeling for a fallen friend is obdurated and perceived no more! The gratitude is obliterated; and your just indignation at iniquitous hostility, merges in puerile servility to the minions of place, power, and authority.

Oh, ingratitude unparalleled! Oh, preposterous selection! Never was such a choice made as you have made and enforced.

> "Blow, blow, thou wintry wind,
> Thou art not so unkind,
> Nor is thy tooth so rude,
> As man's ingratitude".

Yes. If the English Catholics follow your lordship, the biting, chilling, bitter blasts of ingratitude were never so basely blown and so keenly felt, as they will be by every disinterested friend and lover of the generous emotions.

You have, however, your reasons for this desertion of your friends and selection of your enemies. You endeavour to persuade the Catholics of England to abandon those friends and to select those enemies. Your business is to justify a mode of action so repugnant to every right feeling, and so derogatory to every sense of political honour or honesty. It could be palliated only by the most overpowering necessity.

Such was the task you imposed upon yourself. Heavens! how miserably have you failed! Your reasons are to be found in the 4th, 5th, and 6th pages of your letter. I am compelled to say there never was anything more flimsy, more fantastic. It is with pain I must add that drivelling idiocy, or childish folly, could scarcely attain to anything so weak—so mawkish. I will endeavour to analyse the puny material.

First; you allege that "all the great, paramount

"reforms are accomplished" (oh! most sapient sage!)—"and that there is now only *a mere distinction without a difference* between Whigs and Tories."

Let me admit your facts—a matter of some difficulty—in order to admire the conclusion you draw from those premises. Your logic is indeed of a rare quality. What! because there is "only a distinction without a difference" between Whigs and Tories,—*therefore* the English Catholics should, according to you, abandon the Whigs, their consistent friends, and support the Tories, their unrelenting enemies!

Such a specimen of reasoning is not, I believe, to be found among "the royal and noble authors" of any other century or country.

Secondly—as your second argument you state—"That the Tories have adopted the late reforms as an "integral part of our institutions: *and even profess a* "*willingness to concede such changes as the altered circum*-"*stances of society might still require.*"

I cannot concede your facts here; because you told me just now "that *all* the great paramount reforms were actually *accomplished*." Nor do I believe that the Tories intend in anything to ameliorate our institutions. At all events you *must* admit, that the Whigs are at least equally desirous of political improvement. How, then, can you be so preposterous, as to expect that the English Catholics should consider this a reason to abandon their tried friends the Whigs—and to support their known enemies the Tories!

Thirdly—Your third argument insinuates that "the "powers of mischief of a Tory government are sufficiently restrained both by the established reforms "themselves, and by the continually growing force of "public opinion."

I leave, without a single observation, this third sagacious reason why the English Catholics should desert their tried friends the Whigs, and support their known enemies the Tories.

Fourthly—Your fourth argument is accurately abstracted thus; you say,—"If a larger measure of reform "be needed, which it CERTAINLY is in Ireland, the new "men, in the joy and generosity of their triumph, may "POSSIBLY compromise, upon a sound and equitable ad-"justment."

There, my lord—there are your words; not *all* your words; but still, as far as they go, *ipsissima verba*. We have it that a larger measure of reform is "*certainly needed*" in Ireland. But gently—gently, good my lord! Told you not me just now, that *all* the great paramount reforms are accomplished?

There is a class, indeed, of whom the proverb says, that they have occasion for good memories. *You*, my lord, are a truthful man; and therefore you dispense with remembering what you wrote but so short a time before.

Let me now just analyse this last specimen of reasoning:—*Because* the Tories may "*possibly*" in their joy and generosity do some justice to the Irish, *therefore* the

English Catholics ought to grovel in the mire of deep dark ingratitude to the Whigs!

I remember an Irish barrister, who, when addressing a jury, requested of them "not to be carried away by *the dark oblivion of a brow.*" He was stopped by the judge, who exclaimed, "Why, sir, that is nonsense!" "Oh, my lord," returned the unabashed counsellor, "I know it is nonsense,—but it is *good enough for a jury.*"

Thus, good my lord, your inference that the Tories may possibly in their generosity and joy do something for the Irish, is stark nonsense. But upon a matter of political treachery, you deem it good enough for the English Catholics.

Fifthly—Your fifth and last argument may be condensed thus: you say "the times are so menacing and "so unsettled, that it is a problem for futurity to solve, "whether Whig or Tory rule might be better or worse "for the country."

Bravo! So, *because* there may be a problem for futurity to solve as to the comparative merits of Whigs and Tories, *therefore* the living English Catholics are in the interim to decide the point for themselves, by wallowing in the mire of ingratitude and desertion of friends!

I rejoice that I have got through these miserable attempts at persuasion. I cannot, however, avoid saying that they fill me with ineffable disgust. Fortunate, my lord, indeed is it for you, that the weakness of your head may detract but little from the goodness of your heart.

I have thus followed you through the two leading objects of your pamphlet;

First, your attempt to array the English Catholics and Catholicity itself in favour of the grinding bread-tax.

Secondly, your attempt to bring over the Catholics of England, and even to arm Catholicity itself, in the cause of the Tories.

By the first, tainting the sacred banners of apostolic Christianity with the guilt of starving the poor, in order to satiate the avarice of the rich. In the second, inflicting a black spot upon English Catholicity, by making it exhibit the most profligate ingratitude to high-principled (but now powerless) friends; and, with the most abject servility, sharing in the ungenerous joy of malignant enemies.

